MODELS, TRUTH, AND REALISM

Models, Truth, and Realism

BARRY TAYLOR

CLARENDON PRESS · OXFORD

OXFORD

UNIVERSITY PRESS

Great Clarendon Street, Oxford OX2 6DP

Oxford University Press is a department of the University of Oxford.
It furthers the University's objective of excellence in research, scholarship,
and education by publishing worldwide in

Oxford New York

Auckland Cape Town Dar es Salaam Hong Kong Karachi
Kuala Lumpur Madrid Melbourne Mexico City Nairobi
New Delhi Shanghai Taipei Toronto

With offices in

Argentina Austria Brazil Chile Czech Republic France Greece
Guatemala Hungary Italy Japan Poland Portugal Singapore
South Korea Switzerland Thailand Turkey Ukraine Vietnam

Oxford is a registered trademark of Oxford University Press
in the UK and in certain other countries

Published in the United States
by Oxford University Press Inc., New York

© Barry Taylor 2006

The moral rights of the author have been asserted
Database right Oxford University Press (maker)

First published 2006

British Library Cataloguing in Publication Data

Data available

Library of Congress Cataloging in Publication Data

Data available

Typeset by Laserwords Private Limited, Chennai, India
Printed in Great Britain
on acid-free paper by
Biddles Ltd., King's Lynn, Norfolk

ISBN 0-19-928669-8   978-0-19-928669-0

1 3 5 7 9 10 8 6 4 2

For my mother
Edna Elaine Mary Taylor
1919–2002

Preface

This is a short book, but it is the product of more years of thought on its topics than I care to enumerate. It covers a good deal of ground, but is written in rather a compressed style; so, on the advice of the Press, I have included an Overview, which I hope will be of use to a reader in following the twists and turns of the book's argument.

Chapter 5 in large part reproduces a paper I first published in *Mind* ('On Natural Properties in Metaphysics', *Mind*, 102 (1993), 81–100); its provenance is hereby acknowledged. The argument of Chapter 3 also has its origins in a former paper (' "Just More Theory": A Manœuvre in Putnam's Model-theoretic Argument for Antirealism', *Australasian Journal of Philosophy*, 69 (1991), 152–66), which I now find barely intelligible myself. This version is entirely rewritten, considerably enlarged, and, hopefully, also considerably improved.

This work was assisted by a research grant from the Australian Research Council in 2000–1, which is gratefully acknowledged. Thanks are due for comments from members of various seminars at the Universities of Melbourne and Adelaide, Monash and La Trobe Universities, and the Australian National University, where versions of various parts of this work were presented; and for comments from two anonymous readers for the Press. Finally, special thanks are due to my colleagues Graham Priest and Greg Restall, both of whom read and commented on an earlier draft of the book in its entirety; and extra special thanks to the second of these, who, a glutton for punishment, did the same thing again for a revised version. Despite their efforts of all the above, I am afraid I must assume full responsibility for the defects which remain.

B. M. T.

Melbourne, April 2006

Contents

Overview: The Argument of this Book

This book falls into three parts, along with a Coda. Part One argues that traditional realism can be explicated as a doctrine about truth—that truth is objective, that is, public, bivalent, and epistemically independent. Part Two argues that a form of Hilary Putnam's model-theoretic argument demonstrates that no such notion of truth can be founded on the idea of correspondence, as explained in model-theoretic terms (more traditional accounts of correspondence having been already disposed of in Part One). Part Three argues that non-correspondence accounts of truth—truth as superassertibility or idealized rational acceptability, formal conceptions of truth, Tarskian truth—also fail to meet the criteria for objectivity; along the way, it also dismisses the claims of the latter-day views of Putnam, and of similar views articulated by John McDowell, to constitute a new, less traditional, form of realism. The Coda bolsters some of the considerations advanced in Part Three in evaluating formal conceptions of truth, by assessing and rejecting the claims of Robert Brandom to have combined such an account of truth with a satisfactory account of semantic structure. The book concludes that there is no defensible notion of truth that preserves the theses of traditional realism, nor any extant position sufficiently true to the ideals of that doctrine to inherit its title. So the only question remaining is which form of antirealism to adopt.

PART ONE

The strategy of this part is to show, by extrapolation and generalization, how traditional realism is associated with objective truth, characterized as above.

Seeking a neutral and uncontroversial starting-point, Chapter 1 begins by examining and adapting a characterization of realism offered by Michael Devitt, settling on an initial formulation (section 1.1) of realism about objects of kind K as the doctrine that objects of kind K exist objectively, and explaining objective existence in terms of intersubjective warrant. The latter notion is structured by assuming a framework of 'possible epistemic standpoints', modelled on the 'points of view' of Leibnizean monads, and each based upon a possible course of experience of the world; these standpoints certify beliefs through the application of idealized epistemology to the experiences they embody. Then objects of kind K are said to exist objectively iff they exist, and the belief that they exist can be certified from at least two such standpoints; and the doctrine that they do exist objectively in this sense is *object realism* about the objects of kind K.

But (section 1.2) object realism is an inadequate framework for the discussion of some debates between realists and their opponents. To do these justice, we need to invoke the apparatus of situations and facts (obtaining situations). Then *fact realism* concerning a range of situations is the doctrine that these situations are objective facts, i.e., that they obtain and can be certified to obtain from at least two epistemic standpoints. Object realism is subsumed under fact realism as a special case.

However (section 1.3), the argument discussed in the literature under various colourful soubriquets—the 'Great Fact Argument', the 'Slingshot'—reveals that the apparatus of situations is too fragile to bear any explanatory weight. But the developing analysis can be freed from reliance on this apparatus by semantic ascent. Applying this technique, fact realism is supplanted by *semantic realism*, where semantic realism concerning a set of sentences of a language L is the doctrine that these sentences are true-in-L, and can be certified to be true-in-L from at least two epistemic standpoints.

Section 1.4 simplifies this definition by replacing the truth requirement, so that the whole definition is cast in terms of certification. It appeals to the Convergence Thesis, according to which good epistemology homes in on the objective truth as information increases. To put this to use, it extends the framework of epistemic standpoints, enabling any finite union of standpoints to count as a standpoint, so that the standpoints form a Hierarchy of Certification with more information available to higher level standpoints. Then Convergence means that a true sentence will eventually be *stably* certified as true by some standpoint s (i.e., certified as true by s and its union with any other standpoint). A notion of 'corroborated certification' is introduced to play, within the context of the extended framework of standpoints, the role previously filled by the requirement of multiple certification. Then the new definition of semantic realism about a set of sentences of L is that it holds all such sentences are objectively true in the sense that they have a stable, corroborated certification as true-in-L from some standpoint s.

Chapter 2 sets out to extract from this account more of the properties of objective truth. To do so (section 2.1), it inquires into the principles governing certification. Principles governing the logical connectives are borrowed from Crispin Wright, and tested for adequacy against intuition, particularly on the question of the distributivity of objective truth across the connectives. This investigation suggests, first, the introduction of further principles governing second-order certification; and, further, the extension of the Hierarchy of Certification to a further, infinite level to be inhabited by the 'Total View', comprising the union of all finite standpoints. This permits further simplifying the definition of objective truth, so that it becomes just certification from the Total View. *Pure* realism concerning a set of sentences of *L* becomes the doctrine that all members of the set are objectively true-in-*L*, and *global* realism about *L* the doctrine that pure realism holds for some maximal set of sentences of *L*.

Section 2.2 now extracts from this final account of objective truth that objective truth is public, bivalent, and epistemically independent (the last specifically in the sense that a theory ideal by the standards of human epistemology might be objectively false). Finally, section 2.3 suggests that the framework of standpoints and its Hierarchy of Certification, exploited to obtain these insights, can be treated merely as a useful device rather than a metaphysical reality, in much the way possible worlds are treated by many as no more than a useful fiction for investigating modality. Thus we can *explicate* objective truth as truth with the hallmark traits, without commitment to the literal truth of the framework which has helped us to identify them. The question for realism is whether there is some defensible notion of truth possessing these traits, and applicable to a language apt for framing serious theory.

PART TWO

The time-honoured way for realists to found objective truth is by appeal to correspondence. The traditional account of correspondence, however, was discredited back in section 1.3, along with the facts and situations it invokes as the second terms of that relation. But model theory, in the spirit of the old account, also explains truth in terms of relations between language and extralinguistic structures, and can be regarded as a conceptually hygienic, precisely formulated, embodiment of the old intuitions. Putnam has, however, advanced a case for thinking model-theoretic truth unsuited as an account of objective truth as we have explicated that notion, a case which this part evaluates.

Chapter 3 sets out what we take to be the relevant core of Putnam's case. Section 3.1 extracts three arguments from Putnam's writings: the Arguments from Cardinality, Completeness, and Permutation. Of these, section 3.2 argues, only the second is of direct relevance. Appealing to the Completeness Theorem, it shows that the ideal theory, provided it can be cast in a first-order language, must have a model M, whence its theses must in some sense be true (since they must be true-on-M), thus threatening epistemic independence. The other two arguments bear less directly on the realism issue as explicated in Part One. Nevertheless, all three arguments in their disparate ways raise the same issue, namely, how to distinguish 'intended' models from the others. If this distinction can be made secure, then, in particular, the Argument from Completeness can be defused, provided the Completeness-guaranteed model M turns out to be unintended, so that truth-on-M is not a serious brand of truth.

At issue, accordingly, is the possibility of framing constraints which will sort out the intended models. The most popular approach is to cast such constraints as Reference Constraints, which seek to restrict the models which satisfy them to those which assign to linguistic terms entities which are, intuitively, their correct referents. One favourite way to devise such constraints is to exploit a reductionist account of reference, and section 3.3 examines attempts to frame constraints based on causal and psycho-behavioural reductions of reference. Section 3.4 investigates the Translational Reference Constraint (TRC), a constraint on reference which does not rely on a reduction of reference but makes essential use of translation (from object language to metalanguage) to sort out the models which get reference right. TRC in turn suggests a stronger constraint on intendedness, the Translational Truth Constraint (TTC), which goes beyond merely constraining reference, being equivalent to TRC combined with a constraint on the domain on quantification, the Translational Domain Constraint (TDC). TTC, it is argued, constitutes the gold standard of constraints on intendedness. The claims made in this section, however, require foundation in a theory of translation, sufficient to sustain the assumptions it makes about that controversial and opaque notion. This foundation is supplied in section 3.5, whose general tenor is Davidsonian, its key notion being that of a 'hermeneutic theory', i.e., a Davidsonian theory of interpretation cast into model-theoretic terms.

With TTC now identified as the most fundamental constraint on intendedness, it remains to see if it will suffice to rule out as unintended all the models of ideal theory whose existence the Completeness Theorem guarantees. The issue is examined in section 3.6. A notorious argument of Putnam's, the 'Just More Theory' Manœuvre, argues that no constraint on intendedness whatever can do this, because a statement of the constraint can be added to the ideal theory, and Completeness guarantees that this enlargement of the ideal theory will itself have a model. Following David Lewis, many find this Manœuvre involves a confusion between satisfying a constraint, and making true a statement which claims to express it.

Upon investigation, it emerges that Lewis's discussion oversimplifies what is involved, because of the metalinguistic nature of constraints on intendedness in general, and of TTC in particular. Nevertheless, taking these complications into account, the locus of the fallacy Lewis claims to detect can be identified. Still, in the special case in which we are interested, where it is models of *ideal* theory which are in question, no fallacy is involved, because of the restricted nature of the metalanguages of the language of ideal theory which we can meaningfully suppose to be available. Thus the Argument from Completeness remains unimpugned by TTC, and other constraints on intendedness which it subsumes.

Chapter 4 investigates other ways the Argument from Completeness might be attacked. Section 4.1 investigates challenging that Argument's assumption that first-order resources suffice for framing the ideal theory. It concedes that there may indeed be reasons for thinking first-order resources must be extended in some way if ideal theory is to be accommodated, but argues that there are—almost—no grounds for thinking the extension will mean the unprovability of Completeness, as it must if the conclusion of the Argument is to be avoided. The hedge in the 'almost' is to acknowledge that there is a case, albeit an underwhelming one, for casting ideal theory as a second-order language, for which Completeness is often held to fail. But, it is argued, the judgement that it fails depends on dismissing as illegitimate and 'unintended' the Henkin model theory for second-order languages; and there is no way of justifying that dismissal which does not beg the question.

Section 4.2 looks at a suggestion by G. H. Merrill, endorsed by David Lewis, that the model theory used to frame the definition of objective truth should take a nonstandard form, with the referents of predicates restricted to 'elite' sets, the extensions of 'natural' properties marking inbuilt cleavages in nature independent of human psychology and convention. Since the proposed model theory is nonstandard, the suggestion is, Completeness will no longer hold, and the problems it engenders will vanish. A problem arises about the formulation of this suggestion. Lewis suggests it can be recast, not as a proposal to adopt nonstandard model theory but as the requirement that standard models satisfy an Eliteness Constraint, which he counts as a constraint on intendedness. For us, this raises the question of the relation of the proposed Eliteness Constraint to the fundamental constraint on intendedness, TTC, and its vulnerability or otherwise to the Just More Theory Manœuvre. The upshot of the discussion is that Merrill's proposal can, indeed, be formulated using an Eliteness Constraint *in combination with* the fundamental constraint on intendedness TTC, and that the Eliteness Constraint itself should be regarded not as a constraint on intendedness but as an additional, metaphysical constraint; and, further, that it is at least arguable that it is not itself subject to the reasoning of the Just More Theory

Manœuvre, since it makes demands on the resources of the metalanguage beyond those made by constraints on intendedness, thus altering the relations between object language and metalanguage crucial if the Manœuvre is to succeed.

These demands on the metalanguage are not self-evidently legitimate, and the credentials of the Eliteness Constraint can be questioned on that ground. But in Chapter 5 they are subjected to a more fundamental scrutiny, through examining the notion of natural properties on which this whole approach is founded. The examination concentrates on the case for natural properties made by David Lewis, their most articulate advocate in the recent literature. Section 5.1 looks at the role such properties play in Lewis's system. Section 5.2 sets out his reasons for believing in them: that they are required to accommodate Moorean facts about the similarity of objects; and that they are indispensable to philosophical theorizing. Section 5.3 proposes an alternative to natural properties: these are the *T-cosy predicates*, defined by the role predicates play in theories. Section 5.4 argues that *T*-cosy predicates can be used to accommodate the Moorean facts as well as natural properties can do; and section 5.5 that where natural properties have an uncontroversially legitimate role to play in philosophical theory, *T*-cosy predicates will once again do the job. The conclusion is that natural properties constitute unnecessary metaphysical baggage, to be rejected along with the Eliteness Constraint they underpin. Part Two accordingly concludes that the Argument from Completeness goes unanswered, and that in consequence the attempt to found objective truth in model theory fails.

PART THREE (INCLUDING CODA)

This part investigates the credentials of non-correspondence concepts of truth to represent objective truth, paying particular but not exclusive attention to latter-day attempts by Putnam to resurrect some form of realism in the wake of his demolition of correspondence truth.

Chapter 6 examines (section 6.1) Crispin Wright's account of truth as superassertibility; and (section 6.2) the account with which Putnam toys in *Reason, Truth, and History*, of truth as idealized rational acceptability. Both of these, it argues, can be represented as attempts to take a version of Part One's Hierarchy of Certification as a serious analytic tool rather than as a disposable heuristic ladder. In the case of Putnam's analysis, to be sure, the relevant version of the Hierarchy is a complex one, based upon a holistic epistemology rather than the simpler molecular epistemology adopted, in the interests of expositional clarity, back in Part One. Nevertheless, in both cases, the account offered can be represented as taking seriously a version of the Hierarchy; moreover, each of them is then revealed as shrinking from exploiting the Hierarchy's full power, and accordingly as yielding only an etiolated notion of truth, falling short of objective truth on the score of epistemic independence (and, in the case of superassertibility, of bivalence as well).

Chapter 7 discusses formal theories of truth—the redundancy theory and its ilk, distinguished by the attempt to characterize truth in terms of its structural properties—in the context of the position adopted by Putnam in his John Dewey Lectures, here styled 'Common-sense Realism'. This position is described in section 7.1: it combines two principles which we call the Thesis of the Internality (according to which the elements of a representational system are internally related to their content) and the Thesis of World-Embeddedness (which holds that content is dependent on the world in a more than causal way), with a formal account of truth. Such a formal account of truth, it is argued, implies no connection with the properties of truth characteristic of realism, as Part One has explicated it. It is conceded, however, that it is perhaps plausible to think that the whole Common-sense Realism package can claim, as its title suggests, to represent some new-fangled version of realism, because of the close connections between representing system and world which its principles entail.

Section 7.2 dismisses this line of thought. Common-sense Realism, it argues, along with all theories comprising a formal account of truth, should be committed to the flames, because they are cut off from exploiting the Fregean model of meaning, based on a recursion on truth; and this means they have no theoretical account to offer of semantic systematicity, there being no alternative to the Fregean model which is capable of doing so. (This sweeping claim is bolstered in the Coda. This examines the system of Robert Brandom in *Making it Explicit*, which claims precisely to offer a non-Fregean account of semantic systematicity of the sort just claimed to be impossible. The discussion focuses on Brandom's account of singular terms, identified as those playing a characteristic inferential role. It is argued that the same role could be played by expressions which function intuitively on a sub-word level, but that no resource available in Brandom's system disqualifies them as singular terms; hence, that Brandom's account of semantic structure will not do, since it is compatible with a bizarre identification of singular terms and hence, within his system, of objects.)

Section 7.3 examines a response to this objection, based on Cora Diamond's reading of Wittgenstein, and hence very much in the spirit of Common-sense Realism, questioning the need for any theoretical account of systematicity. The response is rejected: following Dummett, it is found incompatible with the rationality of linguistic activity.

Chapter 8 turns to scrutiny of the status of Tarskian truth. Section 8.1 argues that, because of its connections with behaviour and psychology through the notion of translation, it is properly classified as a substantial, rather than a formal, account of truth. In itself, however, it does not embody an objective account of truth, being neutral, for example, on the score of bivalence. Nor can it be used as the foundation for a notion of objective truth, by using it as the basis for a correspondence account of truth (leading to the problems raised in Part Two), or by taking objective truth as the Tarskian truth concept deployed by some superior being such as Davidson's Omniscient Interpreter (leading to problems akin to those discussed in section 5.1). The best that can be claimed is that Tarskian truth is compatible with realism; though even this will be challenged by the considerations of section 8.2.

This section takes up a possibility left open by Chapter 7's discussion of Common-sense Realism. This is that Common-sense Realism might be modified by replacing the commitment it made to a formal account of truth, the basis of Chapter 7's objection to the position, by commitment to a substantial alternative capable of playing a part in the Fregean model of meaning. Tarskian truth, with its bland neutrality, is the obvious candidate for the replacement role. The resulting position, dubbed 'Quietist Realism', proves on examination to be that of John McDowell in *Mind and World*; moreover, its characteristic principles, borrowed by Putnam for Common-sense Realism, are no optional extra to Tarskian truth as McDowell deploys it, but play an essential role in his defence of the notion as suitable for use in the Fregean model, against attacks mounted by Dummett.

It was suggested in Chapter 7 that Common-sense Realism may have claims to represent a form of realism, even if not realism in the official terms of Part One. Such claims are inherited by Quietist Realism, its improved successor. But it is argued that Quietist Realism's treatment both of objects and of facts (truth) proves on examination inappropriate to sustain such claims; and, in particular, that Tarskian truth in McDowell's system surrenders all claim to epistemic independence. Thus, Quietist Realism has no genuine claim to the title of realism, traditional or new-fangled. Moreover, if adoption of its principles is the only recourse to save Tarskian truth for the Fregean model against Dummett's attacks, and if, as has been maintained, that Fregean model is a compulsory one to account for the systematicity of language, then even the formal compatibility of Tarskian truth with traditional realism, still apparently preserved at the end of section 8.1, proves to be an illusion.

The book concludes that no defensible notion of truth will sustain the theses of traditional realism as Part One has explicated it, and that the claims of other positions to be represented as worthy heirs to the realist title may be dismissed. But it leaves unresolved the question of the form the best version of antirealism should take.

PART I

THE EXPLICATION OF REALISM

1

Realism and Objective Truth

Writing in 1978, Hilary Putnam remarked favourably on the passing of 'ism' words from philosophical fashion, whilst noting a tenacious tendency for 'realism' to buck this supposed trend.[1] A quarter century of postmodernism, connectionism, functionalism, feminism, and the rest later, we may well wonder whether he did not exaggerate rumours of a general demise of 'ism'-ism. He was undoubtedly right, nevertheless, to note the staying power of 'realism'. For few 'isms' match this one in the deep loyalty they arouse in their adherents; and many a philosophical discussion would peter out to an early and—perhaps—premature end if not sustained by frequent glib references to 'the realist position' on the matter in hand.

For all that, there is far from consensus about precisely what it is that realism involves. As conceived in this work, it is primarily a doctrine about truth—that truth, across the field for which realism is maintained, is bivalent, epistemically independent, and intersubjective. But this characterization is tendentious, and its ties to traditional positions gathered beneath the realism banner less than perspicuous. The task of establishing and clarifying such ties is complicated by the fact that no agreed principle unites the traditional positions themselves, beyond their conformity to various slogans whose interpretation is open to dispute; so it is tempting to dismiss the matter as intractable, define 'realism' one's own way, and get on with discussing its merits. Such a course is, however, unattractive. For, difficult though it may be to isolate the agreed essence of traditional realisms, there is general consensus that they form an interrelated cluster, making strong metaphysical claims which demand assessment with all musterable rigour. To appropriate the label of realism for some doctrine is accordingly to make out its evaluation has a significance commensurate with, and related to, the claims of traditional realisms, and as such requires justification. At the same time, because of the unclarities around the issues involved, it is too much to demand of such a justification that it demonstrate deductive connections between traditional conceptions and the new ones for which the label

[1] Hilary Putnam, 'What Is "Realism"?,' *Proceedings of the Aristotelian Society*, 76 (1975/6), 141.

is appropriated. Rather, it is sufficient to show how traditional preoccupations can, through a natural progress of abstraction and generalization, be transformed into the new ones. That will not show, of course, that the new problems are precisely the same as the old ones—after all, the whole point of the transformation is to take a step forward, by replacing old, vaguely stated formulations by crispier ones which will lend themselves more easily to precise evaluation. Nor will it show that there may not be other, alternative, and equally good ways of transforming old problems into new ones. But it will, it is submitted, be enough to justify appropriation of the old label for the new doctrine. Establishing the credentials, in this way, of the conception of realism adopted in this work is the task of the present introductory, first part of this work. (Readers prepared to take those credentials for granted may accordingly skip it and read on unimpeded, at least until the beginning of Part Three, when some reference to the framework developed here will be made to help structure the discussion.)

It is not uncommon for those attempting to articulate what realism involves to appeal to the notion of a God's-Eye View of the world, where all the facts of any conceivable observation are laid bare and made grist to the mill of perfect theorizing.[2] A similar appeal will be made here in charting a course from traditional realism to the version here favoured. The strategy will be to show how, starting from a reasonably anodyne formulation of traditional realism, generalization and refinement lead naturally—note there is no claim of compulsion—to reformulation in terms of a God's-Eye View, here more secularly termed a Total View, to still any atheistic qualms; and how natural assumptions about the way things look from such a lofty perspective then entangle realism with a doctrine of truth having the characteristics listed above as the hallmarks of realism, as herein conceived.

1.1 OBJECT REALISM

Michael Devitt's views on realism could hardly be more hostile to those favoured here; faced with the suggestion that realism is fruitfully seen as a doctrine about the nature of truth over the domain for which realism is maintained, he snorts, with Michael Levin, that 'Truth, like Mae West's goodness, has nothing to do with it'.[3] All the more reason to begin our

---

[2] See e.g. Michael Dummett, *The Logical Basis of Metaphysics* (Cambridge, Mass.: Harvard University Press, 1991), 348–51; and 'What Is a Theory of Meaning? (II)', in his *The Seas of Language* (Oxford: Clarendon Press, 1993), 60–2; also Hilary Putnam, *Meaning and the Moral Sciences* (London and Boston: Routledge & Kegan Paul, 1978), 77.

[3] Michael Devitt, *Realism and Truth*, 2nd edn. (Oxford: Basil Blackwell, 1991), 39.

discussion where he does, so that our starting-point at least is one we share with even our most diehard opponents.

Objective existence is a key notion in Devitt's analysis. He glosses it in terms of (epistemic) independence, and writes that 'an object has objective existence, in some sense, if it exists and has its nature whatever we believe, think, or can discover: it is independent of the cognitive activities of the mind'.[4] One might expect him then to take realism to be the thesis that there are objects which, in this sense, exist objectively. But, in fact, his characterization is more complicated.

The complications arise out of Devitt's concern with the external physical world, and his desire to formulate realism as a doctrine specifically concerned with the status of that domain.[5] Devitt recognizes that there are some views of the mental according to which mental objects could be held to exist objectively according to the above definition, but, being reluctant to allow any view of mental items to count as realist because of this desire to limit realism's scope, he tacks on a further clause to what realism must maintain: it should hold not merely that its objects exist objectively but also that they exist independently of the mental.[6] For brevity, let us express this by saying that it should hold that its objects enjoy 'gold-class existence'.

Realism thus apparently becomes the thesis that there are objects which enjoy gold-class existence. In fact, though Devitt does accept this as one form of realism, it is one he disparages. This is mere Weak or 'Fig Leaf' Realism,[7] a pale shadow of the red-blooded realism Devitt is out to defend. This red-blooded version—'Devitt's Realism', in our book, though he calls it 'Realism' *tout court*—maintains that gold-class existence is enjoyed not just by some unspecified objects but specifically by (most of) the physical objects of common sense and science. Thus Devitt's Realism is the thesis that 'tokens of most current common sense and scientific physical types objectively exist independently of the mental'.[8]

We may distinguish two projects in Devitt's discussion: that of characterizing realism; and that of isolating the thesis he wants to defend. It suits Devitt's purposes to conflate the two, but our own current interests, lying just with the former, are better served by teasing them apart. Now, despite his appropriation of the unqualified term 'Realism' for his own favoured position, Devitt does seem to acknowledge that Weak Realism is, in some sense, a form of realism, whilst at the same time framing his official definitions in such a way as to preclude us from saying so. A suggestion which enables us to acknowledge that Weak Realism is a realism, whilst differentiating it from the thesis Devitt is out to defend, is to take the key notion as being

4 Ibid., 15.   5 Ibid., 13.   6 Ibid., 15–16.
7 Ibid., 17 and 23.   8 Ibid., 23.

realism concerning (purported) objects of kind K, this being the thesis that there are, indeed, objects of that kind, and that they enjoy gold-class existence. Then Weak Realism is just realism concerning objects of some unspecified kind or other, whilst Devitt's Realism is realism concerning objects of most common-sense and scientific kinds. Cutting the cake like this accordingly loses none of the distinctions Devitt is out to draw. Moreover, it yields a more general characterization of realism which promises to be more suited to the ends of the present inquiry. For we shall in the sequel be concerned with particular objections to so-called realism, objections which, being highly abstract, will apply, if at all, to a more general position (or set of positions) than Devitt's Realism. Our present interests lie primarily, as explained, in defending the claims to the title of our preferred account of realism; but we have a subsidiary interest, too, in identifying and characterizing the targets of the objections which will later preoccupy us, and this renders less restrictive accounts of what realism involves more attractive.

Similar considerations point against following Devitt's version of what gold-class existence involves—objective existence plus independence of the mental. Devitt adds the second requirement, as we saw, explicitly to rule out any position on the mental from counting as realism, even though, as he concedes, some positions (for example, reductive physicalism) construe mental entities as existing objectively. But it seems perversely restrictive to rule out definitionally the possibility of any realism about the mental, with little to motivate it save Devitt's desire to reserve the prized title of realism for his favourite thesis, which we style Devitt's Realism, and which applies only to the external world; and again our current interests favour a more liberal characterization. This suggests we should take realism concerning objects of kind *K* just as the thesis that objects of that kind objectively exist, leaving realism about the mental as a viable possibility.

But what now of Devitt's account of objective existence itself? Couched as it is in terms of epistemic independence, one of the salient marks of the truth which our present project hopes to associate with realism, it may well seem a welcome and promising starting-point. But Devitt says little about just what this independence involves, and how precisely it is to be cashed; and what he does say suggests a disquieting radicalism which suggests his conception of epistemic independence may carry commitments we may be reluctant to undertake. Thus, he maintains that 'the extent to which and the manner in which we can come to know about an object are, for the realist, epistemic issues which are *quite distinct* from ontological questions about the object',[9] a doctrine which suggests that we should countenance

---

[9] Michael Devitt, *Realism and Truth*, 2nd edn. (Oxford: Basil Blackwell, 1991), 15, emphasis added.

the intelligibility, at least, of the existence of objects which are entirely and in principle unknowable—Kantian things-in-themselves. This suggestion is borne out in his discussion of Weak Realism, which is dismissed as involving too insubstantial a commitment to represent the realism Devitt wants to defend, because its requirements are met by a position countenancing merely these Kantian oddities[10]—a dismissal which presupposes that the existence of such entities makes sense, and would constitute objective existence. Yet we may well not want to follow Devitt in such a commitment, particularly if the unknowability of these noumena applies not just to real warts-and-all fallible humans restricted to the familiar five senses but carries over to our idealized and generalized counterparts. Devitt's stance on these matters is unclear. Worse, there is no way to amplify the notion of independence, and resolve these issues, which is sufficiently obvious and uncontroversial to yield the comfortable and agreed foundation on which we would like our characterization of realism to rest.

These considerations point towards seeking an alternative account of objective existence. Devitt's proposal took one of the traits we eventually aim to associate with realism-constitutive truth—epistemic independence—as the mark of objectivity. If, as it now seems to have emerged, an alternative to his proposal is needed, a natural suggestion is that we might seize upon another such trait to play the same role, and the suitable candidate is *intersubjectivity*—that is, in principle public accessibility. After all, it is a notion frequently associated in the literature with objectivity. Such an association can be found even in Devitt's discussion. For it is the denial of special first-person access which he takes as the touchstone of those theories which accord objective existence to mental items.[11] He, of course, links this with epistemic independence; but it also involves an affirmation of intersubjectivity.

Out of this examination of Devitt, then, we have extracted the view that realism concerning (purported) objects of kind K should be taken as the thesis that entities of kind K objectively exist, with the proposal that objective existence be somehow explained in terms of intersubjectivity, along with the obvious task of fleshing out the explanation. As a start, we might try this: object x objectively exists iff x exists, and its existence is in principle accessible to more than one possible observer. But the terms of the explanation could stand expansion and refinement.

To start with, the term 'observer' may be less than happy; for we should allow that there may be avenues other than observation through which the existence of an object is accessible. Let us then abandon it, replacing it by the more neutral, if less idiomatic, expression '(epistemic) standpoint'. But

10 Ibid., 17.   11 Ibid., 15.

we want to allow that observation is always *a* way in which at least *some* things become accessible to an epistemic standpoint; thus, epistemic standpoints always incorporate, and are based upon, some course of experience 'of the world', and to any such possible course of experience there corresponds some possible epistemic standpoint. (The shudder-quoted phrase means no more—but no less—than that a course of experience be constituted by genuine perceptions, exclusive of foundationless hallucinations; so elliptical-looking pennies may figure in such a course of experience, along with red-seeming pillarboxes, but the phantasmagorical daggers of a disordered mind are excluded. Doubtless this requirement can be analysed causally—roughly, a course of experience is of the world iff the experiences which constitute it are caused by the world; but to avoid counterexamples we must add that the experiences are caused 'in the right way', and murky waters lie ahead when we attempt to specify just what this 'right way' might be.[12] Still, the problem is a general one, which we may safely shelve as tangential to the current enterprise.) The experiences available to an epistemic standpoint constitute the raw materials for the manufacture of beliefs. Since we are interested in what is available 'in principle' to epistemic standpoints, we shall conceive of the manufacturing process as proceeding through a flawless application of the principles of the best epistemology—whatever these may be; for our discussion will proceed at a level of lofty generality intended to apply whatever the truth on such matters of detail may turn out to be. Thus, through the application of ideal epistemology to experiences of the world, an epistemic standpoint comes to *certify*, as we shall put it, certain beliefs. These beliefs will be bound to be reasonable, given the information available to the standpoint, but, of course, they are not guaranteed to be true.

These possible epistemic standpoints are not without philosophical pedigree: they belong in the same broad tradition as the 'perspectives' of Russell's *Our Knowledge of the External World*[13] and, hence, of the 'points of view' of Leibnizean monads on which these perspectives are modelled. Using them, we can sharpen the formulation of realism foreshadowed above: realism about objects of kind *K* holds that entities of kind *K* objectively exist, i.e., that such objects exist, and that the belief that they exist is certified from more than one possible epistemic standpoint. Call realism as thus characterized *object realism*.

[12] See P. F. Strawson, 'Causation in Perception', in his *Freedom and Restraint, and Other Essays* (London: Methuen, 1974), 66–84; and subsequent literature, e.g. Christopher Peacocke, *Holistic Explanation: Action, Space, Interpretation* (Oxford: Clarendon Press, 1979).

[13] Bertrand Russell, *Our Knowledge of the External World* (London: George Allen & Unwin, 1926), 94 ff.

Some of the epistemic standpoints we may label *human* standpoints: these are those based on the course of experience of the world of some actual or possible human being, who we may say *occupies* the epistemic standpoint in question. But even though a person—Descartes, say—may occupy an epistemic standpoint *s*, and though when in thoughtful mood Descartes may certify various beliefs, there need, of course, be no coincidence between the certifications Descartes endorses and those endorsed by *s*. To start with, Descartes has the job of sorting out genuine experiences of the world from hallucinations produced by a mind which malfunctions from time to time, a problem *s* never has to confront. Further, Descartes may make mistakes when processing sensory evidence, or appeal to the wrong principles in doing so; but *s* operates flawlessly according to the tenets of ideal epistemology. So even human standpoints are idealized versions of actual human beings who may occupy them. For all we have said, indeed, the idealization may go further. For ideal epistemology, on some conceptions, may presuppose a methodology which it is not even in principle possible for a human being to implement, such as the ability to complete an infinite survey; in which case *s* may issue certifications Descartes could never be in a position to match. On this and other matters concerning epistemological detail, such as whether ideal epistemology is molecularly empiricist or holistic, we shall, as far as possible, remain noncommittal, preferring a neutrality in keeping with the largely diagnostic aims of the present introductory chapters. Similarly, we shall keep an open mind about the possibility of nonhuman epistemic standpoints—those based on courses of experience analogous to our own, but constituted out of the alien sensory modalities of bats, flounders, or Martians.

Even on a niggardly conception admitting only human epistemic standpoints as possible, and using a human-sized measure of epistemology, object realism, as we have explained it, pretty clearly counts naïve common sense about middle-size material objects as a realist position, as of course it should. For naïve common sense construes the tree in the quad as something whose existence is certifiable from a host of possible human epistemic standpoints; that is, by the lights of our proposed analysis, it construes the tree as existing objectively. Less clear is how our proposed analysis classifies Berkeley's position on the same everyday material objects. For they are, on Berkeley's construal, congeries of mental ideas, and it was urged a little while back, *contra* Devitt, that we should remain open-minded about the possibility counting some views of the mental as realist. So we are well advised to address that issue before turning to Berkeley.

Physicalism is perhaps the obvious candidate for a view of mental objects to be counted realist. But it is a reductionist theory, a consideration which imports complications making it less than ideal as a paradigm to expose the bones of the issues involved. Consider, then, instead a classical dualism about the mind—specifically, let us say, about sensations, to keep things simple—complete with a doctrine of incorrigibly correct privileged access. Does this count as realist position? On the current account, the issue turns on the possibility of the certification of the existence of sensations from some epistemic standpoint other than the privileged one of the first person. Of course, any dualism which wants to avoid explicit scepticism about other minds is going to maintain that the existence of my pain can be certified in some sense or other from other epistemic standpoints, and by human ones at that. A classic problem with dualism is, then, whether the certification offered from outsider standpoints, differing radically in kind and authority from that offered by the privileged standpoint, is really certification enough. In the present context, the question becomes whether such certification passes the tests imposed by ideal epistemology; if not, then there is a problem about providing for the double certification of the existence of sensations which object realism requires, at least so far as possible *human* standpoints are concerned. But, suppose our dualism posits nevertheless that sensations could be apprehended directly, perhaps in much the same way as they present themselves to the privileged standpoint, from other *non*human and nonprivileged standpoints; that God, or some suitably equipped Martian, could look into my mind and there see and certify what I was thinking of and feeling, like looking at a beetle in a box into which I alone among humans have the privilege of peeking. This may be a silly theory of the mind, but it is not evidently incoherent; and the current theory does not seem at odds with intuition in deeming it a realist one. By contrast, according to the account under canvass, a dualism which construes sensations as irremediably accessible only from the one privileged epistemic standpoint surrenders all realist pretensions. Again, this seems in accordance with intuition; for, according to such a dualism, sensations evidently become mere features of an epistemic standpoint, rather than independent items upon which the standpoint is directed.

We can now return to Berkeley, and apply the foregoing considerations to his position. If the tree in the quad is a congeries of ideas, and those ideas are construed on the 'beetle in the box' model (so that God can perceive them too), then the position is a realist one; but if my ideas are irremediably accessible only to me, so that God's ideas can at best resemble mine, realism is rejected.

A possible refinement of the position emerging is perhaps worth pointing out. This is that it can allow for gradations of objectivity, and so allow that a theory may treat some objects more realistically than others. Thus, objectivity as we have treated it so far—certifiability from more than one epistemic standpoint—could be regarded as objectivity at the minimal level; and entities are regarded as increasing in objectivity the more possible *kinds* of epistemic standpoint are able to provide certifications of their existence.

So far, then, so good. But object realism provides us with too restrictive a framework, and it is time it was transcended.

1.2 FROM OBJECT REALISM TO FACT REALISM

For Devitt, realism is primarily a thesis about the way objects exist, and our object realism reflects its origins in preserving this feature. But, in fact, many of the issues between realists and their opponents transcend mere disputes about the existence of objects. A simple, albeit manufactured, example will illustrate the point. (We shall turn to some more complicated, less artificial, cases in a moment.) Consider two versions of beetle-in-the-box dualism about sensations, differing in their view of the status of some property P which sensations can bear: View One holds that the Martian view which, in addition to mine, can certify the existence of my sensations, is also able, and with equal authority, to certify that some sensation of mine S has property P; whereas View Two restricts the certifications of the Martian view to certifications of the *existence* of my sensations, and leaves me alone as the sole true certifier of the possession by my sensations of P. Then it seems clear that View One embodies a more thoroughgoing realism about sensations than does View Two. But each is equally realist on the existence of all the individuals in play, as measured by the standards of the object realism; hence the apparent need to go beyond those standards.

It may be responded that no real extension of the old account is required, just a more thoroughgoing exploitation of its potential. For, an objector may urge, there is no reason to regard the definitions of the last section as applying only to individuals; they can be extended to properties as well, and the difference between the two views canvassed is just that View Two is realist about the individuals alone, whereas the more thoroughgoing View One also asserts the objective existence of property P. Actually, the extension of object realism to properties is less straightforward than just made out, since it is not clear what the criteria are for a property to exist, nor *a fortiori* for a certification of its existence to be warranted. Suppose for the sake of argument, however, that we take an Aristotelian view, and regard a property as existing iff it is instantiated. Then the objector's proposed diagnosis of the difference between our two views is still inadequate: for we can modify View Two so that it enables the Martian view to certify both that sensation S exists and that property P exists (i.e., is somewhere-or-other instantiated, or even is somewhere-or-other instantiated among my sensations), whilst leaving it as the sole privilege of my special stand-point to issue a certification that sensation S has property P. A similar point can be made if other standards of property-existence are adopted.

Object realism, accordingly, appears to lack the resources to differenti-ate between our two views. But resort to a familiar metaphysical framework appears to supply the lack. The framework in question is that of *situations* (aka *states of affairs*), such as the situation of Socrates being wise. These situations manifest themselves in language as whole sentences; thus the sample manifests itself as 'Socrates is wise' (contrast the individual Socrates, which manifests itself as the singular term 'Socrates', and the property of wisdom, which manifests itself as the predicate 'is wise'). Some of these situ-ations—those manifesting themselves as true sentences—*obtain*; and such situations are *facts*. Using this terminology, we can say that our two Views differ in the status they attribute to the fact of S's having P. Only View One treats that situation as obtaining objectively, where a situation obtains objectively iff it obtains, and the belief that it obtains can be certified from more than one possible epistemic standpoint.

Generalizing, it seems that realism should accordingly be treated primar-ily as a doctrine not about the objective existence of a purported domain of objects but about the objective obtaining of a range of situations, or alleged facts: realism about such a range is the doctrine that each element of the range obtains objectively, where objective obtaining is explained as above. Let us call realism of this sort *fact realism*. Then object realism can be recovered from realism as thus more broadly conceived as a special case. The simplest way is just to take object realism about a purported domain D of objects as fact realism about the range of alleged existential facts concern-ing each of the elements of D. The broader framework of fact realism can, however, also be exploited to yield a richer account of object realism than that hitherto available. Thus, an alternative account which may appeal to some is to take object realism about a purported domain D as fact realism about the range not just of alleged existential facts about elements of D, but also of the alleged *essential* facts about those elements.[14]

Number theory provides a further and less contrived example of the need for the shift to the perspective of fact realism. There are several ways realism

[14] An alternative version of the theory of situations makes the contrast between object realism and fact realism appear less dramatic. On this version, there are no situations other than those which obtain, so that all situations are facts, and the contrast between obtaining and existing vanishes. This makes fact realism turn out to be just a special sort of object realism, namely, object realism about a set of purported facts. Still, the contrast with the last section remains: we are forced take a new set of purported entities as the focus of debates about realism, and this new focus supersedes and encompasses earlier preoccupations.

about the natural numbers can be rejected. One (nominalistic) way is to deny numbers exist at all. A second (idealistic) way is to construe them as private mental objects, and so to deny that the numbers of which I speak can be certified to exist from any perspective other than mine. Both of these may be unlovely options, facing obvious difficulties in explaining, in the first case, how number theory can be simultaneously false and useful; in the second, how arithmetic can be common knowledge—but in any case, both are denials of realism even by the standards of object realism. But constructivism provides us with a third, and more interesting, way to reject realism about the numbers. According to the constructivist, certifications about the numbers, no matter where the epistemic standpoint which issues them, can only take the form of proofs in principle constructible by a thinker subject to the constraints which govern the human thinker. A certification of the existence of a number n thus consists of an appropriate proof that n exists. Such a proof may, for example, take the form of a proof of the existence of n from the Peano postulates, a procedure equivalent in practice to counting until the numeral for n is reached. Clearly, there is an upper limit to the counting any actual human mind can carry out, and so an upper bound on the numbers it can certify to exist; but the constructivist, unlike the strict finitist, regards any such limit as transcendable in principle, so that a certification of the existence of any number can be made by any possible epistemic standpoint (whose certifications are all those which ideal epistemology permits). Thus, by the standards of object realism, the constructivist is a realist about the numbers. But the constructivist denies that the ability to transcend in principle the limitations of actual human thinkers extends, for example, to the capacity to survey an infinite domain. Thus, the constructivist holds that there may be no certification to be issued, by any epistemic standpoint, either for an undecidable proposition such as Goldbach's Conjecture, or for its negation, and (loath to countenance facts whose obtaining cannot in principle be certified) will also deny the existence of a fact corresponding to either. In contrast, platonism construes certifiability-in-principle more liberally, affirming that one or other of the pair of propositions in question is certifiable from any epistemic standpoint, and with it the existence of a corresponding fact. Clearly, constructivist and realist divide over some question of realism; yet even the constructivist is a realist about the numbers by the lights of object realism. Hence the need to advance to fact realism for the distinction to be drawn.

Reductive positions, too, are more easily situated and classified within the broader framework of fact realism than within the confines of the object version. In the last section, Berkeley's object–object reduction of material objects to congeries of ideas was considered. But the modern cousin of that position, phenomenalism, is couched as a fact–fact reduction, a reduction of facts about material objects to facts (albeit sometimes counter-factual facts!) about human sensation, and if it fails as a realism at all—we shall briefly return to the issue below—it fails as a *fact* realism, by not treating the facts of the reducing class as objective. And, for similar reasons, the framework of fact realism will be required for the classification of scientific instrumentalism.

Finally, the possibility, envisaged in the discussion of object realism, of a graded scale of objectivity increasing with the number of kinds of certifying standpoints, can be made in the environment of fact realism to do some serious work. Thus, facts about the shapes of things may be seen as more objective than facts about their colours because, though both are object-ive in the minimal sense, the obtaining of the former but not the latter is also certifiable from *outré* standpoints like those of bats. And, perhaps, to take a case which worries Crispin Wright,[15] facts about what is funny will be less objective even than facts about colours, because their certifiab-ility varies with culture and background, the joke not being visible even from all human perspectives. Relative objectivity of this sort will not figure largely in the sequel, which will be concerned with objectivity and real-ism in their more elemental forms; but it is an advantage of the present perspective in its fact realism metamorphosis that it gives promise of such further development.

1.3 FROM FACT REALISM TO SEMANTIC REALISM

Loudly though the praises of the fact realism framework have just been sung, it suffers from a fatal defect: the 'facts' to which it is wedded are brittle things, incapable of bearing the explanatory weight placed upon them.

Afire with the spirit of Ockham, Quine has taught those who have learned his lessons to beware the spurious charms of purported explanatory power bought at the cost of ontological inflation. What precisely are these so-called facts? How are they counted? How do they relate one to the other, and to more mundane things? These are uncomfortable questions, admitting no ready answer. Adrift in this sea of metaphysical uncertainty, it seems we can, however, clamber up on one rock, the Truth–Fact Link, as we shall style it: if situations and facts exist at all as an ontological category, and are to subserve the functions attributed to them in the philosophical tradition, then obtaining situations or facts are items to which true sentences correspond, in much the same way as existent individual things correspond to nonvacuous singular terms. We may formulate the Link

---

[15] Crispin Wright, *Truth and Objectivity* (Cambridge, Mass., and London: Harvard University Press, 1992), *passim*.

as a biconditional: a sentence is true iff it corresponds to a fact. But Davidson,[16] citing an argument he attributes to Frege—an argument refined by Church, and now variously known in the literature as 'the Frege Argument', 'the Great Fact Argument', and 'the Slingshot'—contends that even this minimal and key characteristic is fatal for facts. The argument in question begins by maintaining that if true sentences really are to relate to facts as nonvacuous singular terms relate to objects, then two principles should apply: logically equivalent truths should correspond to the same fact; and the fact corresponded to by a true sentence should be robust under substitution of codesignative singular terms in the sentence. From these premises, the argument purports to establish that any two true sentences must correspond to the same fact—the One Great Fact stood for by all true sentences. But this makes fact theory so indiscriminating as to be useless for almost all analytical purposes—including those of explicating realism, since the discussion of the previous section would make little sense if the facts enshrined in various mathematical truths could not be distinguished from each other, let alone from facts of quite different kinds, such as facts about the physical world.

If facts are to be consigned to the wastebasket of metaphysics, the right-hand side of the Truth–Fact Link collapses. So the analysis we attempted using the chimerical concepts of the right-hand side had best be recast in the everyday, if philosophically notorious, terms deployed on the left-hand side. So realism must be recast as a doctrine not about the objective *obtaining of situations*, but about the objective *truth of sentences*; fact realism must be reshaped as *semantic* realism.

Effecting this transformation is complicated by the way truth, considered as a predicate of sentences, must be indexed to the language in which the sentences are regarded as cast. This indexing of a crucial term in the *anaylsans* will infect the *analysandum*: thus, semantic realism is, strictly considered, *L-realism concerning a set S of sentences of L*. It holds that these sentences are *objectively true-in-L*; where, transforming our account of objective obtaining in the obvious way, a sentence A counts as objectively true-in-*L* iff A is true-in-*L*, and the belief that A is true-in-*L* is certifiable from at least two epistemic standpoints. Two worries about semantic realism, as thus explained, need to be addressed.

[16] See Donald Davidson, 'Truth and Meaning' and 'True to the Facts', both in his *Inquiries into Truth and Interpretation* (Oxford: Clarendon Press, 1984), 37–54; and many other of his papers. See also Alonzo Church, *Introduction to Mathematical Logic*, Vol. 1 (Princeton, NJ: Princeton University Press, 1956), 24–5. For the—admittedly vague—Fregean credentials, see Gottlob Frege, 'On Sense and Meaning', in his *Collected Papers on Mathematics, Logic, and Philosophy*, ed. by B. F. McGuinness (Oxford and New York: Basil Blackwell, 1984), 162–3.

The first is its apparent commitment to the existence of *languages*: after all, it may be said, it is all very well to inveigh against facts on Quinean grounds, but the pot calls the kettle black if we replace a commitment to facts by a commitment to languages, which as intensional entities call down Quine's sternest strictures. In response, it may be urged that the commitment to languages as entities is illusory: 'true-in-*L*' is a one-place predicate, with the '*L*' strictly speaking as a mere syntactic part, not a variable occupying a quantifiable argument-place;[17] similarly, the position occupied by the index in '*L*-realism' should not be regarded as accessible to quantifiers. Thus the analysis indicates what it is to be an *L*-realist relative to sentences *S*, as distinguished from a realist relative to *L* and *S*.

A second worry arises out of uncertainty over what the certification of semantic beliefs might involve. For it seems that, to certify the belief that A is true-in-*L*, a standpoint should not only certify a belief *b*(A) with the content that A, according to *L*, possesses but should also certify beliefs enshrining semantic principles about *L* sufficient to derive from *b*(A) the belief that A is true-in-*L*. But when does a standpoint certify such semantic principles? The key to a response is to recognize that semantic principles are a priori—that, for example,

'der Schnee ist weiss' is true-in-German iff snow is white

holds because truth-in-German is what it is, and so can be certified just on the basis of acquaintance with concepts. (What is not a priori and requires hard-won empirical knowledge is that any particular utterance is to be evaluated for truth-in-German, or that German is the language of a given speaker or population.) Being a priori, we may take semantic principles as in principle certifiable no matter what course of experience may occur, and, hence, as always certifiable from any of our idealized epistemic standpoints. It follows that we may, in general, take an epistemic standpoint to be in a position to certify the belief that A is true-in-*L* iff it can certify the belief *b*(A).

Fact realism, from the present perspective, is thus revealed as no more than a detour on the trip from object realism to the semantic version. It is a detour worth making, nevertheless, lest diehards like Devitt, for whom realism is a purely metaphysical issue,[18] should be given opportunity to accuse

[17] This logical parsing is, of course, compulsory, on pain of paradox; see e.g., Donald Davidson, 'The Structure and Content of Truth', *The Journal of Philosophy,* 87 (1990), 285.

[18] See e.g., his Maxim 3 (*Realism and Truth,* 4): 'Settle the realism issue before any semantic or epistemic issue'; and compare p. 39: '*Realism says nothing semantic at all*' (his italics). In fairness to Devitt himself, it should, however, be added that he is no fan of

us of cavalier introduction of semantic apparatus to handle complexities which could be resolved without leaving the level of ontology.

This rejection above of the fact framework will rightly puzzle a small but rather distinguished group. These are readers familiar with earlier work of the present writer.[19] For, in the past, he argued that the Great Fact argument is of doubtful validity. Whether it goes through, and in what form, for the sentences of a particular language depends (he argued) on highly specific features of the language—notably, the presence within it of a primitive description operator, and on the semantic treatment accorded to failed descriptions. Further, even when it goes through, its effect can be circumvented provided 'logical equivalence' is construed strictly enough in the requirement that logically equivalent truths should correspond to the same fact. And not only did he thus question the credentials of the fact-destroying Great Fact argument, and point to the way around it, he actually proposed a set-theoretic construction of facts as part of a wider range of situations (there called 'states of affairs'), and then proceeded to urge their use as a tool in semantic analysis, specifically of adverbial constructions. And now, like Hal ascending the throne, he has the gall to repudiate entirely the old chums with whom he heard midnight chime!

In fact, rejecting the appeal to facts in the current context remains consistent with that earlier position. True, the Great Fact argument is not as devastating a weapon against facts as Davidson makes it appear; but the discussion above carefully refrained from saying that it is. What the argument does show is that intuitions in the area are untrustworthy, and the theory of facts needs to tread carefully if disaster is to be avoided. Further, the sensitivity of the argument to the nuances of language shows how the theory of facts must display a similar sensitivity; so facts are more like ontological shadows cast by language than robust, independent items which can be used to illuminate how language works. (Compare Strawson's view that we have no independent handle on facts other than as 'what true statements state'.[20]) This means that, while the Truth–Fact link can be maintained, we cannot use its right-hand side ('*S* corresponds to a fact') to *explain* its left ('*S* is true'), in the way the Correspondence Theory of

facts (see p. 27). This leaves mysterious what his preferred method would be for handling the pressures which seem to force an advance beyond object realism.

[19] See Barry Taylor, 'States of Affairs', in Gareth Evans and John McDowell (eds.), *Truth and Meaning: Essays in Semantics* (Oxford: Clarendon Press, 1976), 263–84; or ch. 2 of *Modes of Occurrence: Verbs, Adverbs, and Events* (Oxford: Basil Blackwell, 1985).

[20] P. F. Strawson, 'Truth', in his *Logico-linguistic Papers* (London: Methuen, 1971), 190–213.

Truth attempts to do. All of this is entirely consistent with the construction of facts which was proposed in the earlier work to which we have referred. For that construction made no attempt to explain truth in terms of facts. Rather, it used model-theoretic methods to explain both truth and facts, in such a way as to preserve the Truth–Fact link; and the point of introducing the facts was not meant to be the illumination of truth, but to provide some items alleged to be helpful in some of the other antics of semantics.

1.4 FROM TRUTH TO STABILITY

The aim of the present part is to link realism, traditionally conceived, with a commitment to the applicability, across the field for which realism is maintained, of a concept of truth which is intersubjective, epistemically independent, and bivalent. In arguing for a construal of realism as semantic realism, the preceding sections have attempted to link realism with truth, and with intersubjectivity; but no connection with epistemic independence is evident, and bivalence is nowhere on the horizon. To forge these further connections, we must first recast the definition of objective truth on which the characterization of semantic realism is based. That definition, in its current form, defines the objective truth-in-L of A in two clauses: one requiring outright that A be true-in-L; the other imposing conditions on how the belief that A is true-in-L must be certifiable. The aim of the recasting is to find a unitary characterization which will dispense with the first clause, and be stated entirely in the terms of the second clause; that is, to characterize the objective truth-in-L of A entirely in terms of how the belief that A is true-in-L is certifiable from various epistemic standpoints. Evidently, this project can succeed only if we can somehow capture the force of first clause, requiring that A be true-in-L, in appropriate terms; or, at least, if we can effect this trick whenever A is an appropriate candidate for being objectively true-in-L.

The clue for doing this lies in the *Convergence Thesis*. This is the notion that, as information increases, good epistemology will always tend to home in on the objective truth. As such, it predicts that no matter how diverse the initial informational bases of two theories may be, and no matter how diverse their initial theses accordingly, the two will increasingly tend to converge in their findings as the information available to them grows; further, that as new theories grow from old ones in striving to accommodate accumulating information, theses of the old theories will tend increasingly to be preserved as approximations (since the old theories, like the new, converge on the objective truths). It is a thesis congenial to realists, especially those sometimes called the 'convergence realists',[21] who, claiming to discern that real theories do, in fact, behave as the Convergence Thesis predicts, use this as evidence that objective truth prevails in the domain of the theories in question. For present purposes, its relevance is that invoking it promises to give a characterization in terms of certification for what it is for a sentence A to be true-in-L, at least when A is apt for *objective* truth-in-L: roughly, such a sentence A is true-in-L just when the belief that A is true-in-L will eventually and definitively be certified as such, from any epistemic standpoint, as evidence accumulates.

The problem with this rough formulation is its dependence on the notion that the evidence available to an epistemic standpoint may expand; but that idea is a literal nonsense as epistemic standpoints have been hitherto construed, since a single and fixed course of experience of the world has been regarded as constitutive of each such standpoint.

To address the difficulty, we need to expand the framework of epistemic standpoints. Thus, let the epistemic standpoints appealed to so far be rechristened *basic* or *individual* ones; and let us allow further that whenever s_1 and s_2 are epistemic standpoints, so, too, is their union $s_1 \cup s_2$, formed by pooling the information available to each. Issuing certifications on the basis of the pooled information will then be a further task for ideal epistemology; *inter alia*, this will involve using its principles to adjudicate between incompatible claims severally certified by the pooled standpoints, sometimes utilizing its principles to plump for one of the alternatives, at other times judiciously refraining from endorsing either. The new epistemic standpoints thus form a hierarchy, with the old basic standpoints at the bottom level 1, and with level n comprising all unions of n basic epistemic standpoints.

Now let an *expansion* of a basic epistemic standpoint s be any nonindividual standpoint $s \cup s_1 \cup \ldots \cup s_n$; further, let us say that a standpoint s *stably certifies* that p iff s certifies that p, and moreover for any s', $s \cup s'$ certifies that p. Then to say that 'the belief that A is true-in-L will eventually and definitively be certified as such, from (individual) standpoint s, as evidence accumulates' is to say that s has an expansion which stably certifies the belief that A is true-in-L; so our old account of what it is for A to be true-in-L (at least, where A is a candidate for being *objectively* so true) boils down to saying that every individual standpoint has such an expansion. Equivalently,

[21] See e.g., Richard Boyd, 'Realism, Underdetermination, and a Causal Theory of Evidence', *Nous*, 7 (1973), 1–12; William Newton-Smith, 'The Underdetermination of Theories by Data', *Proceedings of the Aristotelian Society Supplementary Volume*, 70 (1978), 71–91; and the earlier Putnam, as represented by e.g., the papers in Hilary Putnam, *Mind, Language and Reality: Philosophical Papers Volume Two* (Cambridge and New York: Cambridge University Press, 1975).

and more simply, it can be expressed by requiring just that there be some standpoint s which stably certifies that A is true-in-L. For it is trivial that this is entailed by the more complex requirement; and conversely, if it is true, then so too is the more complex requirement, since any individual standpoint must have an extension which is $s \cup s'$ for some s'.

The first clause of the definition of objective truth in the last section, imposing the outright requirement of the truth-in-L of an objectively true sentence A, can thus accordingly be supplanted by a requirement that A be stably certified from some subjective standpoint. Such a modification is evidently entirely in the spirit of the original definition; for the key idea of that definition was to connect objectivity with intersubjectivity, which teams happily with stable certification, since both, in their own way, require certification to be linked to a more extensive epistemic base.

Now the way to the unitary characterization of objective truth this section set out to find is open: we need just replace the first clause of the old definition with its new counterpart, obtaining the formulation: a sentence A counts as objectively true-in-L iff the belief that A is true-in-L is stably certifiable from some epistemic standpoint, and certifiable from at least two epistemic standpoints. Fidelity to the old definition suggests, however, that we had better specify further that the epistemic standpoints of the second clause be *individual* ones, since those were the only ones envisaged when that clause was originally formulated. Moreover, a moment's thought shows that this specification is indeed necessary if the second clause is to have any bite, since it follows trivially from the definition of stability that anything stably certified from one epistemic standpoint will be certified from multiple nonindividual epistemic standpoints. So our unitary characterization becomes: a sentence A counts as objectively true-in-L iff the belief that A is true-in-L is stably certifiable from some epistemic standpoint, and certifiable from at least two individual epistemic standpoints.

But it is necessary only to state this characterization to perceive its defects. For why should it not be that there are beliefs which are certifiable only on the basis of a vast body of information, greatly exceeding that available to any individual standpoint? If so, then there would seem to be no reason why such beliefs should not, depending on their content, turn out to be objectively true, despite failing the second clause of our proposed definition.

That second clause was designed to express the requirement of intersubjectivity; the problem is that it goes beyond its brief, and imposes too strong a condition, once it is set inside the wider framework of a hierarchy of epistemic standpoints, to which we have now moved. A more modest and well-motivated condition should impose the requirement of multiple certification only on *individual* standpoints, and demand of nonidividual standpoints only that they never rely on information passed on by constituent individual standpoints unless it is so secured. Thus, let us say that a certification of a belief *b* by a standpoint *s* is *corroborated* iff *s* is an individual standpoint, and some other individual standpoint *s'* also certifies *b*; or *s* is a nonindividual standpoint, and *s* in certifying *b* relies on no certifications from other standpoints save for corroborated ones. Then we incorporate the requirement of intersubjectivity by requiring that certification be corroborated, and define: A is objectively true-in-*L* iff the belief that A is true-in-*L* has a stable and corroborated certification from some epistemic standpoint *s*.

Before moving on, let us pause briefly to introduce some conventions to simplify terminology, which threatens to become unwieldy under the increasing burden of qualifications and indices. First, we shall allow ourselves to suppress the language parameter on the truth-predicate: 'A is true-in-*L*' will become just 'A is true'. Second, we shall allow ourselves to talk of certifying *sentences*: '*s* certifies A' will mean '*s* certifies [the belief] that A is true' (that is, '*s* certifies the belief that A is true-in-*L*'). Finally, because we shall henceforth be concerned almost exclusively with corroborated certification, certification should henceforth be taken always to be corroborated, unless otherwise stated. Of course, these conventions are overridable, and full-dress terminology will be reintroduced where it seems necessary to avoid ambiguity, or to remind ourselves of complexities which shorthand might obscure.

2

Realism Explicated

2.1 THE STRUCTURE OF CERTIFICATION

The uniform characterization of objective truth which the last section set itself to find is now to hand. The payoff promised was that this would aid in discerning connections between realism, epistemic independence, and bivalence; but these, it must be admitted, are still below the horizon. Perhaps there are some grounds for discerning progress in linking realism with epistemic independence—after all, the uniform account is at least cast in the epistemic language of certification; but the way forward is admittedly obscure. And the uniform characterization at first sight may seem to offer nothing at all towards connecting realism with bivalence.

But, upon reflection, the latter judgement may be too pessimistic. If bivalence is a property of objective truth at all, it is clearly connected with the way objective truth interacts with the logical connectives, and in particular with negation; for to say objective truth is bivalent is to say every sentence is objectively true or false, and a sentence is false iff its negation is true. And the uniform characterization of objective truth in terms of certification suggests that these matters, in turn, will depend on the way certification behaves with respect to the connectives; so by investigating the principles governing the logical behaviour of certification, we may hope for illumination on the bivalence issue. Moreover, in this investigatory task, we may hope to derive some succour from an increasing convergence of our analytic apparatus with other notions available in recent literature on issues of realism and antirealism, and in particular with devices deployed in the work of Crispin Wright.[1] For to say the truth of a sentence is certifiable from an epistemic standpoint, in the terminology of the present work, is closely akin to saying with Wright that it is 'assertible in' a corresponding 'state of information'. (True, we have made more of the intersubjective nature of certifiability than does Wright of assertibility; but the difference may be only one of emphasis.) With that parallel drawn, the connections

---

[1] Crispin Wright, 'Can a Davidsonian Meaning Theory Be Construed in Terms of Assertibility?' in his *Realism, Meaning and Truth* (Oxford: Blackwell, 1993), 411–18.

become closer, since our notion of objective truth stands to certifiability just as Wright's 'superassertibility' stands to assertibility. We shall persist with the present quaint terminology, emphasizing that we reserve a right to insist on differences in detail; but the parallels will prove more than handy in illuminating the formal properties of certification.

A common assumption in the literature on the theory of assertibility which we hope in this way to exploit is that the underlying epistemology is essentially molecular. Under this assumption, the assertibility of the simplest (atomic) sentences is held to be determined directly in some way dependent on the their structure out of predicates and singular terms; and the assertibility of these simplest sentences, in turn, determines the assertibility or otherwise of all more complex formulae. This assumption is motivated, at least in part, by a desire to assign to assertibility a key role in the explication of meaning, a burden our own notion of certifiability has not been asked to carry; further, we have to date been keen to preserve as much neutrality on matters epistemological as possible, and, hence, in particular have made no commitment to molecularity. Nevertheless, it will simplify our discussion if we now agree *pro tem* to confine our account to a framework of a molecular epistemology, postponing to a later chapter (Chapter 6) an investigation of the complications which result from allowing epistemology to take a more holistic form.

Within the molecular framework thus adopted, certain atomic sentences are singled out as 'core'. The certifiability or otherwise of a core, atomic sentence from an epistemic standpoint s is then determined by rules derived from the meanings of the predicates and terms comprising the sentence, and specifying when experiential content and epistemic manipulations available to s warrant the sentence's certification. (Should the language also contain core but nonobservational atomic sentences, there will be further rules determining the certifiability of these, too, on the basis of their structure; for example, in the case of mathematical equations, these will take the form of specifying calculations, determined by the structure of the singular terms figuring in a given equation, and of outcomes these calculations must yield to confer certifiability.) Boundary rules then stipulate when further atomic sentences are certifiable, on the basis of the certifiability or otherwise of clusters of the core ones. Finally, it is the role of the formal principles of certification to determine when complex sentences become certifiable, in a way determined by the certifiability of their parts.

What shape should these principles of certification take? For conjunction, at least, there seems an obvious and uncontroversial candidate to hand:

[CONJ] A conjunction A&B is certifiable from epistemic standpoint s iff both of its conjuncts A and B are certifiable from s.

Two points about this. First, 'certifiable' in it, and subsequent provisions, means 'corroboratedly certifiable', in accordance with the abbreviatory policy recently announced; though in this and the other cases the more general principle with unrestricted certifiability would seem equally acceptable. Second, and again in this and subsequent provisions, a classical reading is taken as the default for the connectives and operators of the metalanguage. In view of the common connection drawn between classical logic and realism, it may be wondered whether questions are not begged by this assumption; but it is hard to see why that should be so. For our current project is, after all, to characterize realism, not to defend it; adopting principles friendly to realism, at least *pro tem*, is arguably indispensable for such a project. And, in any case, part of what we hope such a characterization may illuminate is the validity of the alleged connection between classical logic (in particular, bivalence) and realism; so the existence of such a connection cannot be antecedently assumed as a basis for criticism.

What next of disjunction? Again, there is an obvious suggestion: to take a disjunction as certifiable from a standpoint iff either of its disjuncts is so certifiable. Upon reflection, however, this appears too stringent—a standpoint should surely count as certifying a disjunction when it does not itself afford a certification of either disjunct, but does certify that one disjunct or the other will eventually be certifiable, as information accumulates. Adapting a formulation of Wright's,[2] accordingly, we might offer

[DISJ] A disjunction A ∨ B is certifiable from *s* iff at least one of its disjuncts A or B is certifiable from *s*, or it is certifiable from *s* that there is an *s'* such that either A is certifiable from *s* ∪ *s'* or B is certifiable from *s* ∪ *s'*.

(It might be objected—indeed, has actually been objected, by Greg Restall—against this provision that it offends against molecularity in its final clause. After all, we are trying to say when a disjunction is certified from *s*; and the third clause tells us this is so when *another* disjunction (this time buried under a quantifier) is so certified. This may seem to make the provision as a whole look if not exactly circular, then suspiciously spiraliform; at any rate, dubious in its claims to underwrite molecularity. But these worries are ill founded. The third clause of our provision introduces *second-order* certification: certification concerning what standpoints certify. We shall turn below to the task of enunciating

---

[2] Crispin Wright, 'Anti-Realism and Revisionism', in his *Realism, Meaning and Truth*, 442. (But we ignore as irrelevant to present ends the subtleties of 'effective transformation' in Wright's original.)

some of the characteristics of second-order certification, and the principles which govern it. For the moment, let it suffice to say that it is to be guided by information about the rules which govern first-order certification of object-language formulae, about the nature of epistemic standpoints, and about the structure of the hierarchy they inhabit. This is admittedly vague enough, and our provision may be open to legitimate charge on that ground. But it does not evidently anywhere make the certifiability of a disjunction from standpoint *s* depend on information concerning the certifiability of any object-language formulae beyond those disjoined; and that is what would need to be shown to sustain the charge that it sins against molecularity.)

Negation and the conditional prove yet more problematic than disjunction, since in these cases there is a dearth even of prima facie candidates; once again we turn with gratitude to Wright's[3] work for some suggestions we can adapt to our purposes. The thought underlying the negation rule is to count ¬A as certifiable in a standpoint affording enough information to rule out the idea that any further accretion of information could certify A. So we have:

[NEG] A negation ¬A is certifiable from standpoint *s* iff it is certifiable from *s* that there is no standpoint *s'* such that A is certifiable from $s \cup s'$.

The rule for the conditional counts a conditional as certifiable iff enough information is at hand to warrant assurance that, should further information be acquired sufficient to certify the antecedent, the consequent will also be certifiable:

[COND] A conditional A → B is certifiable from standpoint *s* iff it is certifiable from *s* that for any standpoint *s'*, if A is certifiable from $s \cup s'$, so also is B.

Obviously, these clauses governing the logical connectives need supplementation to cover the quantifiers. But these will not loom large in the discussion to follow, and, having plenty of material to work with, we shall forbear from attempting details (though it will be a presupposition of discussion to follow that some satisfactory supplementation can be found).

How adequate are these provisions governing certification and the connectives, viewed from the perspective of the conception of objective truth which they underpin? A strong, if not universal, intuition about objective truth is that it should distribute across the connectives; so one way of answering the question is to see how objective truth fares on this score when underwritten by the suggested provisions.

---

[3] Crispin Wright, 'Truth Conditions and Criteria', in his *Realism, Meaning and Truth*, 62; and 'Can a Davidsonian . . .', 412–15.

Embarking on this project, we strike immediate gold; for it turns out to be easy enough to show, appealing to [CONJ], that a conjunction A&B is stably certifiable iff each of the conjuncts A and B are stably certifiable, that is, that A&B is objectively true iff A is objectively true and B is objectively true. [Proof. *Sufficiency.* Suppose A&B is certifiable from s; then by [CONJ] each of A and B are certifiable from s; and each of these certifications must be stable. (For suppose one of them, say that of A, is not. Then A is not certifiable from $s \cup s'$, for some standpoint s'; hence by [CONJ], A&B is not certifiable from $s \cup s'$, contradicting the assumption that it is stably certifiable from s.) *Necessity.* Suppose A stably certifiable from some standpoint s, and B from s'. Since both these certifications are stable, A and B are both certifiable from $s \cup s'$, so by [CONJ] A&B is certifiable therefrom. Further, this certification is stable. (Suppose it is not. Then for some s'', A&B is not certifiable from $(s \cup s') \cup s''$; so by [CONJ] either A or B is not certifiable from $(s \cup s') \cup s''$. But since $(s \cup s') \cup s'' = s \cup (s' \cup s'') = s' \cup (s \cup s'')$, this contradicts the assumptions that A is stably certifiable from s, and B from s'.)]

Unfortunately, after this promising start, the project stalls as soon as disjunction is confronted. True, half of the desired result is forthcoming: it is simple to show that if either A or B is objectively true, so is the disjunction A ∨ B (because [DISJ] guarantees that if a disjunct is stably certifiable from a standpoint, so is the disjunction). But the converse is impossible to prove. (Suppose A ∨ B is objectively true, i.e., stably certifiable from some standpoint s. We must show that one of its disjuncts has a stable certification from some standpoint s'. The obvious ploy is to attempt to do so taking s' as s itself. But even if we suppose that one of the disjuncts (say, A) is certifiable from s—an oversimplification in itself, due to the complications we saw fit to incorporate into the statement of [DISJ]—we cannot conclude, from the stability of the certification of the whole disjunction A ∨ B from s, that this certification of the disjunct A from s is stable; for the stable certification of the disjunction is compatible with the circumstance that, for some standpoint s', it is the other disjunct B which is certifiable from $s \cup s'$.)

Given such problems with disjunction, it is unsurprising, given the complexity of the statement of their associated rules of certification, that negation and the conditional should also prove recalcitrant.

In particular, examining the problems which arise in the case of negation proves to be instructive. Before proceeding to discuss the details, however, we need to agree on some further principles governing certification; this time, on principles governing the second-order certification of statements about the certification of first-order formulae, a notion deployed in the rules we have introduced. First, whilst we have emphasized that certification from a standpoint is in general defeasible, it seems reasonable—bearing in mind the idealized way in which certification is meant to operate—to assume that each standpoint is a reliable authority at least about its own certifications; so that we have

[SECOND-ORDER RELIABILITY] If p concerns nothing beyond the certifications which are or are not available to s, and s certifies that p, then p.

Second, and with the idealized nature of the way standpoints issue their certifications still very much in mind, we shall assume that each standpoint is in a position to undertake a *complete* survey of the certifications of object-language formulae available to it, and so to certify that such a certification is available to it whenever that is so, and, conversely, whenever no such certification is available to it, to certify that that too is so. Hence we have

[SURVEYABILITY] If A is (or is not) certifiable from s, then it is certifiable from s that A is (or is not) certifiable from s.

Adopting with these second-order principles, let us return to the problem of the distributivity of objective truth across negation. To be shown is that a negation $\neg$A is objectively true iff A is not objectively true. Left-to-right, the result goes through easily enough. (For suppose $\neg$A is objectively true, i.e., stably certifiable from some standpoint s; and, for *reductio*, that A is objectively true, i.e., stably certifiable from some standpoint s^*. From the latter, we have that A is certifiable from $s^* \cup s = s \cup s^*$, by the definition of stability. But from the former, by the definition of stability once more, we have that $\neg$A is certifiable from $s \cup s^*$, and, hence, by [NEG] that it is certifiable from $s \cup s^*$ that there is no s' such that A is certifiable from $(s \cup s^*) \cup s'$; *a fortiori*, it is certifiable from $s \cup s^*$ that A is not certifiable from $s \cup s^*$ itself, and, hence, by Second Order Reliability, A is not certifiable from $s \cup s^*$. This gives a contradiction; so A is not objectively true.) Right-to-left, however, the story is different, the recently adopted second-order principles notwithstanding. For suppose A is not objectively true. Then there is no standpoint from which A is stably certifiable. But from this there is no evident way to prove that there exists a standpoint from which $\neg$A *is* stably certifiable, i.e., that $\neg$A is objectively true.

These difficulties, both with disjunction and negation, are existential—our problem in both cases is to find a standpoint with the desired property existing somewhere on the hierarchy. This suggests that the difficulties may be overcome by extending the hierarchy. So far, we have allowed any *finite* union of individual standpoints to count as a further, nonbasic standpoint; the extension which suggests itself is to allow that any infinite union should also so count. The immediate motivation for the extension is, of course, that it will set our definition inside a framework adequate to ensure that objective truth possesses the intuitively right properties in relation to the connectives. But, in any case, the proposal is an entirely natural one, not only because there is no evident independent reason to favour a truncation of the hierarchy which limits it to merely finite levels but also because, as we saw back in the opening sections of the preceding chapter, it is in the spirit of realism to be generous in drawing the boundaries when countenancing possible epistemic standpoints.

Suppose, accordingly, we extend the hierarchy of standpoints by admitting as further standpoints the infinite unions of individual standpoints. It follows as a consequence, of course, that the hierarchy of standpoints has a topmost level κ, where κ is the cardinality of the set of individual standpoints; and at level κ there will exist the Total View **TV**, the union of *all* the individual epistemic standpoints. Moreover, with **TV** in place, we can simplify the definition of objective truth: a sentence is objectively true iff it has a corroborated certification from **TV**. (For any certification from **TV** is stable, since the union of the **TV** with any standpoint is identical with **TV** itself; thus, if A has any certification at all from **TV**, it is *stably* certifiable from **TV**, and thus is objectively true under the old definition. And if A is stably certifiable from some lesser standpoint s, then A has a certification which survives into the union of s with any other standpoint, and thus survives into **TV**; so any sentence which is objectively true under the old definition has a certification from **TV**.)

But does the proposed extension really suffice for the task for which it was devised: that of ensuring distributivity of objective truth across the recalcitrant connectives? Consider first the case of negation, in the troublesome right-to-left direction. Then it appears that the answer is affirmative, provided we make one further plausible assumption about idealized certifiability and standpoints. We may call this the assumption of Self-Location; it holds that, the information available a priori to any standpoint, and hence in particular to **TV**, includes information about the structure of the hierarchy of standpoints, and about the location of the standpoint within that structure. (For suppose this principle of Self-Location granted, and that A is not objectively true, i.e., not certifiable from **TV**. Then, by Surveyability, it is certifiable from **TV** that A is not certifiable from **TV**. Since the union of **TV** with any standpoint is **TV** itself, it follows that A is not certifiable from the union of the **TV** with any standpoint; and, granted Self-Location, this inference can be traced within **TV** itself. Hence, by [NEG], ¬A is certifiable from **TV**, i.e., ¬A is objectively true.)

Similarly, the enriched framework, supplemented once more by Self-Location and the other second-order principles, permits demonstration of the distributivity of objective truth across disjunction. (To revisit the difficult half of the proof, suppose A ∨ B is objectively true. Then by [DISJ] either (1) A is certifiable from **TV**, or (2) B is certifiable from there, or (3) it is certifiable from **TV** that there is a standpoint s such that either A is certifiable from **TV** $\cup$ s or B is certifiable from **TV** $\cup$ s. But because the identity of **TV** with **TV** $\cup$ s is, by Self-Location, demonstrable in **TV** itself, if (3) holds, then it is certifiable from **TV** that either A is certifiable from **TV** or B is certifiable from **TV**; and from this, by Second Order Reliability, it follows that either A or B is indeed certifiable from **TV**, i.e., that either (1) or (2) holds. Thus either (1) or (2) holds; that is, either A is objectively true, or B is objectively true.) And, finally, the distributivity of objective truth across the conditional—ignored hitherto in our discussion—follows from this result for disjunction, together with that for negation.

Let 'pure realism' be our name for the construal of realism that emerges when the hierarchy of standpoints takes the unrestricted form just envisaged, extending sufficiently far to incorporate the Total View. To be fully specific, then, we may bring to a close a chain of definitions stretching back to our original characterization of object realism: *pure realism* concerning a set S of sentences of a language L is the doctrine that the sentences of S are objectively true in L, when a sentence A is construed as objectively true in L iff it is certified as true-in-L from the Total View **TV**. It will be useful, too, to define the doctrine of *global* pure realism, concerning the whole of L; this we take as the doctrine that there is a maximal consistent set of sentences of L—a set which contains any sentence A of L iff it does not contain its negation—for which pure realism holds.

2.2 PURE REALISM, BIVALENCE, AND EPISTEMIC INDEPENDENCE

The strategy of this introductory Part One, as outlined in the opening paragraphs of the last chapter, is to draw out from the traditional conception of realism a characterization which enmeshed that doctrine with a God's-Eye View of the world, and show how realism, as thus characterized, involved a commitment to a doctrine of intersubjective, bivalent, and epistemically independent truth. The last section delivered the characterization promised, with the God's-Eye-View appearing in secular garb as the Total View; and it is time to deliver on demonstrating the commitments to the properties of truth which realism as so characterized allegedly undertakes.

A connection between pure realism and intersubjectivity is presumably clear enough, given the origins of its definition in the conception of objectivity as intersubjectively certifiable truth surviving into the requirement that certification, as construed in the final definition, is to be corroborated. But bivalence, too, emerges out of that definition, in the sense that, inasmuch as the rules of certification apply universally across the sentences of L, every sentence of L is either objectively true or false. For those rules ensure that any sentence A is either certified from a standpoint, or not; hence, it is either certified from **TV** or not, i.e., is either objectively true or not; hence, by the distributivity of objective truth across negation, either A or its negation is objectively true, i.e., A is objectively true or false. Since our definitions obviously preclude the possibility that a sentence be *both* objectively true and objectively false, it further follows that, inasmuch as the rules of certification apply universally across the sentences of L, global pure realism applies to L. Moreover, the rules of certification combined with the unrestricted hierarchy characteristic of pure realism also guarantee the preservation of classical logical principles of the object-language. In particular, Excluded Middle is preserved, in the sense that any instance thereof will be certifiable from any standpoint. (For, for any standpoint s, either A is certifiable from $s \cup$ **TV**, or $\neg$A is certifiable from there; by Self-Location, this last fact is certifiable from s; so by the third clause of [DISJ], A $\lor \neg$A is certifiable from s.)

The fact that our definitions thus, as advertised, connect their favoured conception of realism with bivalence does not obviously entirely commend them. For it implies that any rejection of bivalence must be a repudiation of realism. But it is admittedly not always obvious that this is so, a fact which may revive lingering suspicions as to the claims of pure realism, the considerations urged above notwithstanding, to represent realism as traditionally conceived. Moreover, the position we have reached entails that any rejection of bivalence must at the same time involve an objection to the application of some feature of the model of hierarchical certifiability, and, again, it is not always easy to pinpoint the focus of such an objection. Here we may look for assistance to the writings of Michael Dummett, with whom the link between bivalence and realism is, of course, famously associated.[4] His analyses of the way specific rejections of bivalence involve repudiations of realism directly address the first of our difficulties. They can also assist in the second, that of locating the focus of the objection to the application of the hierarchical model which a given rejection of bivalence involves.

Consider, for example, Strawson's repudiation of bivalence in introducing truth-value gaps for sentences containing 'rotten' singular terms—those which fail of unique reference. Whilst at first blush we here have a repudiation of bivalence involving no concomitant repudiation of realism at all, Dummett ingeniously suggests that this impression is false:

---

[4] The references are legion. But see, especially, Michael Dummett, 'Truth', in his *Truth and Other Enigmas* (London: Duckworth, 1978), 1–24; and 'Realism', in his *The Seas of Language*, 230–76.

for, as he points out, it can, after all, be construed as a rejection of an unlovely realism about Meinongian objects serving as the referents of such failed descriptions.[5] This also suggests one plausible ground which may be advanced for the belief that such sentences cannot be accommodated within the hierarchical model of certification. For it is plausible to take an atomic sentence $F(t)$, where F is an observational predicate, as certified from an individual standpoint s when (a) the referent of t is presented to s observationally, and (b) a test associated with F, and applicable to observationally presented objects, is successfully applied to the referent thus presented. From this it is a short step to thinking that the negation $\neg F(t)$ of such a sentence should count as certified from s when (a) holds, but the F test yields an *un*successful result. If this step is taken, then, if the hierarchical model is to apply universally, so that either $F(t)$ or its negation is certified from TV even when t is a rotten singular term, we must be prepared to admit standpoints to which Meinongian referents of rotten singular terms are observationally presented. Now we have noted a tendency to profligacy in the admission of epistemic standpoints as a characteristic trait of realism; but even those most reckless in embracing the consequences of their philosophical convictions are liable to balk at admitting epistemic standpoints to which the present King of France is somehow observationally presented. Note, however, that it is not structural features alone of the hierarchical model of certification which lead to its apparent failure to accommodate sentences with rotten singular terms; rather, that failure springs from a combination of those structural features along with a natural, but superimposed, picture of certification of atomic sentences and their negations.

Linguistic vagueness is another phenomenon often thought to mandate a rejection of bivalence. Without too much strain, this rejection also can be read as involving a rejection of realism—this time of realism concerning the existence of sharp boundaries between the extensions of predicates. Again, this failure of bivalence can be portrayed as arising out of the awkwardness of fitting vague statements onto the grid of the hierarchical model of certifiability, this time because of structural features along with the limitations of the 'good epistemology' which guides certifiability. Thus, consider the statements 'the blob is red' and 'the blob is orange', said of a borderline-case blob. We should, perhaps, allow that the former can count as certified from some individual standpoint s_1, and the latter from other individual standpoint s_2; but what are we to say of the certifications of their union $s_1 \cup s_2$? That both should be certified by the union seems impossible, given that

⁵ See Michael Dummett, 'Realism and Anti-Realism', in his *The Seas of Language*, 462–78, at 468.

they are contradictory and that the combination of [NEG] and [COND] evidently implies that if a contradiction is certifiable from any standpoint, so is every other statement. On the other hand, 'good epistemology', no matter how much information it is supplied with, is, in the nature of the case, unable to decide between the claims for certification of the two conflicting candidates, which suggests perhaps that neither of the two should be certified by $s_1 \cup s_2$, or by its further union with any other standpoints. But that means that neither statement will be certified from **TV**, a finding which, by [DISJ], is inconsistent with the strong intuition that if the blob is indeed a borderline case, then at least the disjunction 'the blob is red or orange' should count as objectively true, and thus *should* be certified from **TV**.

Thus it is plausible, at least prima facie, that global bivalence should be rejected in the face of the phenomena of rotten singular terms and of vagueness; in both cases, this rejection can be construed, as our evolving account demands, as a rejection of realism, and can be traced to an apparent difficulty in imposing the rules of certification upon sentences exhibiting the phenomena in question, in the context of an unrestricted hierarchy of certification. But various reactions to this situation are possible. A diehard realist may insist the prima-facie difficulties these phenomena raise are not intractable. It might be maintained, for example, that apparent rotten singular terms are a superficial artefact of the grammatical superstructure of language, which disappears under Russellization; so the debate about realism operates at a linguistic level at which the problem of rotten singular terms may be presumed to have dissolved. As for vagueness, a possible line is that, whilst 'good' epistemology—that implementable by mere mortals—may be unable to decide between the claims to certification of 'the blob is red' and 'the blob is orange' in a borderline case, given enough information *superlative* epistemology can always do so; hence, construing certification, at least at the ultimate level, as proceeding by the standards of superlative epistemology, one member of this pair of statements will be certified at **TV**, removing the objection to construing vague statements as marching in accordance with the normal rules of certification. On the other hand, it might be maintained that the problems posed by one or other of these phenomena are sufficient to force exempting them from the scope of the normal rules of certification. That will involve a retreat from global pure realism concerning a language in which the troublesome phenomenon is exhibited. It will also, of course, incur an obligation to articulate the way certification for statements of the troublesome class does indeed work, given that it does not operate in accordance with the standard rules.

What, finally, of the last of the troika of properties of objective truth we claimed at the outset to be connected with realism, namely, epistemic independence? In one sense, our construction emphasizes that there are indeed connections between objective truth and epistemology, since objective truth is introduced via the epistemic notion of certification. Nevertheless, the same construction vindicates that objective truth is epistemically independent, when epistemics are taken to be limited to *human* ways of finding the truth; more specifically, it vindicates the view that an ideal theory, constructed on the basis of all past, present, and future human observation using the best epistemology, might not be objectively true. To see this, reflect that the information available to a human at a time can be identified with that available to an individual standpoint; that accordingly the information available to a human being in a lifetime can be identified with the union of the informationally different standpoints occupied by the human being across time; and that the union of all such unions (call it the Human Total View, **HTV**) accordingly represents the sum total of information ever available to the human race. Plausibly, **HTV** will be merely a finite union (if we assume there will only ever be finitely many humans, and that each human, despite surviving through infinitely many times, occupies only finitely many informationally distinct standpoints in a lifetime). But even if it is infinite, it clearly falls far short of the Total View **TV**, which includes all possible standpoints, including those never, in fact, occupied by humans plus possibly some inaccessible to them. If we identify a (humanly accessible) ideal theory with the set of sentences certified at **HTV**, it is accordingly clear that this need not coincide with, or even be a subset of, the set of sentences certified at **TV**; that is, that some of its sentences need not be objectively true.

2.3 THE STATUS OF THIS ACCOUNT

The foregoing pages are our attempt to clarify the issues at stake in the debate over realism, and, in particular, to vindicate the connection between the concerns of contemporary debate with more traditional metaphysical questions. But what is the status of the account that has been offered?

Can we, to begin with, claim to have offered an *analysis* of the doctrine of realism? Not, at any rate, if we take the aim of analysis to be the provision of a philosophically respectable equivalent of the *analysandum*, couched in unimpeachable terms and ironing out any unclarities in the original, and so establishing its metaphysical and epistemological credentials—not, in short, if we take analysis to aspire to the standards Frege wanted his account of the natural numbers to meet. For the apparatus that our account invokes, specifically the 'possible individual epistemic standpoints' and our various vaguenesses about what sorts of them exist and the ways in which they certify, is hardly suited to figure in the *analysans* of so ambitious an analysis. But the goals of analysis can be set less vaultingly, and our account may perhaps be fairly counted an analysis by these less exacting standards. Thus, the account of necessity in terms of possible worlds and an accessibility relation between them provides, in one good sense of the term, an 'analysis' of the notion, despite the tendentious nature of its analytical apparatus which, indeed, clearly raises many interpretative problems of the same kind as are raised by the *analysandum*. The point of an analysis of this sort is not to establish the credentials of the *analysandum* beyond doubt, by resting it on a conceptually firmer footing. Rather, it is to locate the target concept within a wider conceptual system, with the aim that, even if the denizens of the conceptual neighbourhood in which it is thereby located share some of the murkier features of the target itself, still a map of the neighbourhood can reveal features of the target which are obscured if it is studied in isolation. In the modal case, a payoff is the diagnosis and deeper understanding of the ambiguities in the senses of necessity articulated by the various modal axiom systems. In the realism case, our claim will be that discussion of realism using the apparatus of certification and epistemic standpoints reveals and elaborates the connection of realism with objective truth, and the further connections of the latter with bivalence, classical logic, and epistemic independence.

An analysis of the second, lower-grade variety thus has virtues of its own. But these virtues can be magnified if the analysis can be built upon, and converted into an analysis of the first and higher grade, by showing how the apparatus of the *analysans* can, after all, be rendered respectable by the highest philosophical standards. This is the heroic task which David Lewis undertakes in the modal case; with what success it is beside our present brief to determine. A similar conversion might be attempted for our own lower-grade analysis, but no such attempt will be made here. The apparatus we have invoked is, hopefully, clear enough for the purposes of the lower-grade analysis in which we have indulged; but the task of polishing it up to meet the standards of full metaphysical and epistemological respectability is one we may well, and with considerable justification, judge to be hopeless.

As we shall see below (Chapter 6), others may be read as taking a more optimistic view of this matter. The important point is that we need not be committed to the possibility of conversion to a higher grade to make use of our lower-grade analysis. Rather, we can use it as the basis of an 'explication' of the problem of realism, in Quine's technical sense of the term.[6] Explication involves, not (like analysis in both its forms) the spinning-out

---

[6] W. V. Quine, *Word and Object* (Cambridge: Technology Press of the Massachusetts Institute of Technology, 1960), § 53.

of a concept in greater conceptual detail, but rather the *replacement* of a concept which we find wanting by the best philosophical standards by a hygienic new substitute, one serving the same purposes as the old one, but more suited to proper philosophical debate and evaluation. In devising such an explication, we must, in Quine's words, 'fix on the particular functions of the unclear expression that make it worth troubling about, and then devise a substitute, clear and couched in terms to our liking, that fills those functions'.[7]

Applying this to the case of realism, the first part of Quine's recipe calls for the identification of the critical functions and doctrines that explication of that notion should preserve. And evidently our low-grade analysis can be put to work to do just that: thus, we may propose that what is important about realism is that it is a doctrine about a set of sentences, holding that they are objectively true, where objective truth is bivalent, epistemically independent (in the sense that an ideal theory may still fail by its standard), and intersubjectively certifiable. (In selecting just these properties we may, perhaps justly, be charged with playing favourites. Still, they are distinguished ones: one involved in the original motivation for our analysis, and the others important formal and material properties which emerge as characteristic as that motivation is pressed to its limit in the construction of the Hierarchy of Certification.) Any doctrine preserving these theses we may deem worthy of the name of realism, in the explicated sense; failure to preserve other theses associated with traditional realism can be dismissed as a Quinean 'don't care'.

It remains to complete Quine's task, and actually 'devise a substitute, clear and couched in terms to our liking', which will play the role assigned to objective truth in the above account. Note that the task of doing so can hardly be separated from defending the thesis that realism is actually true, at least as far as a large class of sentences is concerned; for it would hardly be possible to defend the credentials of some candidate as a genuine truth-predicate with the desired properties unless it could be shown to have some genuine and wide application within language. The rest of this book will be devoted to assessing the chances of defending realism, in the explicated sense. More precisely, our concern will be with the assessment of the claims of *global* realism, construed as realism about a maximal consistent set of sentences of a given language—the doctrine that precisely one of each pair of a sentence and its negation is objectively true. The task is, thus, to assess the philosophical respectability of a notion of truth meeting the standards for objectivity, and arguably capable of such global application. Of course, we have seen that there may be special reasons for abandoning

[7] Ibid., 258–9.

global realism, reasons to do with special features of some sentences in the language. But we shall not be concerned in the sequel to cavil at global realism on the grounds of concessions which may be wrung from it on the basis of such local peculiarities. We have bigger fish to fry, and more general considerations to advance. Accordingly, we shall profit from simplifications to be gained by gearing our discussion to realism in its most ambitious and unqualified form. At the same time, we should bear in mind that a realistic realism would probably incorporate qualifications of detail which disappear from view from the lofty perspective we have chosen to adopt.

PART II

MODEL THEORY AND CORRESPONDENCE

3

Putnam's Model-theoretic Arguments

Realism, according to the findings of Part One, is a doctrine about the objectivity of truth. As such, it makes substantive philosophical claims, which require elaboration and defence; and the natural place to look for these is in the analysis of truth, seeking to establish firm credentials for a notion of objective truth with global range. Traditional affiliations suggest a congenial underpinning may be sought in the Correspondence Theory of Truth. But the view put forward in Chapter 1 is that we lack a clear enough conception either of the notion of correspondence, or of the domain of correspondent facts, for these to bear the burden which the Correspondence Theory places upon them in explicating the notion of truth. Rather, the direction of explanation flows in the opposite direction: to the extent that the notions of correspondence and of facts are useful at all, they are to be understood in terms of truth, or, more precisely, in terms of truth as model theory explains it.[1] This suggests that realism should look for its foundations not in the outmoded Correspondence Theory, but rather in the model theory which supplants its role. After all, model theory apparently proceeds in the spirit of the Correspondence Theory, seeking to explicate truth in terms of the relations between language and extralinguistic structures; and if it can do so without importing the metaphysical baggage characteristic of the theory it displaces, more power to its elbow.

Seminal work by Putnam, however, in what we might with more confidence call his 'middle period' if we were better informed about the number of periods to come, suggests that any promise for setting realism on model-theoretic foundations is illusory, and, indeed, that fundamental results of model theory are, in fact, actually hostile to the tenets of realism. This part is devoted to the examination, and ultimately the defence, of this currently unfashionable view.

---

[1] For attempts by the present author to explore one way in which notions of (I-relative) correspondence and facts can be extracted from a model-theoretic account of truth-on-I, see 'States of Affairs', 263–84; or *Modes of Occurrence*, ch. 2.

3.1 ROUNDUP OF THE USUAL SUSPECTS

Exegesis of Putnam is never an entirely straightforward matter. Still, it seems tolerably clear that we may distinguish three arguments (or argument families), the origins at least of which are to be found in Putnam's writings, and which merit consideration and evaluation. (These arguments, it should be emphasized, are directed against *alleged* features of realism, and it will not always be apparent that these are genuine features of that doctrine as Part One construed it. The next section will be devoted to the task of initial assessment of the claims of the arguments this section expounds; and part of that task will be to evaluate the legitimacy of their targets.)

First, let us review the basic concepts of model-theoretic semantics. (Such a review will be useful to standardize the terminology and symbolism of the present discussion. Readers totally unfamiliar with model-theoretic ideas may like to consult the appropriate pages of a standard logic text for fuller explanation.[2]) Let L be a first-order language, formulated with individual constants but without function symbols (so we shall suppose, as a convenient but eliminable simplification), and with conjunction, negation, and universal quantification as its logical primitives. Then an *interpretation* I for L is a pair $\langle D_I, \mathrm{Ref}_I \rangle$, where D_I (the *domain* of I) is a nonempty set of objects, and Ref_I (the *reference relation* of I) is a function which assigns, to each individual constant of L, some element of D_I, and to each n-place predicate-letter of L, an n-ary relation over D_I (set of n-tuples of members of D_I). An interpretation I for L is *normal* if L contains the identity predicate $=$, and Ref_I assigns to that predicate the identity relation over D_I; trivially, I also counts as normal if L does not contain the identity predicate. Subscripts indexing D and Ref to I will be suppressed in the sequel when ambiguity seems unlikely to result.

Let s be a denumerable sequence of elements of D. Then we define when s *satisfies* a formula A of L according to I—in symbols, when $I, s \models$ A— by the following induction:

(1) If A is atomic $= P^n \tau_1 \ldots \tau_n$, then
$I, s \models$ A iff $\langle \mathrm{Val}(s, \tau_1) \ldots \mathrm{Val}(s, \tau_n) \rangle \in \mathrm{Ref}(P^n)$

where, if τ_i is an individual constant, $\mathrm{Val}(s, \tau_j) = \mathrm{Ref}(\tau_i)$; and, if τ_i is an individual variable—specifically, that coming in the j-th place in some

[2] See e.g., Geoffrey Hunter, *Metalogic: An Introduction to the Metatheory of Standard First-order Logic* (Berkeley and Los Angeles: University of California Press, 1971); or Elliott Mendelson, *Introduction to Mathematical Logic* (Princeton, NJ: Van Nostrand, 1964).

standard alphabetical ordering of L's variables—then $\text{Val}(s,\tau_i)$ is the object occupying the j-th place in s.

(2) If A is ¬B for some B, then
   $I, s \models$ A iff not: $I, s \models$ B
(3) If A is (B & C) for some B and C, then
   $I, s \models$ A iff $I, s \models$ B and $I, s \models$ C
(4) If A is $\forall v$B, for some formula B and variable v—specifically, the j-th variable in the alphabetical ordering—then
   $I, s \models$ A iff $I, s\# \models$ B for each j-variant $s\#$ of s
where $s\#$ is a j-variant of s iff s and $s\#$ have the same objects in all places save possibly the j-th.

We now say that A is *true* according to I—in symbols, $I \models A$—iff $I, s \models$ A for every s. Finally, we define a *model* for a set Γ of sentences of L as an interpretation for L according to which all elements of Γ are true; and take a first-order *theory* of L to be a set of L's sentences which is deductively closed (under some standard proof theory).

Preliminaries in place, let us return to the adumbration of model-theoretic arguments alleged to undermine realism. The first and simplest of these we may dub the *Argument from Completeness*.[3] The model-theoretic result on which it trades is Gödel's—a proof will be found in standard texts:

COMPLETENESS THEOREM: Any consistent first-order theory has a model (and a normal model).

Armed with this result, we can argue as follows: consider an ideal theory T^*, crafted by generations of superscientists. Being ideal, T^* accords at least as well as any competitor with the methodological constraints on theories—for example, its mix of ontological parsimony and conceptual simplicity is at least as impressive as that of any alternative; further, it meets all 'operational constraints', i.e., it jibes with all empirical evidence, past, present, and future. Meeting these lofty standards presupposes that T^* also possesses the humble virtue of consistency. Suppose also that first-order resources suffice to express T^*—Quine has, after all, made a strong case for thinking such means are enough to say anything reputable science needs to say. Then by the Completeness Theorem, T^* has a model M^*. So, though realism holds that T^*, for all its ideality, may be false, we have established that all of its theses are true, in one clear sense of 'true'; for all of them are true-on-M^*.

---

[3] See Hilary Putnam, 'Models and Reality', in his *Realism and Reason: Philosophical Papers Volume 3* (Cambridge and New York: Cambridge University Press, 1983), 13.

Whilst the Argument from Completeness uses model theory to argue that there is no room for the ideal theory to be *false* in the way realism requires, the next two arguments suggest instead that model theory shows there are too many ways, by the lights of realism, in which a true theory, ideal or otherwise, can be true. The first of this pair we shall call the *Argument from Cardinality*; whilst its Putnamian credentials are shakier than either of its cousins, it hovers in the background of the discussion in 'Models and Reality', and makes explicit appeal to the Löwenheim–Skolem Theorem, whose relevance to the realism issue that paper advertises. This theorem, which concerns the cardinality of models (i.e., the cardinality of their domains), comes in an Upward and a Downward version. The Upward version is that directly involved here (though the Downward version is indirectly implicated through an intimate connexion between its proof and that of the Completeness Theorem):

UPWARD LÖWENHEIM–SKOLEM THEOREM: If a set Γ of first-order sentences has, for each natural number n, a normal model whose cardinality is at least n, then it has, for each infinite cardinal κ greater than or equal to the cardinality of Γ, a normal model of cardinality κ.

(Again, a proof can be found in standard texts.) Assume now we are dealing with a true theory T written in a first-order language with a countable vocabulary. (This is hardly a drastic restriction, since there are well-known reasons for thinking that any language we could learn must have a vocabulary which is not just countable, but finite. Accordingly, it is also a restriction even the ideal theory T^* can be assumed to meet, if we suppose it is one capable of being forged by beings who implement our capacities ideally well, as distinct from transcending them altogether.) Then T, as a set of sentences of such a language, is at most denumerable; and, being a deductively closed set, it is at least denumerable; so T is precisely denumerable. Further, since T is true, it is consistent; so by Completeness it has at least one normal model. There is, moreover, no finite upper bound on the cardinality of these models. (For suppose there were such an upper bound n. Since T is true, it will remain consistent if augmented by a further truth. Such a truth is that there are at least $n + 1$ objects—for example, numbers. Augment T to $T+$ by adding this truth, expressed using quantifiers, logical connectives, and identity. Then $T+$ has a normal model, which must have a cardinality of at least $n + 1$; and since $T+$ extends T, this is also a model of T, contradicting the supposition that n is an upper bound on such models.) Therefore, by Upward Löwenheim–Skolem, T has models of every infinite cardinality.

But realism, it is urged, requires that there is a *unique* total state of the world which makes for the truth of T. Now, models of T are not themselves total states of the world. To start with, as models of the language of T, they will be subject to limits imposed by the expressive power of that language, and so cannot pretend to be total. More importantly, models are abstract sets, whereas states of the world (or, at least, of its nonabstract regions) are concrete. Still, a model of T is an abstract skeleton of a total world state, abstracting from that state the totality of objects which comprise the world, and a structure of relations over that totality which is necessary and sufficient for the theses of T to be true. Now, models of T of the sort we have demonstrated to exist, so drastically different as to diverge even in cardinality, cannot even by the loosest conceptual standards be counted as abstracted skeletons of a single total world state. So, it is maintained, the existence of such models for T contradicts realism's demand for a unique truth-making state of the world to which T corresponds.

A final argument, turning once more on an alleged *embarrass de richesses* of truth-makers, derives from Putnam's later presentations of model-theoretic problems for realism in *Reason, Truth, and History*.[4] This one we shall call the *Argument from Permutation*. Let a *permutation* on a nonempty set S be a one–one function from S onto S. Where π is a permutation on the domain D_I of interpretation I for L, let the permutation $\pi(I)$ of I be that interpretation I^* of L such that:

1. $D_{I^*} = D_I$
2. $\mathrm{Ref}_{I^*}(c) = \pi(\mathrm{Ref}_I(c))$, for each individual constant c of L
3. $\mathrm{Ref}_{I^*}(P^n) = \{\langle \pi(x_1), \ldots, \pi(x_n)\rangle | \langle x_1, \ldots, x_n\rangle \in \mathrm{Ref}_I(P^n)\}$, for each n-place predicate-letter P^n of L.

Then we have the following:

PERMUTATION THEOREM. For each formula A, interpretation I, and permutation π of D_I, $I \models$ A iff $\pi(I) \models$ A.

(*Proof.* Where s is a denumerable sequence of elements of D_I, let $\pi(s)$ be the sequence resulting by replacing each element x of s by $\pi(x)$. By induction on the length of A, show that we have $I, s \models$ A iff $\pi(I), \pi(s) \models$ A. Derive the result as a consequence.)

Let T once more be a true theory, written in a first-order language. This time the tenet of realism with which model theory allegedly conflicts is that the truth of T's theses is underwritten by a unique and determinate reference relation obtaining between the individual constants and predicate-letters of its language and the world. But the Permutation Theorem shows that, even if we can somehow discount the problems raised by the Cardinality Argument, and settle on models with one fixed domain as those

⁴ Hilary Putnam, *Reason, Truth, and History* (Cambridge and New York: Cambridge University Press, 1981).

which can truly claim to be abstractions of the world—even then, there are as many different reference relations holding between the subsentential expressions of *T*'s language and the world as there are nontrivial permutations of the fixed domain, all of which underwrite the truth of exactly the same sentences, and, hence, equally subserve the truth of the theses of *T*. There being no basis for preference between these reference relations, realism's doctrine that there is a unique, privileged such relation is apparently discredited.

[*Digression:* The Permutation Theorem just appealed to goes back, in a truth-theoretic rather than a model-theoretic form, to John Wallace,[5] and is discussed by Davidson;[6] in its model-theoretic version it is stated, proved and discussed by Bob Hale and Crispin Wright[7] under the title 'Weak Permutation'. It is not, however, the result on which Putnam depends in his discussion in *Reason, Truth, and History*. Instead, both in his informal discussion in the text and in the more formal Appendix, he moves beyond the framework of first-order model theory in which we have operated, and into the territory of world-based modal semantics.

To follow him, we must accordingly expand our own framework and terminology. Let a *world-interpretation I* for a first-order language *L* be a quadruple $\langle D_I, W_I, \phi_I, \text{Ref}_I \rangle$ where—omitting the indexing subscripts—D is, as before, a nonempty set of objects, W is a nonempty set (intuitively, a set of possible worlds), ϕ is a function assigning, to each element w of W a nonempty subset of D (intuitively, the set of objects which inhabit w), and Ref is a function assigning appropriate world-relative referents to the proper symbols of *L*—so that $\text{Ref}(c, w)$ is some member of $\phi(w)$ for each individual constant c of *L*, and $\text{Ref}(P^n, w)$ is a set of n-tuples of elements of $\phi(w)$ for each n-place predicate P^n of *L*. We can now extend the definitions of satisfaction and truth of a formula A according to *I*, where *I* is a first-order interpretation, to obtain definitions of notions of satisfaction and truth of A relative, this time, to a world w, and according to a world-interpretation *I* (in symbols, $I,s,w \models A$ and $I,w \models A$, respectively). (Take satisfiers as denumerably long sequences of elements of $\phi(w)$. Then just add a world-parameter throughout the clauses of the old definition of

[5] John Wallace, ' "Only in the Context of a Sentence Do Words Have Any Meaning" ', in P. A. French, T. E. Uehling, and H. K. Wettstein (eds.), *Midwest Studies in Philosophy 2: Studies in the Philosophy of Language* (Morris: University of Minnesota Press, 1977), 305–25.

[6] Donald Davidson, 'The Inscrutability of Reference', in his *Inquiries into Truth and Interpretation*, 227–41.

[7] Bob Hale and Crispin Wright, 'Putnam's Model-theoretic Argument against Metaphysical Realism', in Bob Hale and Crispin Wright (eds.), *A Companion to the Philosophy of Language* (Oxford: Blackwell, 1997), 427–57, at 448–9.

satisfaction, and define truth-in-w on the old pattern, as satisfaction-in-w by all sequences.) Now let a *regular* permutation π of D, according to I, be a permutation which never maps any inhabitant of a world onto an object which does not itself inhabit the same world—i.e., one in which for each x in D and w in W, if $x \in \varphi(w)$, then $\pi(x) \in \varphi(w)$. Then (restoring index-ing subscripts), where π is such a permutation of D_I, let the permutation $\pi(I)$ of a world-interpretation I for L be that world-interpretation I^* for L such that

(a1) $D_{I^*} = D_I$, $W_{I^*} = W_I$, $\varphi_{I^*} = \varphi_I$
(b1) $\text{Ref}_{I^*}(c, w) = \pi(\text{Ref}_I(c, w))$, for each individual constant c of L and $w \in W_I$
(c1) $\text{Ref}_{I^*}(P^n, w) = \{\langle \pi(x_1), \ldots, \pi(x_n)\rangle | \langle x_1, \ldots, x_n\rangle \in \text{Ref}_I(P^n, w)\}$, for each n-place predicate-letter P^n of L and $w \in W_I$.

And now the modal result on which Putnam relies[8] can be stated:

STRONG PERMUTATION THEOREM. Let I be a world-interpretation for L and π a permutation of D_I which is regular according to I. Then for each formula A of L and $w \in W_I$, $I, w \models A$ iff $\pi(I), w \models A$.

Proof of this parallels that of the unadorned Permutation Theorem.

The pertinent question is whether this more complicated permutation result presents sharper difficulties for realism than does its simpler prede-cessor. Since Putnam never bothers stating the simple Permutation The-orem, the issue is not one he ever explicitly addresses; still, his discussion makes it clear that he regards the world apparatus deployed in his favoured, strong version of the theorem as endowing it with additional philosophical weight. (Cf. *Reason, Truth and History*, 33: '[N]o view which only fixes the truth-values of whole sentences can fix reference, even if it fixes truth-values for sentences *in every possible world*' (italics Putnam's), where the last clause emphasizes the significance attached to the role of worlds.) Bob Hale and Crispin Wright do address the comparative issue explicitly. On their dia-gnosis,[9] the issue turns on the precise form of the realist commitment to a tie between truth and the determinacy of reference. This should properly be interpreted as the view that sentences have the truth-*conditions* (and not merely the truth-*values*) which they do in virtue of a unique, determinate reference-relation holding between their subsentential parts and appro-priate bits of the world. If—following Putnam, according to Hale and Wright—we interpret the truth-condition of a sentence, according to an

  [8] *Reason, Truth, and History*, 217–18; and see Hale and Wright, 'Putnam's Model-theoretic Argument', 449–51, on which presentation the present one is modelled.
  [9] 'Putnam's Model-theoretic Argument', 428 and 448.

interpretation, as the set of worlds in which that sentence is true according to that interpretation, then the Strong Permutation Theorem asserts, in effect, that there can be interpretations assigning the same truth-*conditions* to all the wffs of *L*, yet based on divergent reference-relations; and this clashes with the claims of realism, properly construed. But the unadorned Permutation Theorem says no more than that there can be interpretations of *L* agreeing in their assignments of truth-*values* to its wffs, but incorporating different reference-relations; and this is nothing realism need deny.

This evaluation seems, however, to depend on an unsustainably weak construal of the significance of the simple Permutation Theorem. To speak of 'truth-conditions' is to deploy a term of art which can be cashed in many ways, and to do so by appeal to possible worlds is to enmesh it more deeply with murky ontology than many find appealing. Another way to cash it would be to say that two interpretations assign the same truth-conditions to a wff if they not only assign the same truth-value to the wff, but *demonstrably* do so, on the basis of set-theoretically provable properties of the interpretations, and of the semantic rules which govern them; and with truth-conditions so construed, the humble Permutation Theorem comes to have all the significance previously held to be reserved to the strong version.

Upon reflection, it should be clear that very little can hang on the difference between the two theorems. For the strong version comes from the simple Permutation Theorem just by adding some superfluous structure onto interpretations, and then tacking an idle world-parameter onto all semantic predicates in the statement of the theorem, and in its proof; and it is entirely implausible to think that anything of genuine philosophical significance can turn on such superficial decoration. Accordingly, the argument based on the more austere result will be taken as canonical for the present discussion. This is not, however, to deny all merit to the strong version of the theorem. By introducing world apparatus, it paves the way for an extension of the Permutation Theorem to the case of languages which enrich first-order apparatus by adding various forms of modal operator—i.e., to cases where the world-parameter ceases to sit idle, and the additional structure added to interpretations is exploited in forging new clauses for the inductive definition of satisfaction, to handle the additional operators.[10] So the complications of world apparatus may come into their own further down the track, to combat an objection that the Permutation Argument somehow depends on an illegitimate concentration on the pure first-order case. But when the first-order case *is* the one under consideration, the apparatus of

[10] 'Putnam's Model-theoretic Argument', 451–2; and compare Putnam, *Reason, Truth, and History*, 218, Third Comment.

worlds merely complicates discussion, without compensating illumination. *End of digression.*]

3.2 SORTING SHEEP FROM GOATS

Let us return, first, to the Argument from Cardinality. One point on which it may appear vulnerable is in its breezy assumption that there are more than finitely many objects, so that we can be assured that a true theory T can always, and for every n, be consistently and truly augmented by a statement to the effect that there are at least $n + 1$ objects. That assumption was justified, when the argument was sketched above, by pointing to the numbers. To the same end, appeal could be made to sequences of sets—if you prefer, *other* sequences of sets, accepting the set-theoretic account of the numbers—such as i, $\{i\}$, $\{\{i\}\}$, ... for some individual i. But both of these may seem a bit of a cheat. How, it may be asked, does the argument fare if we stop counting numbers, and abstract entities in general, among the objects?

In the absence of cogent argument for doing so, however, there is no real reason we should feel impelled to pander to this prejudice for the concrete. It is true that complications we have hitherto suppressed, in the interests of simplifying exposition—complications to which we shall later return—require that the theories T we are considering, be they ideal or merely true, and the languages in which they are cast, fall short of the resources to express *all* the facts about the abstract world, in particular of its set-theoretic component. But that does not mean the abstract universe should be ruled out of consideration entirely, or even that we should limit attention merely to a finite fragment thereof. Further, even if, carried away by a spirit of concessionary tolerance, we do choose to concentrate on the concrete, it is by no means obvious we are left with a finite totality. It is at least arguable, for example, that the concrete world is best conceptualized as containing continuum-many concrete space–time points. All in all, realists would be ill advised to leave the fate of their cherished metaphysic to turn on a commitment to the finitude of the concrete, both because of the uncertain credentials of that commitment itself, and because even if justified it is highly dubious that it is enough to turn the Argument from Cardinality.

A more telling criticism of that argument is that it is based on a false construal of the commitments of realism. For it finds its target by saddling realism with the view that the truth of a theory derives from its reflecting a unique total state of the world. Such a doctrine is presumably derivative from the Correspondence Theory of Truth, that the truth of each constituent statement of the true theory consists in its correspondence to a fact. But we have been at pains to divorce realism from reliance upon this suspect theory; its primordial commitment is to the objectivity of truth, and its ties to the Correspondence Theory are limited to the extent that the claims of that theory can be rendered respectable by model theory. From this perspective, it is indeed an interesting, perhaps mildly surprising, result that the model theory should teach, via its Completeness and Löwenheim–Skolem Theorems, that the notion of truth as it applies to a single theory should so diverge from that the old Correspondence Theory enshrines as to be explicable in a number of nonequivalent ways, each bringing with them their own different accounts of correspondence and of correspondent facts. But it is not a result which bears on the core doctrines of realism, that truth is bivalent, non-epistemic, and publicly certifiable—or, in a word, objective.

Similar remarks apply to the Argument from Permutation. For that argument takes as its target an alleged commitment by realism to a unique, determinate reference relation obtaining between subsentential expressions and appropriate nonlinguistic items. But if, as was maintained in Part One, realism's primordial commitment is to the objectivity of truth, this target is genuine only in so far as a case can be made for thinking objective truth must be subserved by such a determinate reference relation; failing that, interpretations based on distinct reference relations, but on which sentences are assigned equivalent truth-conditions, can be regarded as encapsulating alternative, equally good, systematizations of a single notion of objective truth. Thus Hale and Wright, whilst advocates of the Argument from Permutation as the strongest of the model-theoretic arguments against realism, concede that it is impotent when realism takes shape along the lines here advocated;[11] and Davidson evidently saw the realism he espoused at the time of his papers on reference[12] as compatible with accepting the Permutation Theorem in its truth-theoretic form. (Of course, Davidson was latterly to repudiate the label of realism in his John Dewey Lectures;[13] but the connection with the repudiation of determinate reference is at best remote.)

These reflections leave the Argument from Completeness as the sole model-theoretic argument still standing which engages directly with realism as Part One conceived it. Accordingly, it is that argument which will be our principal focus in the pages to come. But even though the other two arguments are thus dismissed as of less than immediate relevance to the

[11] Hale and Wright, 'Putnam's Model-theoretic Argument', 447–8.
[12] Donald Davidson, 'Reality without Reference', in his *Inquiries into Truth and Interpretation*, 215–26; and 'The Inscrutability of Reference'.
[13] Donald Davidson, 'The Structure and Content of Truth', 304–9.

problem of realism, they do not miss their mark completely; for both of them serve to focus attention on the same issues as arise out of the more central Argument from Completeness. Thus, the Argument from Completeness confronts us with a model M^* which renders true all the theses of the ideal theory T^*, and, hence, with a sense of 'true'—true-on-M^*—according to which all of the theses of T^* are guaranteed to be true, apparently conflicting with realism's commitment to objectivity of truth, specifically to its epistemic independence. To rebut the argument, it is sufficient to find criteria which will rule out truth-on-M^* as providing the proper construal of truth *tout court*, as that notion applies to the language L^* of T^*; and this, in turn, will be achieved if criteria can be found for discounting the claims of M^* to be a genuine or 'intended' interpretation for L^*, where an intended interpretation I is one such that truth-on-I *is* a legitimate construal of truth *tout court* in application to L^*. Now the Arguments from Cardinality and from Permutation invite the same distinction between intended interpretations and the rest, the former in order to disqualify from serious consideration interpretations with the 'wrong' cardinality, the latter those with the 'wrong' reference relation.

The two arguments are, however, on a different footing when it comes to evaluating the constraints they suggest for sorting intended interpretations from the rest. Reflection on the Argument from Cardinality suggests some sort of Cardinality Constraint: an intended interpretation of a language L in which is cast a theory T is one with a cardinality κ somehow determined by the details of L and T. It seems, however, that no such Cardinality Constraint could turn the trick against the Argument from Completeness, by ruling out M^* as an intended interpretation of the language L^* of the ideal theory T^*. For suppose the chosen Cardinality Constraint ruled that an intended interpretation of L^* must have cardinality κ. We may suppose κ is infinite, for reasons given above (there is no finite upper bound on the cardinality of models of a true theory). But then, even if M^* itself is of some cardinality other than κ, the Upward Löwenheim–Skolem Theorem assures us that T^* will also have another model M^{**} which *does* have that cardinality; and the proposed Cardinality Constraint will be useless to rule this one out as an unintended interpretation of L^*. On the other hand, consideration of the Argument from Permutation suggests that unintended interpretations might be filtered out by means of a Reference Constraint: the reference relation of an intended interpretation for L must meet some specified condition, intended to insure the 'right' referents are assigned to subsentential expressions of L. And there is no reason to think that such a constraint, suitably formulated, might not also serve to defeat the Argument from Completeness, by disqualifying M^* as an intended interpretation of L^*.

It may seem, however, that the adoption of a Reference Constraint to filter out unintended interpretations will be entirely arbitrary and unmotivated unless we can find an argument of the sort we earlier found wanting, connecting a determinate reference relation with the notion of objective truth. If such an argument could be found, of course, the claims of the Argument from Permutation as a direct attack on realism would be reinstated. Thus, it may appear, the Reference Constraint tactic is not merely one which reflection on the Argument from Permutation may prompt; rather, its credentials and those of that Argument stand together. In fact, however, independent motivation of the Reference Constraint tactic is perfectly possible. In particular, it may be motivated by considerations connected with truth *in general*, as distinguished from *objective* truth. Thus, it may be argued, any notion worthy of serious consideration as a notion of truth—be it bivalent, epistemically independent, and publicly certifiable, or not—must be underpinned, if not by a determinate reference relation, at least by one meeting the conditions spelt out in the favoured Reference Constraint. One who takes this line can no longer view the Permutation *Theorem* with the lofty equanimity we pictured earlier, and regard 'interpretations based on different reference relations but assigning equivalent truth-conditions as encapsulating alternative, equally good systematizations of a single notion of objective truth'—for not all of them will encapsulate good systematizations of *any* notion of truth at all (assuming the favoured Reference Constraint is sufficiently discriminating to distinguish between the reference relation of an interpretation and of its arbitrary permutations). At the same time, the *Argument* from Permutation itself, which seeks to deploy the Permutation Theorem against a specifically realist doctrine, still lacks a genuine target. For the association of truth with a constrained notion of reference is, on this view, not local to the realist.

3.3 REDUCTIONIST REFERENCE CONSTRAINTS

Reference Constraints have loomed large in the literature as a preferred method for filtering out unintended interpretations, thanks, in part, to their natural connections with the Argument from Permutation on which Putnam has placed so much emphasis. But imposing a Reference Constraint is, independent of such historical vagaries, in any case a natural device to consider; after all, the reference relation is one of just two of the components which go to build an interpretation, and, as such, is a natural focus for a filtering strategy. True, other methods suggest themselves. We might, for example, consider concentrating on the other element of an interpretation, its domain. Our ruminations on the Argument from Cardinality suggest, to be sure, that realism may not be entitled to disqualify an interpretation as second rate or unintended on the grounds of the cardinality of the domain; but perhaps, after all, there is some other criterion whereby the domain of an intended interpretation can be circumscribed. Or we might aim for a constraint operating somehow jointly on both reference relation and domain; or consider a constraint which seeks in some fashion to evaluate an interpretation directly at the level of its output in assignments of truth-values to sentences, rather than by taking as the primary target either or both of the interpretative elements whereby these assignments are determined. Still, we must begin somewhere, and considering possible Reference Constraints is the way to do so. A further natural idea is to found such a constraint on an *analysis* and *reduction* of the relation of reference in some favoured, purportedly more basic, terms; and then to require that an intended interpretation is one whose assignment of referents to proper symbols accords with that determined by the relation of the reduction.

A dominant motive in Putnam's early writings is that words gain their meanings through the causal interactions between speakers and the world, suggesting that a Reference Constraint might be based on a causal reduction of reference. The central idea of such a reduction, in so far as it concerns individual constants or names, is that a primitive association is established between name and referent in a primordial first use of the name, involving a direct causal interaction between referent and user—an act of baptism, in the Kripkean version of the story. Other users of the language then come to use the name to pick out the same referent, in a way causally dependent on the usage of others, and ultimately on the first, primordial use. Much fun is to be had by adherents of this basic strategy for reduction in arguing about how it is best refined, modified, and articulated. What they have in common is the belief that there is a predicate 'Namecause(c,x,G)', definable in causal terms, and holding between a name c, object x, and group G, when and only when x is the 'true' referent of c in the language of the group G. This permits formulation of a

CAUSAL REFERENCE CONSTRAINT ON NAMES. Where L is a first-order language, I an interpretation of L, and $G(L)$ the population of users of L, then I is an intended interpretation of L only if, for each individual constant c of L,

$$\text{Ref}_I(c, x) \text{ iff Namecause}(c, x, G(L)).$$

The causal account can be generalized to encompass at least some predicates, to wit, those which encapsulate 'natural kinds'. One way of developing the idea goes something like this: the predicate is first applied to certain especially salient, stereotypical instances in circumstances involving direct causal interaction, reminiscent of those involved in baptisms in the case of names. Thereafter it is generally used in the language to be true of those things belonging to a natural kind to which the stereotypes belong; such a kind being determined by causal laws which decree natural boundaries between kindred things; and general usage being deferential to, and causally dependent on, the usage of experts on discerning the natural boundaries thus drawn. Once again, there is considerable scope for debate among adherents of the general position about the details of its refinement and implementation; but there will be general agreement among them that it is possible somehow to formulate, in broadly causal terms, a predicate 'Predcause(P,K,G)', holding between a predicate P, natural kind K, and group G when and only when P is 'correctly' construed as a predicate for the natural kind K in the language of G. This clears the way for a

CAUSAL REFERENCE CONSTRAINT ON PREDICATES. Where L is a first-order language, I an interpretation of L, and $G(L)$ the population of users of L, then I is an intended interpretation of L only if, for each predicate P of L for which Predcause is nontrivially defined,

> $\text{Ref}_I(P, X)$ iff Predcause($P, K, G(L)$) and for each x, x is a member of X iff x is of kind K.

A general *Causal Reference Constraint* can now be obtained by combining the versions for names and predicates. Applying it to the special case needed to defuse the Argument from Completeness, of course, involves a hypothetical manœuvre; for we are then asked to apply it to the case of the language L^* of the hypothetical ideal theory T^*, a language spoken by no actual population. But the moral to which it points is clear enough: nothing about the way the model M^* has been constructed gives the slightest cause to think it would satisfy a Causal Reference Constraint at any level, for a hypothetical population whose dealings with L^* replicate those of actual speakers with more familiar languages.

Despite its prominence in the literature, the causal route is not the only one to take in formulating a reductive Reference Constraint. The causal formulation took its motivation from the allegedly pivotal role of causation in semantics; but others see a similar role played by the intentions and other psychological attitudes of language users and associated behavioural dispositions, suggesting a Reference Constraint framed in such psycho-behavioural terms. At its simplest, such a constraint, formulated for singular terms, builds on the thought that the referent of a term is the object to which, by community-wide agreement, speakers intend to refer when they use the term—i.e., the object which they intend to be that relevant for determining the truth-values of sentences they utter containing the term in question, in the manner spelt out, for first-order languages at least, by the rules of model-theoretic semantics. Once again, much refinement and variation is possible. First, there is the question of explicating what 'community-wide agreement' on p among a group G amounts to. (Among suggestions are—building on Peacocke[14]—that p should be 'common knowledge' among the members of G; or—building on Lewis[15]—that action conforming to p be a convention among them, with 'convention' spelt out in terms of mutual expectations and other psychological apparatus; or, more obscurely—following Grice[16]—that such action be a 'procedure in the repertoire' of members of G.) Further, there is the issue of whether it is sufficient to talk merely of a simple intention on the part of speakers to refer to a given object in using a term, or whether more complex attitudes need to be invoked—such as, for example, a subsidiary Gricean intention that this primary simple intention be recognized by an audience. But all adherents of the general position in question will agree that there is some operator

it is K in G that

definable just in psycho-behavioural terms, which explicates the relevant sense of community-wide agreement; and some relational predicate

Namepsych(s, c, x)

definable in similar terms, and specifying the critical relation between speaker s, name c, and object x; such that when and only when x is the 'true' referent of c in the language used by group G, we have

it is K in G that, for each speaker s in G, if s utters a sentence containing c, then Namepsych(s, c, x).

Armed with a version of this schema, we can formulate a *Psycho-Behavioural Reference Constraint on Names*, by requiring that the reference relation of an intended interpretation I for a language L should assign an object x as the referent of a name c of L when and only when the favoured version of the schema holds for c, x, and $G = G(L)$, the population of speakers of L.

Just as Causal Reference Constraints could be adapted to apply to predicates as well as names, so too, and even more straightforwardly, with Psycho-Behavioural Reference Constraints. The trick will be to adapt the favoured account of the critical predicate 'Namepsych(s,c,x)' to form a

---

[14] Christopher Peacocke, 'Truth Definitions and Actual Languages', in Gareth Evans and John McDowell (eds.), *Truth and Meaning* 174.

[15] David K. Lewis, *Convention: A Philosophical Study* (Cambridge, Mass.: Harvard University Press, 1969).

[16] Paul Grice, 'Utterer's Meaning, Sentence Meaning, and Word Meaning', in his *Studies in the Way of Words* (Cambridge, Mass.: Harvard University Press, 1989), 117–37.

predicate 'Predpsych(s, P, X) so that, when and only when the set X is the 'true' extension (referent) of the predicate P in the language of the group G, we have

> it is K in G that, for each speaker s in G, if s utters a sentence containing P, then Predpsych(s, P, X).

Then we can use this schema to frame a *Psycho-Behavioural Reference Constraint on Predicates* parallel to the constraint on names above. Combining the two yields a general *Psycho-Behavioural Reference Constraint*, and it is tempting to think that in the combined form the 'only if' can be strengthened to a biconditional, since it imposes a constraint across the whole domain of the reference relation of an interpretation. (Contrast the corresponding general version of the Causal Reference Constraint, which imposes a less than total requirement on the reference of predicates.) We should, however, recall that even in its general form the Psycho-Behavioural Reference Constraint does not suffice to determine uniquely the other element of an intended interpretation, its domain; so we should strengthen to a biconditional only if happy with that consequence, and otherwise treat it only as a necessary condition for intendedness, one which needs a supplementation to restrict the acceptable domains before being strengthened to a biconditional.

3.4 TRANSLATIONAL CONSTRAINTS

The two forms of Reference Constraint so far considered are reductionistically motivated—each is based on an attempt to spell out, in the favoured causal or psycho-behavioural terms, what it is for an expression, in the language of the group G, to refer to an entity of the appropriate sort. A different sort of Reference Constraint—a *Translational Reference Constraint*, as we may style it—seeks rather to exploit structural properties of the unreduced concept of reference, in much the same way as Tarski's Convention T exploits structural properties of the unreduced concept of truth.

In framing a Translational Reference Constraint, it behoves us to be more explicit than we have been hitherto about the metalanguage *ML* in which the model-theoretic semantics of the object-language L is cast, and in which, too, our various Reference Constraints are written. Clearly, we have been using as *ML* a fragment of English, broadly construed to contain various technical devices. Specifically, a review of our practice reveals that this is a fragment containing enough set theory to go about our model-theoretic business; also, special variables and devices enabling us to discuss the syntax of L, and to form descriptions of its expressions in terms of their structure. (In fact, the device we have used to this latter end is the natural, and unobtrusive, one used in the standard logic texts, that of autonymous use.[17]) Further, we have assumed that causal, psychological, and behavioural terminology are available in *ML*, so that the Causal and Psycho-Behavioural Reference Constraints can be stated in it. Now, to permit statement of the Translational Reference Constraint, we must further assume that the metalanguage is 'expressively sufficient'. This notion we shall, for the moment, be forced to leave unsatisfactorily vague. It is intended, however, to entail that the metalanguage has enough resources to reflect term-by-term the descriptive power of the object-language, by containing translations of all its proper symbols (individual constants and predicate-letters); and also by containing 'translational' variables, i.e., variables which precisely match those of the object-language, enshrining the same notion of 'thing'. These translational variables we shall write as bold, Roman letters $\mathbf{x}, \mathbf{y}, \mathbf{z}, \ldots$, distinguishing them from the italicized general variables of the metalanguage $x, y, z, \ldots$.

The Translational Reference Constraint now arises as follows. The 'correct' reference of (say) a German name can always be given in English by using an English translation, as in

the referent of 'Wien' is Vienna.

Just so, the correct referent of an individual constant of the object-language can always be given in the metalanguage by using its translation into that language; and similarly for predicate-letters. Hence, we have the following

TRANSLATIONAL REFERENCE CONSTRAINT ON NAMES. If *L* is a first-order language, then *I* is an intended interpretation for *L* only if there is, in an expressively sufficient metalanguage, for each individual constant *c* of *L*, a true instance of the schema

$\text{Ref}_I(^{**}) = \underline{\quad}$

in which '**' is replaced by a structural description of *c*, and '__' by a translation of *c* into the metalanguage.

And along with this goes the

TRANSLATIONAL REFERENCE CONSTRAINT ON PREDICATES. If *L* is a first-order language, then *I* is an intended interpretation for *L* only if there is, in an expressively sufficient metalanguage, for each *n*-place predicate-letter *P* of *L*, a true instance of the schema

$\text{Ref}_I(^{**}) = \{\langle \mathbf{x}_1 \ldots \mathbf{x}_n \rangle \mid \underline{\quad} \mathbf{x}_1 \ldots \mathbf{x}_n \underline{\quad}\}$

---

[17] See Church, *Introduction*, 58–63.

in which '**' is replaced by a structural description of P, and '$\_\_\mathbf{x}_1 \ldots \mathbf{x}_n\_\_$' by a translation of $P(\mathbf{x}_1 \ldots \mathbf{x}_n)$ into the metalanguage.

A general *Translational Reference Constraint* is then found by combining these two. As with the general version of the reductionist Psycho-Behavioural Reference Constraint, the question arises as to whether it should be strengthened to a biconditional, raising once again the issue of the extent to which an intended interpretation must be constrained in its selection of domain. This is a matter to which we shall return.

Meanwhile, we may note that there are features of this Translational Reference Constraint which distinguish it from the other reference constraints we have discussed, besides the fact that, unlike them, it is not motivated by a reductionist view of reference. One such feature is that it is a single constraint, schematically stated; unlike the others, it does not come in many versions, depending on the details of implementation which are favoured. More importantly, it does not compete with the others in the same way they compete with each other. True, there is perhaps no formal incompatibility between a Causal Reference Constraint and a Psycho-Behavioural one—no formal reason why, for example, the 'correct' reference of names, as determined by the preferred story of the crucial causal connections, should not in all cases coincide with the 'correct' reference as determined by a favoured psycho-behavioural account—but it would seem to be a staggering coincidence should this turn out to be so. Rather, the two approaches conflict in their assessment of what is essential to reference, and we should expect at most one to give acceptable results. By contrast, it should come as no surprise if the 'correct' referent as determined by one of the other two approaches should coincide with the Translational Reference Constraint by vindicating the bland truisms on which it insists; rather, that is exactly what we should expect to happen, if either of those approaches really is on the right track. Far from competing with the other constraints, it seems, the Translational Reference Constraint lays down a criterion of adequacy for these other, more ambitious, Reference Constraints to meet: they can succeed in specifying the 'right' referent only if they deliver results also conforming to the Translational Reference Constraint. For this reason, too, the Translational Constraint merits outright and unconditional endorsement, whereas its more ambitious colleagues depend for their credentials on reductionist programmes which, however worthy they may appear in the eyes of their devotees, run a risk of discreditation commensurate with their ambition.

A question which now arises is that of whether another Translational Constraint on intended interpretations can be framed at the level of sentential truth, rather than at the level of subsentential reference just considered.

The idea is a natural one, given the Tarskian paradigm which inspired the introduction of translation as a tool for forging new constraints; and we noted at the outset that constraints on intended interpretations need not confine themselves to restricting the reference relation, but could rather impose direct requirements on the way such interpretations assign truth-values to sentences. Moreover, framing such a constraint seems straightforward enough:

TRANSLATIONAL TRUTH CONSTRAINT. I is an intended interpretation for a first-order language L iff there is, in an expressively sufficient metalanguage, for each sentence S of L, a true instance of the schema

$$I \models^{**} \text{iff} \underline{\qquad}$$

in which '**' is replaced by a structural description of S, and '___' by a translation of S into the metalanguage.

We shall refer to an instance of the indicated schema in which '**' is replaced, as before, by a structural description of S, and '___' by any sentence of the metalanguage not containing semantic vocabulary relativized to I, as a T_I-sentence for S, and as a *translational* T_I-sentence if the sentence replacing '___' is a translation of S into the metalanguage. So the Translational Truth Constraint could be rephrased like this: I is an intended interpretation for a first-order language L iff there is, in an expressively sufficient metalanguage, for each sentence S of L, a true translational T_I-sentence for S.

Clearly, 'expressive sufficiency', for the purposes of this latest Constraint, must include the requirement that the metalanguage contain translations of all sentences of the object-language. That this requirement is fulfilled is guaranteed by what we have already required of a metalanguage which is to be expressively sufficient to subserve the needs of the Translational Reference Constraint, namely that it should contain translations of the proper terms of the object-language along with translational variables. For then the metalanguage will contain not just translations of sentences of the object-language but *canonical* translations thereof; where a canonical translation A# of a wff A is defined by the provisions that (i) if A is atomic, A# comes from A by replacing its proper symbols by translations thereof; (ii) if A is ¬B, A# is ¬[B#] for some B#; (iii) if A is (B&C), A# is (B#&C#) for some B# and C#; (iv) if A is ∀vB, A# is ∀vB# for some B#.

It will not go unnoticed that it has been seen fit to cast this Translational Truth Constraint (TTC for short) as a biconditional. That seems right, since what it does is to spell out, in more precise terms, the intuitive idea that an intended interpretation is one which assigns its truth-values to the sentences of L in a way according with the true meanings of those sentences. Grounded as it is on a sure foundation of bland truisms, it appears moreover to merit the same unconditional endorsement we earlier accorded to the general form of the Translational Reference Constraint (TRC). But how, precisely, do the two relate?

Let us ask first whether an interpretation meeting the condition for intendedness set by TRC also satisfies that set by TTC. If so, that would warrant elevating TRC also into a biconditional; but when we posed the question earlier of whether such elevation was warranted, misgivings were expressed that its necessary condition on intendedness may need supplementation by some constraint on domains, before being allowed to be sufficient as well. Judged by the standard set by TTC, such misgivings prove well founded. The supplementation required can be articulated in the same translational terms as those of the constraints currently under review, provided the resources of an expressively sufficient metalanguage are so construed that such a metalanguage must contain a 'translational domain predicate'—intuitively, one translating 'x is a thing' as the object-language uses it, or, more precisely, one translating the object-language formula '$\exists yy=x$'. If the translational variables already assumed to be present in an expressively sufficient metalanguage are taken as primitive, then such a predicate is, of course, already available, in the shape of the formula '$\exists yy=x$'. That, however, requires us to regard the metalanguage as irreducibly many-sorted, and so outside the first-order framework we are taking as the standard one. Instead, then, let us assume that such a predicate is expressible in a sufficiently rich metalanguage by some standard first-order formula OTx. Then, rather than use translational variables to formulate a translational domain predicate, we can use the predicate to explain translational variables away as convenient shorthand for purely first-order formulations, thus:

(1) $\forall vA(v)$ abbreviates $\forall v(OTv \rightarrow A(v))$
(2) $\exists vA(v)$ abbreviates $\exists v(OTv \mathbin{\&} A(v))$
(3) $\{\langle v_1 \ldots v_n\rangle |\, A(v_1 \ldots v_n)\}$ abbreviates $\{\langle v_1 \ldots v_n\rangle |\, OTv_1$
     $\mathbin{\&} \ldots \mathbin{\&} OTv_n \mathbin{\&} A(v_1 \ldots v_n)\}$

Assuming some such translational domain predicate in place in an expressively sufficient metalanguage, we can now state the additional constraint an intended interpretation must meet, in addition to TRC, if the full requirement of TTC is to be matched:

TRANSLATIONAL DOMAIN CONSTRAINT. If L is a first-order language, then I is an intended interpretation for L only if there is, in an expressively sufficient metalanguage, a true instance of the schema

$D_I = \{x \mid \underline{x}\}$

in which '___x___' is replaced by a translational domain predicate of the metalanguage.

Call this constraint 'TDC'. Then any interpretation meeting both of the conditions which this constraint and TRC impose as necessary for intendedness, also meets the condition which TTC decrees to be necessary and sufficient. For if I meets the first two conditions, there is a true translational specification of the domain of I, and the true translational statements of I-relative reference for the proper symbols of the object-language. And these, together with the definitions of model-theoretic semantics, entail the truth of T_I-sentences which are not just translational, but canonically so.

In subscribing simultaneously to TTC, TRC, and TDC, we are, of course, already committed to the converse of this result, that any interpretation which counts as intended by the standard of TTC also meets the necessary conditions for that happy state decreed by TRC and TDC; so we can proclaim a general equivalence between TTC and the cocktail of TRC and TDC. At the same time, the situation is not entirely satisfactory, since our commitment to the converse arises from the decision to formulate TTC as a biconditional. That decision is reasonable enough, perhaps, on the intuitive grounds which prompted it, but we may well seek a deeper rationale to motivate this converse commitment. Any such rationale, however, must turn on an issue which we have said nothing to illuminate to date, namely that of how sentence-level translation, of the sort with which TTC traffics, relates to the term-by-term translation figuring in TRC and TDC; and we should be careful not to oversimplify the question by gratuitously assuming that sentence translation will always take the canonical shape lately identified. This issue combines with others which the discussion has skirted rather furtively—such matters as the question of just what it is which makes a metalanguage 'expressively sufficient' to frame translational constraints on the object-language, or of just what is involved in a predicate's 'translationally' circumscribing the domain—to highlight something which, given the philosophical wranglings of the last half century or so, should, in any case, be glaringly obvious: namely, that the whole notion of translation, wielded in this section with bland insouciance, stands in urgent need of scrutiny and clarification. To a brief discussion of that topic we accordingly turn.

3.5 TRANSLATION AND HERMENEUTICS

Our thesis will be that the key to the analysis of translation lies in the notion of a 'hermeneutic theory', which is just a fancy Greeked-up alternative name for the adaptation to model-theoretic semantics of what Davidson calls a 'theory of interpretation'. (We deviate from his terminology with reluctance, but for the good reason that in the present context 'interpretation' has been pre-empted as a term of art for the set-theoretic semantic structures of preceding pages, and only confusion can result from mixing this with Davidson's different semi-technical use.) A hermeneutic theory, in turn, is a 'truth theory', forged to meet special standards according to a method of 'radical interpretation', as Davidson calls it, or 'radical hermeneutics' as our deviant terminology will prefer to say. Our first task accordingly is to explain what a truth theory is.

We begin with the notion of a *truth theory* for a first-order language L cast in the metalanguage *ML*. Such a theory we shall take to consist of the axioms and definitions of model theory, along with further axioms spelling out the details of one specific interpretation, the *distinguished interpretation* of the truth theory.[18] These axioms take the form of the schemata figuring in the statements of the Translational Domain and Reference Constraints, without the restriction to translational form. Thus, if $Tt(L)$ is a truth theory for L having I as is its distinguished interpretation, $Tt(L)$ will contain a 'domain axiom', of the form figuring in the Translational Domain Constraint, but with '__x__' supplanted by some metalinguistic predicate metalanguage true of all and only the members of the domain of I. And it will contain a 'reference axiom' for each proper symbol of L, these taking the same shape as the schemata figuring in the Translational Reference Constraints on Names and Predicates, save that to qualify as a reference axiom it is not, in general, required that the expressions used on the right be *translations* of those mentioned on the left; rather, they will be expressions of the metalanguage designating the referent assigned by the designated interpretation I to the proper symbol mentioned on the left. The *T-sentences* of a truth theory $Tt(L)$ are the same as the T_I-sentences for its distinguished interpretation I; thus T-sentences flow as theorems from the axioms of the truth theory.

But truth theories thus explicated are insufficient to explain the workings of hermeneutic theories. This is because, as we shall see, the hermeneutic method cannot grip unless it can discern the deployment of indexical apparatus by its subject; hence, a hermeneutic theory, as the output of the hermeneutic method, is perforce a truth theory not for a first-order

---

[18] So a truth theory in our sense is not a Davidsonian one—like his, it generates T-sentences (see below), but it permits itself a luxurious use of set theory to do so, whilst the Davidsonian alternative makes do with more frugal means (see e.g., Donald Davidson, 'The Method of Truth in Metaphysics', in his *Inquiries into Truth and Interpretation*, 205–6). The difference arises because we are working already in a set-theoretic context; no point is served by denying ourselves free appeal to its resources, and integrating the new notion into our ongoing framework.

language unadorned, but for an *indexical extension* thereof. We shall take the indexical extension $L+$ of a first-order language L is to be formed by supplying it with a stock of 'demonstrative terms' $that_1, that_2, \ldots that_n \ldots$, behaving syntactically like individual constants. Semantically, we suppose available in the metalanguage the notions of a set U of (potential) utterers and a set T of times, and a predicate $\text{Dem}(u,t,n,x)$, read as: x is an object demonstratively indicated by u in u's utterance during t of the n-th demonstrative term. Then an interpretation I for $L+$ is the same as an interpretation for L, but semantic notions are redefined in their application to $L+$: all such notions are relativized to utterers u and times t, the intuitive idea being that

$$I, u, t \models A$$

should hold just in case, if each constituent demonstrative term $that_n$ in A is regarded as referring to the object x in D_I such that $\text{Dem}(u,t,n,x)$, then $I \models A$ holds.

Implementing this intuitive idea formally is straightforward enough. The chief modification required to the standard first-order semantics, as outlined above in the opening paragraphs of section 3.1, is to the first clause in the definition of satisfaction, dealing with atomic sentences, which should now read:

(1') If A is atomic $= P^n t_1 \ldots t_n$, then
$I, s, u, t \models$ A iff $\langle \text{Val}'(s, u, t, t_1) \ldots \text{Val}'(s, u.t, t_n) \rangle \in \text{Ref}(P^n)$
where $\text{Val}'(s, u, t, \tau) = \text{Val}'(s, \tau)$ unless τ is a demonstrative term; if τ is the n-th demonstrative term, then $\text{Val}'(s, u, t, \tau) =$ the object x in D_I such that $\text{Dem}(u, t, n, x)$.

(Note that this clause leaves the fate of demonstrative terms unmatched with suitable objects by appropriate demonstrations to depend on the fate of rotten descriptions in the metalanguage; for concreteness and simplicity we might suppose this is Fregean, so that some unfortunate dummy element is singled out to be the referent of all such descriptions.) All the remaining clauses in the definition of satisfaction need now only be relativized to u and t throughout. Relativized truth emerges from relativized satisfaction in the standard way.

A truth theory $Tt(L+)$ for $L+$ with designated interpretation I now consists of domain and reference axioms on the old style suitable for simple nonindexical L, supplemented by semantic axioms in this new, relativized fashion. Such a theory will yield T-sentences for indexical sentences on the pattern

$I, u, t \models \text{Rot}(that_1)$ iff the object demonstrated by u in u's utterance of '$that_1$' during t is red in which the sentence used on the right of the biconditional gives a nonindexical statement of relativized truth-conditions for that mentioned on the left. It will be handy below to have a way of referring to the indexical sentence of the metalanguage which comes from the T-sentence's nonindexical right-hand side by replacing its definite descriptions of demonstration by the corresponding demonstratives—in the example, this would be the metalinguistic sentence '*that*₁ is red'; let us call this the *indexical reconstruction* of the T-sentence's right-hand side.

For a proper exposition and defence of the method of radical hermeneutics, the reader is referred to the writings of Davidson;[19] but a brief recapitulation of its main points will be useful to highlight the features of relevance in the present context. The method aims to devise a hermeneutic theory for a speaker U,[20] and is erected on evidence gleaned from U's behaviour about the sentences U believes true and the causal stimuli by which such believings-true are prompted. It must presuppose no prior knowledge on the part of the theorist about the meanings of U's words or of the specific content of U's beliefs; its aim is to identify an indexical extension of a first-order language as the language U speaks, then to construct a truth theory for that language, in such a way that rational sense is made of U's behaviour if U is construed as having beliefs whose content derives from the truth-conditions appearing on the right-hand of the T-sentences which the theory generates for U's believed-true sentences. Construction of the theory proceeds in three stages. (1) A tentative theory of the logical syntax of the language of U is constructed, under the assumption it must have the structure of an indexical extension of a first-order language if semantic methods are to be brought to bear. The evidence here is classes of sentences always held true or always held false (potential logical truths) and patterns of inference. This first step 'identifies predicates, singular terms, quantifiers, connectives, and identity; in theory, it settles matters of logical form'.[21] (2) Concentrating on indexical sentences in U's language, identified as those which U is prompted to hold true by changing circumstances, the theorist seeks to identify the prompting circumstances. A constraint on the target truth theory for U's language is, then, that it should generate,

---

[19] See, in particular, 'Radical Interpretation' and 'Belief and the Basis of Meaning', both in his *Inquiries into Truth and Interpretation*, 125–40 and 141–54; and 'The Structure and Content of Truth', § 3.

[20] Davidson vacillates on the issue of whether a hermeneutic theory applies principally to a group of speakers ('Radical Interpretation', 135; 'Belief and the Basis of Meaning', 151) or to an individual speaker, eventually comes down on the latter side ('The Structure and Content of Truth', 311). We follow faithfully, though the former decision would sit more easily with our earlier emphasis on speaker groups.

[21] 'Radical Interpretation', 136.

for each such indexical sentence S, a T-sentence whose right-hand side describes the obtaining of such circumstances, whilst U during t makes suitable acts of demonstration, as the condition for the truth of S at U and t on the designated interpretation. Further, those circumstances should be so described that the indexical reconstruction of the describing sentence is one which the theorist also is prompted to believe true by the same circumstances, and when making the same demonstrations as U during t. (3) Finally, the truth theory is to be completed under the constraints of the Principle of Charity: sentences held true or false by U at t are to be assigned truth-conditions on the designated interpretation which the theorist believes to obtain or not at t.

We can now put hermeneutics to work to clarify the apparatus used in developing the translation constraints of the last section. Suppose radical hermeneutics identifies $L+$ as the language of some speaker U. Then a metalanguage is expressively sufficient for $L+$ (and, hence, for the contained first-order L) iff within it can be cast a truth theory for $L+$ adequate as a hermeneutic theory for U; and a sentence S' of the metalanguage is a translation of the sentence S of L if S' occurs on the right-hand side of a T-sentence for S which that truth theory generates.[22] Less obvious is how to extend this account of translation to subsentential expressions, and any resolution smacks of stipulation. But the most natural idea is to take a translation of a proper symbol as given by a term on the right-hand side of the reference axiom (or other similarly structured provable identity) for the symbol in question, in the same carefully crafted truth theory as that mined for sentence translations; and to take a translational domain predicate as one apt to figure in the domain axiom of the same truth theory. Under these definitions, it will transpire that every object-language sentence has a canonical translation into an expressively sufficient metalanguage, though not that every metalinguistic translation is canonical.

Explaining translation this way, however, reveals a complexity in the notion which was not acknowledged in the formulation and discussion of the translational constraints of the last section. This is that translation is *indeterminate*: the restraints governing the operation of the hermeneutic method are sufficiently loose to certify many hermeneutic theories for the same object-language, including even some which will assign translations

---

[22] This definition has the consequence that any logical equivalent of a translation of S is itself a translation of S; for some purposes, we may want the notion of translation to cut finer than this. One way of doing so is to define a canonical method whereby a truth theory can produce its T-sentences, take the *critical* T-sentence for S as the first T-sentence generated by this canonical method in the approved truth theory, and use the right-hand side of the critical T-sentence to define translation. But a looser standard of translation will suffice for present purposes, so we can be spared these contortions.

of opposite truth-value to the same sentence. Translation, then, is best seen as relative to a hermeneutic theory, or 'translation-schema' as we may also put it—but note that to adopt a translation schema in this sense is, because of the way hermeneutic theory works, not merely to assign meanings but also to attribute beliefs. This relativity of translation to a translation-schema should accordingly be understood retrospectively as implicit in the statements of both the Translational Reference and Truth Constraints, and also to be inherited by the notion of intendedness they enshrine: interpretations are, strictly speaking, not intended *tout court*, but only relative to a translation-schema. Similarly, when our earlier discussion has spoken of Translational Constraints operating in tandem, or of the relations between Translational Constraints, that discussion should now be understood as operating against the background assumption that a single translation-schema governs the operation of all constraints in play.[23]

A problem still unresolved, and which provided an immediate spur to these reflections on translation, was that of gaining insight into why it should be that an interpretation judged to be intended by the standard of the truth-level Translational Constraint TTC should also meet the constraint imposed by the reference-level requirement TRC, along with the domain constraint TDC—all relative to the same translation-schema, as we now hasten to add. To that problem, our account of translation supplies a ready-enough answer. For suppose interpretation I for first-order L satisfies TTC under some translation-schema. Then relative to that schema there is a true translational T_I-sentence for each sentence S of L. That means there is a truth theory adequate by hermeneutic standards for some indexical extension of L and having all these T_I-sentences as theorems (else they would not be translational). The referential and domain axioms of this theory will, in turn, be by definition translational relative to the same translation-schema; and they are also true, since they have the status of stipulations defining I.

The Translational Truth Constraint with which we conclude is thus equivalently formulable as the constraint that an interpretation is intended iff it satisfies the requirements of both the Translational Reference and Domain Constraints. The latter formulation has its uses, as we shall see; but, of the two, the former is evidently the more fundamental conceptually.

---

[23] The relativity of translation to a translation schema should also serve to dispel any appearance of inconsistency between our adoption of the TDC and earlier rejection of the claims of a Cardinality Constraint. For it may seem that TDC, by constraining the domain to be the extension of a privileged translational domain predicate, conceals a Cardinality Constraint, by favouring models with a cardinality determined by that predicate. But this need not be so, since there can be many equally good translational domain predicates determining domains of deviant cardinalities.

For it is only in the light of the clear standard it set that the insufficiency of an unadorned Reference Constraint became manifest. Moreover, the fact that hermeneutic theory takes as its primary goal the interpretation of whole utterances means that the notion of translation applies primarily to sentences, as the unit of utterance, and, hence, that the fundamental and primary form of translational constraint is the version operating at the level of sentences and truth. Moreover, there are strong grounds for thinking that this Translational Truth Constraint also subsumes the claims of the *reductionist* reference constraints discussed two sections back. For, first, it inherits from the Translational Reference Constraint, which we have seen it to subsume, that constraint's credentials, already remarked, to operate as a criterion of adequacy on ambitious reductionist reference constraints. Further, it can claim, too, to have accommodated the role of the causal and psycho-behavioural components of meaning which motivate the reductionist reference constraints, without committing itself to their perhaps overweening endorsement of outright reductionism. For the hermeneutic method underpinning translation has as one of its key foundations the causal promptings of subject and theorist to the believings-true of sentences; and the outcome of the whole enterprise is the construction of a theory enabling a coherent story to be told of the psychology of the subject, by attaching contents to the subject's believed-true sentences which are reasonable by the interpreter's own best cognitive standards. All in all, then, the Translational Truth Constraint seems to emerge as that supplying the definitive standard whereby the intendedness of an interpretation stands or falls.

3.6 CONSTRAINTS ON INTENDEDNESS—'JUST MORE THEORY'?

Emerging, then, from this lengthy disquisition on constraints armed with a definitive standard for intendedness, let us revisit the question which prompted this examination of the notion in the first place. How does the Completeness-guaranteed model M^* for the ideal theory T^* fare on the score of intendedness, as measured by the standard which has emerged?

Rather poorly, at first blush. Details will vary depending on the version of the proof of the Completeness Theorem presupposed. But suppose for concreteness we take the Henkin–Hasenjaeger proof[24] as the one in play. Then M^* is defined in terms of a consistent, closed, negation-complete

[24] See Mendelson, *Introduction*, 62–9; or Hunter, *Metalogic*, 173–86.

extension $T^{*}+$ of T^{*}. The result will validate such $T_{M^{*}}$-sentences as

> $M^{*} \models \exists x F x$ iff there is some closed term τ in the language of T^{*}
> $+$ such that $F\tau$ is a theorem of $T^{*}+$.

But we might also suppose the object-language so used that our best shot at hermeneutic theory warrants the translation of the object-language sentence '$\exists x F x$' as an existential assertion concerning which even ideal theory is agnostic—as it may be, one concerning the existence of some mundane object at some inaccessible location in space or time. Then not only is the displayed $T_{M^{*}}$-sentence not only not translational itself but its right-hand side so diverges from a translation that the two may well differ in truth-value. Suppose, in fact, they do; then the truth of the displayed $T_{M^{*}}$-sentence actually precludes the truth of any translational one, and M^{*} fails the Translational Truth Constraint. This, however, shows nothing more than that we have oversimplified our statement of the problems posed for realism by the Argument from Completeness, specifically by indulging in sloppy talk of 'the' model for the ideal theory whose existence Completeness demonstrates. For, of course, it follows from that theorem not merely that the ideal theory is modelled by the canonical interpretation which figures in the proof of the theorem; there are also the myriad models isomorphic to the canonical interpretation, and the models emerging from these by applying the inflationary techniques adverted to in proving the Upward Löwenheim–Skolem Theorem. And realism is committed not just to the claim that the canonical interpretation itself may fall short of intendedness, but that it provides a standard which *none* of these models, for which the canonical interpretation provides the template, may turn out to meet, relative to any reasonable schema of translation. So constraints on intendedness do not secure for the realist the immediate victory a first glance might suggest. At the same time, the onus is on the antirealist to provide grounds for thinking they will prove too weak a reed for realist aspirations.

Putnam deploys a number of arguments to defuse proposed constraints on intendedness. Most of these are local to particular constraints, aiming, for example, to undermine the reductionist proposals upon which reductionist Reference Constraints depend for their credentials. There is, however, one argument which, although deployed by Putnam himself only against specific forms of the Causal Reference Constraint, promises more general application—if it works, it evidently provides reason for thinking no constraint on intendedness at all could do the job the realist must require it to do, that of providing a standard which all models of ideal theory may fail.

Writing with a version of the Causal Reference Constraint derived from Gareth Evans's analysis of reference in mind, Putnam says:[25]

The problem is that adding to our hypothetical formalized language a body of theory entitled 'Causal Theory of Reference' *is* just adding more *theory*. But Skolem's argument, and our extension of it, are not affected by enlarging the theory.

Here the reference to 'Skolem's argument' may appear obscure, until we are reminded that Putnam tends to run together the Completeness Theorem and the 'intimately related' (Downward) Löwenheim–Skolem Theorem,[26] so we can take this as a reference to the Argument from Completeness. The leading idea here is that the Causal Reference Constraint can be defused by treating it as 'just more theory', to be added to the original ideal theory to form a new, enlarged theory which can be modelled in the same way as the original. Whatever the merits of this idea, it clearly does not depend on the detail of Evans's causal analysis of reference; indeed, it does not apparently depend on the constraint at which it is directed being *causal* or about *reference* at all, but looks like it should apply with equal validity to any constraint whatsoever. David Lewis agrees, and states the reasoning in its generality, with his characteristic limpidity, as follows:[27]

Suppose we say that it is constraint *C* that saves the day—a causal constraint, perhaps, or what have you. We offer an account of how constraint *C* works, a bit of theory in fact. If this bit of theory works, it will deserve to be incorporated into total theory. Suppose it is. Then an intended interpretation must make *C*-theory come true, along with the rest of total theory. But it will still be true, as much as ever, that (almost) any world can satisfy (almost) any theory. [This is Lewis's folksy, deflationary way of saying the Completeness Theorem will continue to apply to the enlarged theory—B.T.] Adding *C*-theory to the rest of total theory doesn't help. ... And the point is general: it applies to any constraint (or at least to any otherwise satisfactory constraint) that might be proposed. Constraint *C* is to be imposed by accepting *C*-theory, according to Putnam. But *C*-theory is just more theory, more grist for the mill; and more theory will go the way of all theory.

He goes on, however, to claim to discern a confusion in the reasoning sufficient to vitiate it entirely:

---

[25] 'Models and Reality', 18. See also *Reason, Truth, and History*, 45–6, where the same reasoning is employed in the context of a version of Causal Reference Constraint based on Hartry Field's account of reference.

[26] 'Models and Reality', 13.

[27] David K. Lewis, 'Putnam's Paradox', in his *Papers in Metaphysics and Epistemology* (Cambridge and New York: Cambridge University Press, 1999), 62.

To which I reply: *C* is *not* to be imposed just by accepting *C*-theory. That is a mis-understanding of what *C* is. The constraint is *not* that an intended interpretation must somehow make our account of *C* come out true. The constraint is that an intended interpretation must conform to *C* itself.

Lewis's diagnosis has been greeted with a chorus of approval[28] sufficient to suggest that he has, indeed, succeeded in pinpointing a grievous fault in Putnam's reasoning. Let us nevertheless persist, by seeing in detail how Put-nam's manœuvre is to be spelled out when *C* is our favoured Translational Truth Constraint, and checking that it does indeed fall foul of Lewis's cri-tique.

The first step, as Lewis explains it, is to enrich the ideal theory T^* by incorporating into it a statement of our favoured constraint. Immediately, it becomes clear that this incorporation is a less straightforward matter than Lewis's exposition makes it appear. Forget for the moment the constraint we really favour, the Translational Truth Constraint, which, as we shall see, raises some additional problems of its own, and concentrate for the moment on the simplest of the constraints we have discussed, the Causal Reference Constraint. Even this, with its semantic vocabulary, belongs not to the language L^* of the ideal theory, but rather to a metalanguage thereof; so there can be no question of simply tacking a statement of the Constraint onto the ideal theory T^*. Rather, 'incorporating' the Constraint must involve ascent into a metalanguage, as Putnam's own discussions of the manœuvre in the places cited above emphasize: the theses of T^* must first be translated into a metalanguage before the Constraint can be appended.

This raises the question of just what shape the envisaged metalanguage ML^* of the language L^* of the ideal theory should take. Hitherto, we have had a bet each way in the matter of metalanguages, treating them as frag-ments of semi-English tortured as convenient into canonical shape; but ML^*, if it is to be a vehicle for a revamped and extended version of the formalized ideal theory T^*, had best now be regarded of as fully formalized itself, and in similarly first-order terms. As for the resources it contains, to be apt to articulate constraints on interpretations, it must contain the familiar appurtenances of metatheory, including devices for structural

---

[28] See e.g., Hale and Wright, 'Putnam's Model-theoretic Argument'; James van Cleve, 'Semantic Supervenience and Referential Indeterminacy', *The Journal of Philosophy*, 89 (1992), 349; Igor Douven, 'Putnam's Model-theoretic Argument Reconsidered', *The Journal of Philosophy*, 96 (1999), 486, applying the criticism to the 'standard realist analysis' of the argument. Moreover, whilst Lewis's crisp statement has provided a natural reference-point for subsequent writers, he himself emphasizes that essentially the same criticism, directed at more specific targets, was made by others before him, and singles out for mention Michael Devitt, 'Realism and the Renegade Putnam', *Nous*, 17 (1983), 291–301.

description of the expressions of L^*, and the resources to describe its model theory; importantly, the latter, of course, entails on pain of paradox that its variables be construed as ranging over a richer set-theoretic universe than do those of L^*, and for concreteness we suppose it to be a universe augmented by containing all sets and relations of things in the universe of L^*. Further, ML^* must contain the expressive power of L^*, both in order to be capable of articulating a revamped version of T^* and if it is to hope to be expressively adequate for formulating the Translational Truth Constraint. It appears we have no real alternative than to conceive ML^* as doing so by incorporating L^* itself, that is, by using the same symbols in the same way as that in which they are deployed in L^*. After all, L^* is the hypothesized vehicle for the ideal theory T^*, a distillation of all human experience and wisdom; so no sublunary language of the sort with which we are currently familiar will presumably be able to match its expressive capacity, unless reformed, extended, regimented, and refined beyond recognition.

An alternative may be to use some language L^{**}, also apt for ideal theory but distinct from L^*. Why we should bother, however, is unclear, if we have already gone to the bother of forging L^* itself. Moreover, the alternative means that translation between object-language and metalanguage cannot be homophonic. Yet, as already noted, the vagaries of hermeneutic theory mean that adoption of a translation-schema involves attribution of belief to object-language speakers. Now homophonic translations—those couched in the same vocabulary, identically used—make manifest how the beliefs attributed are identical with those of the metalanguage-using interpreter; as, indeed, they should be in the present case, where we should not trust interpreters who differ from the wisdom enshrined in the ideal theory of the object-language. True, nonhomophonic translations *can* be compatible with a similar concordance of belief between object theory and metalinguistic interpreter; but their form does not make such a commitment manifest, and it would be perverse to pursue such alternatives in the absence of other advantages.

Accordingly, we shall assume ML^* to contain the proper symbols of L^*, and take translation from L^* into ML^* to be homophonic. Or almost so; for the last paragraph has glossed over a small complication. This is that we need some means of indicating that variables in the translations are more restricted in their range than the unrestricted variables of ML^*. We shall, accordingly, continue to use translational variables $\mathbf{x}, \mathbf{y}, \mathbf{z} \ldots$ in this role, explaining them, as before, in terms of the translational domain predicate OTx; and our translations will supplant ordinary variables of the object-language with translational ones in the metalanguage. Call this the schema of translation *virtually* homophonic.

The first part of the first step of Putnam's constraint-defusing 'just more theory' manœuvre, as reconstructed out of Lewis's generalized recipe, is accordingly to begin construction, in ML^*, of an extension T^*+ of the ideal theory T^*, by annexing to T^*+ the metalinguistic, virtually homophonic translations of the theses of T^*. To continue with the first step, we must further supplement T^*+, by adding to it a statement of our favoured constraint on intendedness. But now we face a further problem: unlike the Causal Reference Constraint we have lately considered in the interests of simplification, whose statement belongs, as we noted, to the metalanguage, the constraint we truly favour, the Translational Truth Constraint, belongs rather in the metametalanguage—for it speaks of the truth of instances of various schemata of the metalanguage as the condition for intendedness. So there is still no adding a statement of *this* constraint to the evolving metalinguistic theory T^*+.

We could confront this problem head-on by ascending further into the metametalanguage as the true home for the extended ideal theory we are out to construct; but there is a simpler, and better, way. For, with a translation-schema into the metalanguage now identified, we can use semantic descent to obtain an equivalent, but metalinguistically stateable constraint. Thus, had we the ability to form infinite conjunctions in the metalanguage, we could formulate an infinitary metalinguistic version of the Translational Truth Constraint as indicated by the following pattern:

I is an intended interpretation for L^*. $\leftrightarrow$.

$$I \models \text{'Fa'} \leftrightarrow \text{Fa}$$
$$\& \, I \models \text{'Fb'} \leftrightarrow \text{Fb}$$
$$\& \, \ldots$$
$$\& \, \ldots$$
$$\& \, I \models \text{'}\neg\text{Gab'} \leftrightarrow \neg\text{Gab}$$
$$\& \, \ldots$$
$$\& \, \ldots$$
$$\& \, I \models \text{'}\forall x(\text{F}x \rightarrow \text{G}x)\text{'} \leftrightarrow \forall x(\text{F}x \rightarrow \text{G}x)$$
$$\& \, \ldots$$
$$\& \, \ldots$$

(To illuminate the structure of the clauses here, structural descriptions are formed by quotation rather than our standard convention of autonymous use. The intention is, of course, that there be one conjunct on the right of the biconditional for each sentence of the object-language.) Lacking these infinitary resources as we do, we can get the same effect by finite means by reverting to the equivalent, if less perspicuous, statement of the Translational Truth Constraint as a cocktail of the Translational Domain and Reference Constraints before taking the step of semantic descent, obtaining:

I is an intended interpretation for L^*. ↔.

$$D_I = \{x \mid OTx\}$$
$$\&\ Ref_I(\text{'a'}) = a$$
$$\&\ Ref_I(\text{'b'}) = b$$
$$\&\ \ldots$$
$$\&\ \ldots$$
$$\&\ Ref_I(\text{'F}^1\text{'}) = \{\mathbf{x} \mid F^1\mathbf{x}\}$$
$$\&\ Ref_I(\text{'G}^1\text{'}) = \{\mathbf{x} \mid G^1\mathbf{x}\}$$
$$\&\ \ldots$$
$$\&\ \ldots$$
$$\&\ Ref_I(\text{'F}^2\text{'}) = \{\langle \mathbf{x}, \mathbf{y} \rangle \mid F^2\mathbf{x}\mathbf{y}\}$$
$$\&\ \ldots$$
$$\&\ \ldots$$

(Quotation is used, once again, to form structural descriptions; and the intention is, of course, that there be a conjunct on the right of the biconditional for each proper symbol of the object-language L^*.) We are going to need a name for this last; let us call it the *Homophonic Constraint*.

Thus T^*+, the extended, metalinguistic version of the ideal theory T^*, is to contain (1) virtually homophonic translations of the theses of T^*, and (2) the Homophonic Constraint. Finally, we should round the theory off, by adding to it further well-attested truths which belong in ideal theory, but because of their metalinguistic nature were not apt for inclusion in its object-language formulation T^*. Notably, these will include any principles appropriate to the additional sets in the range of the variables of ML^*, and the principles and definitions which formulate the model theory of L^*.

With the construction of T^*+ completed, the next stage of Putnam's manœuvre, as described by him and articulated by Lewis, is somehow to reapply the Completeness Theorem to defuse the favoured constraint on intendedness. Here is an attempt to construct such an argument in detail:

Suppose that the set theory of T^*+ is enough to show that the objects satisfying the translational domain predicate form a set—that '$\{x|OTx\}$' is a non-rotten description, if we assume a set theory which eschews proper classes. (We shall see below reasons for thinking this is something which should indeed be demonstrable.) Then the clauses on the right-hand side of the Homophonic Constraint—its translational domain specification, along with its homophonic specifications of reference—define what is provably one interpretation I for L^*. Call this the 'homophonic interpretation' (*HI*), whilst remembering it is a perfectly extensional object, entirely open for specification in nonhomophonic terms.

Trivially, this interpretation is also demonstrably an intended one, according to T^*+; moreover, it is also demonstrably a model for T^*. (For all the virtually homophonic translational T_{HI}-sentences for L^* are provable in T^*+; so are virtual translations of all theses of T^*; hence $HI \models A$ is provable, for each thesis A of T^*.) So according to T^*+, T^* is full-bloodedly true, its theses validated by an interpretation certifiable as an intended one.

Evidently, the anodyne additions made to T^* in forming T^*+ constitute no threat to its consistency. Hence, the Completeness Theorem applies once more: T^*+ must have models M^*+. Hence, it must be true that T^* has not just a model, but an *intended* model, in one good sense of 'true': it must be true-on-some-M^*+.

As a first step in evaluating this reasoning, let us ask whether it contains the confusion Lewis claims to discern: that of confusing the demand that an intended interpretation should conform to a constraint with the demand that an intended model should 'somehow make true' a statement of the constraint. Certainly, it does not make such a confusion literally. For the model claimed to be an intended model for T^* is HI; in the offing there are also the models M^*+ for T^*+, which 'somehow' make true a statement of the Homophonic Constraint (and, more to the point, a statement that it is met by HI); but at no point does the argument turn on the claim that any M^*+ is an intended interpretation of T^*, or of anything else, by virtue of its somehow making these statements true. Still, it may seem there is something in Lewis's complaint. For the reasoning above still only establishes that there must be a model M^*+ which, as Lewis would put it, 'somehow makes true' the statement that HI is a model for T^* which is intended by the standard of the Homophonic Constraint. And, it may be urged, there is still a step from that to the conclusion that HI must indeed really be a model for T^* which is intended by that standard; and, hence, that the ideal theory T^* must be (full-bloodedly) true, contravening realism.

There is indeed such a step. The question of whether it can legitimately be taken is the same as that of whether some M^*+ (let it be M^*+) is intended by the lights of the Translational Truth Constraint. To see this, suppose our metalanguage for ML^* is the one in which the discussion of the last few paragraphs has, in fact, been employing, namely, tortured and technified English; and let **H** be the statement of ML^* itself which is designed to be its formal statement that HI is a model for T^* which is intended by the standard of the Homophonic Constraint. Then if M^*+ meets the Translational Truth Constraint, we have

$M^*+ \models$ **H** $\leftrightarrow HI$ is an intended interpretation for L^* by the standard of the Homophonic Constraint & HI is a model for T^*

and this truth mediates the step mooted. What this raises is, of course, the question of whether T^*+ does, indeed, have intended models, of which M^*+ may be one. And the attempt to settle *that* issue leads into formalizing the metalanguage for ML^*, constructing within that the theory T^*++ incorporating a statement of the Homophonic Constraint on interpretations for ML^*, and reduplicating the reasoning in which we have lately indulged.

We are thus led to the picture of a hierarchy of languages $L_0 = L^*$, $L_1 = ML^*$, $L_2 = MML^*$, ... and theories $T_0 = T^*$, $T_1 = T^*+$, $T_2 = T^*++$, ... With a reservation to be made in a moment, L_0 is our old attempt at ideal theory, now revealed in its true colours as a *base level* such theory merely, with L_0 as its language. L_{i+1} contains a translational domain predicate $OTL_i(x)$ for L_i, and its variables range over the universe of L_i along with all relations over such things; it also contains all the symbols of L_i, and uses the virtually homophonic schema to translate statements of L_i. T_{i+1} contains virtually homophonic translations of the theses of T_i, principles governing the model theory of L_i and the sets L_{i+1} adjoins to those of L_i, and a statement of the Homophonic Constraint on interpretations for L_i. We can then extend the hierarchy into the transfinite by forming L_ω and T_ω as the unions of the L_i and T_i, respectively, and then continue the construction as before. Since set theory is gradually injected into the construction as the hierarchy is ascended, it is natural now to suppose L_0 and T_0 reformulated—here is the 'reservation' adverted to just before—so as to treat of individuals only; these may, of course, include abstract objects such as different categories of number or syntactic expressions, but they will be treated for the time as *sui generis*, to be reduced to sets only as and when a stage in the hierarchy is reached when enough set theory to do so becomes available. (This assumption that variables of the base-level language range over individuals alone is what justifies our earlier confidence that the objects in this range can be assumed to form a set.) And now, for each level α, the Completeness Theorem can be deployed to show that T_α has models, so that all of its theses must, in a sense, be true. Deploying the Translational Truth Constraint to show that this sense of 'true' may be a frivolous one (because none of these models needs be intended) turns out, then, to depend on the status of the models of $T_{\alpha+1}$. At no point can the contention that some of the models of a given theory may be intended be discounted. But that means that the cocktail of the Translational Truth Constraint (the Rolls Royce of constraints on intendedness, it was argued above), plus model theory, is not enough to found an analysis of truth to underpin the realist contention that the ideal theory might be false. The Argument from Completeness does not, of course, refute realism. But it is enough to show that constraint-bolstered model theory, what may appear to provide an attractive avenue for realism to wander down in search of a rationale for its distinctive doctrines once the way of the Correspondence Theory of Truth has been closed, is, in fact, no more than a blind alley.

A crucial role in the above argument is played by the fact that translation from object-language to metalanguage is taken at each point to be virtually homophonic. For that is what permits the Translational Truth Constraint to take concrete shape as the Homophonic Constraint. Moreover, it ensures that the virtually homophonic translations of the theses of lower level theory can be taken over immediately into theory at the next level up (crucial for proving in that theory that the homophonic interpretation is a model for theory one level lower), whereas genuine deviance from homophonic translation, as a consequence of the hermeneutic construal of translation, must be open to the prospect of some accompanying deviance in theory. This commitment to the virtually homophonic account of translation in the languages in our hierarchy arises from generalization of the considerations arising in the base case, the construction of the metalanguage ML^* of L^*; and these, in turn, depended crucially on the role of L^* as the vehicle for the ideal theory T^*.

Our reconstruction of Putnam's argument thus accounts for one of its features which Lewis finds puzzling,[29] by explaining what warrants the emphasis on *ideal* theory. It is the role of ideal theory, too, which explains and justifies another crucial feature of the argument: namely, the denial to the realist of a *stable* metalanguage, unaffected by interpretative vicissitudes of the object-language, in which to formulate constraints on intendedness. Both Lewis[30] and Hale and Wright[31] see this denial as no more than a cheap dialectical trick; but if the present reconstruction is correct, it has its justification because of the special features of the languages and theories in play.[32]

[29] 'Putnam's Paradox', 69.

[30] Ibid., 62–3.

[31] 'Putnam's Model-theoretic Argument', 441.

[32] Graham Priest has suggested there is an analogy between the hierarchy of languages in which the Translational Truth Constraint is alternatively framed and defeated, and the hierarchy of tenses in which objection to McTaggart's alleged contradiction in the temporal A-series is alternatively made and defeated. The analogy is a welcome one to an author who, following Dummett, sees McTaggart's argument as structurally sound, though properly construed as warranting a somewhat different conclusion to that which was drawn by McTaggart himself. See John McTaggart Ellis McTaggart, 'The Unreality of Time', in his *Philosophical Studies* ed. by Stanley Victor Keeling (London: E. Arnold & Co., 1934), 110–31; Michael Dummett, 'A Defence of McTaggart's Proof of the Unreality of Time', in his *Truth and Other Enigmas*, 351–7; Barry Taylor, 'Dummett's McTaggart', in Richard G. Heck (ed.), *Language, Thought, and Logic: Essays in Honour of Michael Dummett* (Oxford and New York: Oxford University Press, 1997), 183–99.

4

Changing the Rules

The game of the last chapter was played according to rules, set by Putnam, whose legitimacy is open to question. For the problems there described confronting any realist attempt to found its conception of truth on model theory depend on the assumption that the Completeness Theorem will apply to the ideal theory; and there are two promising ways in which realism may seek to rebut that assumption. The first is by rejecting the hypothesis, adopted in the last chapter with breezy off-handedness, that first-order resources suffice to subserve the needs of ideal theory,[1] and arguing instead that its language must take some more complex form which resists proof of Completeness. The second is to argue that, for realism's purposes, model theory itself should take some modified shape, so that Completeness is, once more, blocked. In short, the assumption that Completeness applies to the ideal theory may be subverted by insisting on a revamping either of the theory modelled, or of the structures which model it; and it behoves us to consider the viability of either strategy.

4.1 REVAMPING THE LANGUAGE

The question of the adequacy or otherwise of first-order resources to capture the expressive power of the language of science or of natural language is, of course, an enormous one, complicated by differing conceptions of the criteria whereby an attempted formalization is to be judged successful. A thoroughgoing examination of the issues raised by first of the two approaches mooted is, accordingly, beyond the scope of this work; nor does it seem likely that any discussion, however prolonged, would settle them in detail to the satisfaction of all. Nevertheless, the following considerations will serve, it is hoped, to identify the critical points raised by this approach.

---

[1] See e.g., Ian Hacking, *Representing and Intervening: Introductory Topics in the Philosophy of Science* (Cambridge: Cambridge University Press, 1983), 105.

First: in an important series of papers,[2] Davidson—standing on the shoulders of Quine, but operating with the more clearly defined criteria of adequacy provided by his wholehearted espousal of the disciplines imposed by Tarskian truth theory—has made a strong case that, subject to an important proviso to be discussed in a moment, first-order resources can be stretched to accommodate many constructions which appear at first sight to transcend them entirely. Among the constructions dealt with are tense, adverbial structure, statements of indirect discourse (and, by extension, statements of modality and attributions of psychological attitude), causal statements, and nonindicatives—in short, all the familiar bugbears of the would-be first-orderist. Davidson's work thus provides a first-order benchmark, placing the onus on those who would favour some alternative which breaks first-order bounds to argue the case that theirs is the better way.

Second: where an alternative *is* suggested and defended (as when, for example, a predicate-modifier treatment of adverbs is advanced as superior to Davidson's treatment of them as event adverbs, perhaps on the ground of some perceived virtue in closer cleavage to surface grammar), it behoves its advocate to ensure the proposal comes wrapped in enough semantic and syntactic detail to match the familiar first-order trappings of its Davidsonian competitor. But the normal conventions of semantics interpret this as requiring that some version of Completeness be provable in the case of the proposed alternative, unless some special case can be made for waiving this requirement in a specific instance. Just such a case can, of course, be made in one important instance, where the proposal to depart from the first-order is that the language adopted should be explicitly of second (or higher) order; for then the unprovability of Completeness is actually demonstrable, being a consequence of Gödel's Incompleteness Theorem for arithmetic. But this is a special case, to which we must return. Less far-reaching proposals for departure from the strictly first order, such as its augmentation by predicate-modifiers or modal operators, typically come accompanied by their own versions of Completeness, as a condition of their being properly articulated at all; and, hence, raise all the headaches for realism which arise when the language of ideal theory takes straightforward first-order shape.

In particular, there is no solace for the realist in the concession which even Davidson feels constrained to make, that pure first-order resources must be stretched at least to the point of adding demonstrative terms, i.e., in the terminology of section 3.5 above, of forming an indexical extension of a first-order language. Such a concession seems inevitable, in

---

[2] See Essays 6–8 of Donald Davidson, *Inquiries into Truth and Interpretation*; and Essays 6 and 7 of Donald Davidson, *Essays on Actions and Events* (Oxford: Clarendon Press, 1980).

the first place, if the formalism is to accommodate the most jejune, overtly demonstrative sentences, on the pattern of 'that is red'; but further, it provides the resource Davidson exploits to show how tensed, nonindicative, and psychological attitude statements can be dealt with as well. True, it might be urged that the involvement, explicit or implicit, of demonstrative terms in these constructions, whilst doubtless of interest to theorists of the structure of colloquial language, does not establish that the language of ideal theory need be more than first order, since they are all constructions it can eschew. Such a contention is, however, highly dubious. For, first, it raises the question of whether tenseless, nondemonstrative language is truly independent of the tensed and demonstrative (a negative answer to which is suggested by the need, discussed in section 3.5, for hermeneutic theory to find demonstrative elements if it is to grip); and, second, it depends on a peculiarly narrow view of the scope of ideal theory, under which it is to be permitted to ignore psychological attitudes. The important point is that it is not, moreover, a contention on which much turns in the present context. For even if we concede that the language of ideal theory should be an indexical extension of a pure first-order one, thus allowing it the freedom to express a wider range of constructions, still there seems every reason to suppose that a decent semantics for so modest an extension must permit proof of a Completeness Theorem raising all the problems for realism which arise in the straightforward first-order case. The details will, of course, depend on the specifics of the semantics proposed; but certainly the expectation is borne out for the sample semantics proposed in section 3.5. [Details: Let the indexical version of the ideal theory T^* be cast in an indexical extension L^* of a first-order language L. Consider T^* as propounded by the theorist $\mathbf{u}$ at time $\mathbf{t}$, and based upon demonstrations by $\mathbf{u}$ during $\mathbf{t}$ associated with utterances of the first n demonstrative terms. Now add new constants $d_1 \ldots d_{n+1}$ to L^*, and for each formula A of L^*, construct A# by replacing $that_i$ by d_i for $i \leq n$, and by d_{n+1} otherwise. Then by Completeness, there is a model M such that $M \models$ A# for each A in T^*. Turn M into M' by replacing $\text{Ref}_M(d_i)$ by the x such that $\text{Dem}(\mathbf{u}, \mathbf{t}, i, x)$, for $i \leq n$. Then show, using induction on the length of A, that M', $\mathbf{u}$, $\mathbf{t} \models$ A for each A in T^*.]

It remains to examine the suggestion that ideal theory should be cast in a language of second, or higher, order. We shall concentrate on the second-order case, since there is a good sense in which all higher-order cases are reducible to the second.[3] In detail, then, the proposal is that the language of

---

[3] See Stewart Shapiro, *Foundations without Foundationalism: A Case for Second-Order Logic* (Oxford and New York: Clarendon Press and Oxford University Press, 1991), § 6.2.

ideal theory should be a second-order one $L2^*$, coming from an underlying first-order language $L1^*$ by adding n-place second-order variables for every $n > 0$. These variables we also style 'predicate variables', and differentiate them both from the predicate-*letters* and from the *individual* (or, we may now say, 'first-order') variables of $L1^*$, though they share syntactic characteristics of both: they operate like predicate-letters in the shaping of atomic formulae (so if V is an n-place predicate variable and $\tau_1 \ldots \tau_n$ are singular terms of $L1^*$, $V\tau_1 \ldots \tau_n$ is an atomic wff of $L2^*$), and like first-order variables in being bindable by quantifiers (so $\forall VA$ is a wff of $L2^*$ if V is a predicate variable and A is a wff of $L2^*$). Otherwise the same formation rules govern $L2^*$ as $L1^*$. So all atomic wffs of $L1^*$ are also atomic wffs of $L2^*$; and where A and B are wffs of $L2^*$ and v is an individual variable, ¬A, (A&B), and $\forall vA$ are all wffs of $L2^*$.

The principal grounds urged by its friends in favour of adoption of the second-order framework are that it provides a more faithful reflection of mathematical practice,[4] and that it permits the formalization of statements involving plural quantifiers which resist straightforward first-order encapsulation, such as the 'Geach–Kaplan' sentence 'some critics admire only one another'.[5] These may seem to constitute an underwhelming case for thinking ideal theory must take second-order shape—the important thing, it may be urged, is merely that ideal theory should be able, somehow or other, to record mathematical theory, not that it should faithfully systematize the discourse mathematicians find natural. Nor should it matter if the language of ideal theory does not faithfully mimic all the expressive idiosyncracies of ordinary language such as plural quantification, since it is admitted on all sides that the content of the Geach–Kaplan sentence can at least be *crudely* captured by a first-order sentence involving explicit quantification over classes. On the other hand, it should be conceded that the grounds given do constitute a case for increased expressive flexibility in a second-order framework, and the evaluation of the case for realism should not be made to rest on a pig-headed refusal to budge from a first-order base for any reason short of logical compulsion.

Suppose, then, we let the language of ideal theory be second order: what does its model theory look like? According to the *standard semantics*,[6] an interpretation I for a second-order language $L2$ based on a first-order

---

[4] See Stewart Shapiro, *Foundations without Foundationalism: A Case for Second-Order Logic* (Oxford and New York: Clarendon Press and Oxford University Press, 1991), ch. 5.

[5] George Boolos, 'To Be Is to Be a Value of a Variable (or to Be Some Values of Some Variables)', *The Journal of Philosophy*, 81 (1984), 430–49; and 'Nominalist Platonism', *The Philosophical Review*, 94 (1985), 327–44.

[6] Adapted from Shapiro, *Foundations without Foundationalism*, 72.

language $L1$ is the same as an interpretation for $L1$. Satisfaction on I is now taken as a relation between a formula A and a *denumerably long, denumerably-rowed* sequence s, having in its bottom (0-th) row a denumerable sequence of elements of the domain of I, and in its n-th row a denumerable sequence of sets[7] of n-tuples of elements of that domain. Sequence $s\#$ is a j-variant of s in the n-th row iff s and $s\#$ have the same elements in all places of all rows save possibly in the j-th place of the n-th row. Suppressing subscripts indexing terminology to I, we define:

(1) If τ is a first order term (= term of $L1$), then
$\mathrm{Val}(\tau, s) = \mathrm{Ref}(\tau)$ if τ is an individual constant
= the j-the member of the 0-th row of s, if τ is the j-th individual variable.

(2) If P^n is an n-place predicate symbol (predicate-letter or predicate variable), then
$\mathrm{Val}(P^n, s) = \mathrm{Ref}(P^n)$ if P^n is a predicate-letter
= the j-th member of the n-th row of s, if P^n is the j-th n-place predicate variable.

(3) If A is an atomic wff = $P^n(\tau_1 \ldots \tau_n)$ for some predicate symbol P^n and first-order terms $\tau_1 \ldots \tau_n$, then
$I, s \models$ A iff $\langle \mathrm{Val}(\tau_1) \ldots \mathrm{Val}(\tau_n)\rangle \in \mathrm{Val}(P^n)$.

(4) $I, s \models \neg$A iff not: $I, s \models$ A

(5) $I, s \models$ (A&B) iff $I, s \models$ A and $I, s \models$ B

(6) If v is the j-the individual variable, then
$I, s \models \forall v$A iff $I, s\# \models$ A for every $s\#$ which is a j-variant of s in the 0-th row.

(7) If V is the j-th n-place predicate variable, then
$I, s \models \forall V$A iff $I, s\# \models$ A for every $s\#$ which is a j-variant of s in the n-th row.

Truth is now defined in terms of satisfaction in the usual way. With consistency characterized in terms of the orthodox proof theory for second-order logic, the Completeness Theorem fails relative to this semantics, in the sense that there must be consistent second-order theories which lack a model.[8] Hence, accordingly, the hope that realism may avoid Completeness-induced headaches by insisting that ideal theory take second-order shape.

But this standard semantics is not the only one in the field, there is also the *Henkin semantics*.[9] A Henkin interpretation H for a second-order

---

[7] The precise notion of 'set' in play is tendentious; see Shapiro, ibid., § 1.3. The present discussion is intended to be neutral on the issue.

[8] This result follows from Theorem 4.14 of Shapiro (ibid., 87). By the 'orthodox' proof theory is meant Shapiro's deductive system $D2$ (ibid., 66–7), though Shapiro's proof applies to any sound, effective deductive system.

[9] Ibid., 73–4.

language $L2$ based on an embedded first-order language $L1$ is a triple $\langle D_H, D_H, \text{Ref}_H \rangle$ where (suppressing subscripted indexing of H) $\langle D, \text{Ref} \rangle$ is an interpretation for $L1$, and D is a function from the nonzero integers assigning to each n an appropriate domain for the n-place predicate variables of $L2$. Specifically, let D^n be $D \times \ldots \times D$ (n times), so that $D^1 = D$, and D^n for $n > 1$ is the set of all n-tuples of elements of D. Then $\text{D}(n)$ for $n > 1$ is a nonempty set of subsets of D^n (the set of all n-tuples of elements of D); with the further requirement that $\text{Ref}(P^n)$ is always a member of $\text{D}(n)$, for each predicate letter P^n of $L1$. Satisfiers are again denumerably long, denumerably rowed sequences; the bottom row of such a sequence is, as before, a denumerable sequence of elements of D, whilst the n-th row for each $n > 0$ is a denumerable sequence of elements of $\text{D}(n)$. Precisely the same clauses as operated in the standard semantics can now be used to characterize truth and satisfaction for the Henkin semantics. A *faithful* Henkin interpretation is one which satisfies the axioms of the orthodox proof theory. And now the crucial difference between this semantics and the standard one is that Completeness holds for second-order theories relative to the Henkin semantics: any second-order theory which is consistent by the lights of orthodox proof theory has a faithful Henkin model.[10]

Assuming, then, that the ideal theory is to be a second-order one $T2^*$, written in a second-order language $L2^*$, the question arises as to whether there is just one true 'intended' model theory for $L2^*$, and that the standard semantics, so that embarrassing Completeness-induced questions for realism do not arise; or whether the Henkin model theory is equally legitimate, providing a semantic seedbed out of which Completeness may again spring, to the discomfiture of realism. Now, whilst the constraints of the last chapter were framed for the purpose of choosing between various interpretations *within* a single model-theoretic framework, rather than of choosing between whole model-theoretic systems, it seems nevertheless that the considerations there advanced can be adapted to clarify the issues involved in the present case, too. For the considerations there advanced suggested that translation from the language of ideal theory into the metalanguage must be virtually homophonic, so that an intended interpretation could be defined as one specifiable in the metalanguage by the provisions of the Homophonic Constraint. Similarly, a model-theoretic framework for $L2^*$ may be judged legitimate if it admits intended interpretations for $L2^*$, these being interpretations satisfying a Homophonic Constraint.

The question arises, accordingly, of the shape a Homophonic Constraint for $L2^*$ might take. That, in turn, is brought into sharper focus by considering the Homophonic Constraint not in the final, finitary, form in which it

---

[10] Shapiro, *Foundations without Foundationalism*, 89–91.

was stated in section 3.6, but rather in the infinitary form which preceded that formulation, from which it is apparent that the critical question is that of how virtually homophonic translation into the metalanguage is to be construed. It is clear, moreover, that the hedge in 'virtually' must do more work now than it had to do in the first-order case. Then, the only departure from strict homophony required was to restrict variables of object-language sentences by using a metalinguistic domain-predicate; such a departure will, of course, be required once more, but will need to take a more complex form, since some range-indicating device will be required not for individual variables alone but also for predicate variables in their many forms. But a further departure from pure homophony will also be required. For both forms of semantics envisaged are stated in the first-order language of set theory, and accordingly presuppose a first-order metalanguage. So predicate variables will be replaced in translations by first-order individual variables over sets, and set membership will take the place of predication when predicate variables are involved.

These considerations suggest the form of virtually homophonic translations of sentences of $L2^*$ into a first-order metalanguage $ML2^*$ might be given as follows. First, consider $ML2^*$ formulated as a many-sorted language, with variables v to match the individual variables v of $L2^*$, and further *individual* variables V to match $L2^*$'s predicate variables. Then form the *provisional* virtually homophonic translation of a formula A of $L2^*$ by

(i) replacing each subformula in A of the form
$V \tau_1 \ldots \tau_n$

by

$\langle \tau_1 \ldots \tau_n \rangle \in V$
(identify $\langle \tau \rangle$ with τ for this purpose),

then

(ii) replacing all variables v and V by v and V.

Next, form the virtually homophonic translations out of these provisional ones by cashing formulae with the many-sorted variables as shorthand for straightforward first-order ones with variables restricted by suitable predicates of the metalanguage. The variables of the metalanguage are now of a single semantic sort, and function in the same way syntactically; nevertheless, it is convenient to imagine them coming in two syntactically differentiated upper- and lower-case styles, to simplify statement of the conventions relating one-sorted statements and their many-sorted abbreviations. As for the restricting predicates of the metalanguage, *formally* speaking what is required is a predicate OTx (used for restricting variables v supplanting individual variables v of the object-language) and another REL(X,n) (for use with variables V supplanting n-place object-language predicate variables V). Then we have the following abbreviatory schema:

(1) $\forall v A(v)$ abbreviates $\forall v (OTv \rightarrow A(v))$

(2) $\forall V A(V)$ abbreviates $\forall V (REL(V, n) \rightarrow A(V))$, where n is the number of places of the predicate variable which V replaces, and n is the numeral for n

(3) $\exists v A(v)$ abbreviates $\exists v (OT \, v \& A(v))$

(4) $\exists V A(V)$ abbreviates $\exists V (REL \, (V, n) \& A \, (V))$, where n is the number of places of the predicate variable which V replaces, and n is the numeral for n

(5) $\{\langle v_1 \ldots v_n \rangle \mid A(v_1 \ldots v_n)\}$ abbreviates $\{\langle v_1 \ldots v_n \rangle \mid OTv_1 \& \ldots \& OTv_n \& A(v_1 \ldots v_n)\}$.

The critical question now is whether semantic frameworks under consideration enable flesh to be placed on these formal bones, by allowing room to identify suitable candidates for the restricting predicates OTx and $REL(X,n)$, and, hence, the articulation of a Homophonic Constraint.

The problem of finding a candidate for the predicate OTx is familiar from the first-order case discussed in sections 3.4 and 3.6. There, it was eventually proposed to identify it with the predicate 'x is an individual', and we may simplify discussion by assuming that proposal carries through to the present context. True, it is an assumption we may later choose to abandon, since the proposal was partly fired, in discussing the first-order case, by a need to stratify the ideal theory driven by considerations arising out of the Completeness Theorem, and a different model may suggest itself should the second-order alternative prove to be a way such considerations may be defused. At the same time, accommodating OTx is a problem common to the homophonic translation of $L2^*$ under both the semantic approaches under investigation, and a single solution will evidently be applicable to both (since it is not in their treatment of individual variables that they differ); and it is surely reasonable, at least *pro tem*, to take that solution as the one applicable in the first-order case, whose treatment of individual variables is that which both approaches have carried over.

What, then, of $REL(X,n)$? For the standard semantics, the obvious suggestion is to take it as 'X is an n-place relation between individuals' (identifying a 1-place relation with a set). Virtually homophonic translation into the metalanguage should draw as little as possible on concepts not available in the object-language, and this identification is very much in the spirit of that requirement. For the conceptual freight of $REL(X,n)$ as it construes it is of the abstract, formal nature which may plausibly be reckoned available to any interpreter, and so on hand to be superadded to the concepts imported by the object-language and the ideal theory it houses. Moreover, it is a simple enough matter to show there will be an interpretation of L2* meeting a Homophonic Constraint based on this conception of virtual homophonic translation; such, indeed, will be the Homophonic Interpretation for the first-order language L1* which L2* embeds. Thus, it appears that the standard semantics provides a legitimate framework for the model theory of L2*, inasmuch as it provides a framework within which L2* has intended models.

But as for the standard semantics, so it seems for the Henkin semantics as well. Translation, as understood by the lights of hermeneutics, is not theory-neutral, but constrained by the theory brought to bear by the interpreter. Undiluted set theory is to the fore in determining the translation of predicate variables in the standard semantic framework just canvassed; but it is equally legitimate for homophonic translation to bring to bear the ideal theory $T2*$, as the cradle of the object-language concepts in which such translation trades. Then a suggestion is that REL(X,n) may be read as 'X is an n-place relation between individuals required by $T2*$', i.e., one of the minimal set of such relations which must be counted among the values of the predicate variables of $T2*$ if all its theses are to come out true. Because this suggestion envisages the possibility of predicate variables ranging over less than a full complement of relations of individuals, it articulates a concept of virtual homophonic translation consonant with the framework of Henkin semantics. An intended Henkin interpretation for L2* can accordingly be taken as one which assigns truth-values to wffs which match those of their virtual homophonic translations, or equivalently, as one specifiable by means of disquotational provisions on proper vocabulary and virtually homophonic specifications of domains, on the pattern of the Homophonic Constraint of section 3.6; and because all sets required are subsets of those figuring in an interpretation which is intended by the lights of the standard semantics, the existence of an intended Henkin interpretation follows from the existence of an intended standard one. Conclusion: the standard and the Henkin frameworks provide equally legitimate model-theoretic accounts for L2*, each relative to its own equally legitimate schema of virtual homophonic translation into the metalanguage. But this means that there is no escaping the problems posed for realism by Completeness by casting ideal theory in a second-order language, since Completeness survives in the context of the Henkin model theory, and there are no grounds for thinking that semantic framework any less legitimate than its standard competitor.[11]

---

[11] Compare Putnam's brief comments on second-order languages in 'Models and Reality', 23. The foregoing is intended as an elaboration of these comments, adapted to the line of argument of the present discussion.

We noted some paragraphs back how both the semantic treatments under discussion involved some considerable departure from homophony, inasmuch as both proposed using a first-order metalanguage to interpret the second-order object-language; and we might speculate about the possibility of a different semantic approach altogether, in which the metalanguage itself was second order, and predicate variables were somehow deployed in the metalanguage to explain the semantics of their object-language cousins. Such is the project of George Boolos,[12] who provides a radically different semantics, which takes seriously a reading of predicate-variable/quantifier combinations as plural quantification, and in which predicate variables differ fundamentally from individual ones in not ranging over a domain of entities of any sort. Boolos's semantics is not, however, a model theory, but is presented as a Tarskian truth theory; and, though he shows how to extend it to obtain a definition of the validity (or 'supervalidity', as he calls it) of a single sentence, he finds it impossible to extend it to a full account of logical consequence. For that to happen, '[w]hat we want is some way to explain what it is for some sentences ... to be true under some one interpretation ... There seems no way to do it for an infinite set of sentences, however.'[13] In other words, the Boolos semantics is *irreducibly* truth-theoretic, and incapable of generalization in a model-theoretic elaboration of what it takes for the ideal theory to be true. As such, it will fall in the scope of the discussion to come, of the hopes for realism in a purely truth-theoretic analysis of truth (see below, Chapter 8), but is beside the point of the present discussion, where the claims of a model-theoretic analysis are at issue.

4.2 MODIFYING THE MODELS

This chapter began by identifying two strategies which the realist might deploy in order to avoid the difficulties engendered by the applicability of the Completeness Theorem to the ideal theory. The first, on which we have concentrated so far, is to insist that the theory be cast in some non-first-order language which resists Completeness. We turn now to examine the second strategy: to allow ideal theory to continue to be rendered in first-order form, but to argue for a semantics in which interpretations take such a new shape that there is no longer any guarantee that any consistent theory has a model in the new sense.

---

[12] Boolos, 'Nominalist Platonism'.   [13] Ibid., 343–4.

G. H. Merrill[14] has a proposal, heartily endorsed by David Lewis,[15] which fits the pattern. His leading idea is to exploit the thesis that the world is *inherently* structured—structured, not by classifications imposed on it by thought or language, but by inbuilt cleavages entirely independent of human psychology and convention. This structure is imposed by a system of 'natural' properties, both non-relational and relational,[16] founded on immanent, mind-independent similarities between things. Subscription to some such doctrine of structuring natural properties is, Merrill urges, a familiar component of traditional realist thought. Hence, it is entirely in the spirit of realism to invoke it in a model-theoretic explication of realist truth, by reconstruing interpretations so as to require that the referents of predicates should always be extensions determined by natural properties—'elite' sets and relations, as Lewis styles them.[17] So a *Merrill interpretation I* for a first-order language L is like a standard interpretation, save that $\text{Ref}_I(P^n)$ must always be an elite set or relation, of appropriate degree, over D_I. Satisfaction and truth relative to such an interpretation are explained as in the standard case. Clearly, there is no proving that an arbitrary consistent first-order theory has a modelling Merrill interpretation by the standard Completeness Theorem techniques, since there is no guarantee that the referents of predicates in the models yielded by such techniques will be elite. So an explanation of truth by Merrill interpretations apparently faces no challenge to the doctrine that the ideal theory may be false arising from the Completeness Theorem, even allowing that ideal theory may take first-order form.

As noted above, Merrill's general approach wins the support of David Lewis, though naturally this endorsement is not without the imparting of a little additional Lewisian spin. To start with, Lewis formulates the proposal, not as a *reconstruction of* standard interpretations, but as a *constraint which governs* them. In the form in which Lewis originally considers it, and which he takes to be most faithful to Merrill's own conception, this constraint is one met only by standard interpretations I for which $\text{Ref}_I(P^n)$ is always an elite set or relation, of appropriate degree, over D_I. Call this the

[14] G. H. Merrill, 'The Model-theoretic Argument against Realism', *Philosophy of Science*, 47 (1980), 69–81.
[15] See David K. Lewis, 'New Work for a Theory of Universals', in his *Papers in Metaphysics and Epistemology*, 47–9; and 'Putnam's Paradox', 64–8.
[16] By a 'relational property' (of degree n) is meant an n-place relation-in-intension; properties *tout court* can be identified with relational properties of degree 1. We reserve 'relation' (of degree n) to mean relation-in-extension, i.e., set of n-tuples; again, sets *tout court* can be identified with relations of degree 1.
[17] 'Putnam's Paradox', 65.

Eliteness Constraint. What manner of constraint is this? And what are the implications of presenting Merrill's proposals in this alternative form?

Lewis thinks of the Eliteness Constraint as a Reference Constraint, playing a similar role to the Causal Reference Constraint, though, in his mind, superior to it. So (though the terminology is not his) he evidently treats it as a constraint on the intendedness of interpretations. Thus, as Lewis sees things, the impression that Merrill's approach avoids the Argument from Completeness from the beginning is misleading; rather, it is a proposal to defeat that argument with a new constraint on intendedness. This immediately raises the question of whether the new constraint is subject to the 'just more theory' manœuvre discussed in section 3.6, and there hailed as a general defuser of constraints on intendedness. This is not, of course, a question which much troubles Lewis, since he claims to have shown that that manœuvre is inherently flawed. But it is an urgent one from the perspective of the present essay, which has argued that the manœuvre is worthy of more respect.

Perhaps it is not, however, a question that really arises after all. For it is not clear that the Eliteness Constraint can properly be counted as a constraint on the intendedness of interpretations at all. An intended interpretation is one truth relative to which can be identified with truth *tout court*, and the various constraints on intendedness introduced in the last chapter were all attempts to circumscribe the interpretations which are intended in this sense. In the context of the discussion in that chapter, these constraints were of interest to investigate the status of Completeness-guaranteed models of the ideal theory, to see if they could be excluded from the inner circle of intended interpretations; but quite independently of that context, it is essential for any model-theoretic explanation of truth to be supplemented by an account of intendedness, to extract an account of truth *simpliciter* from the fundamental, interpretation-relative concept which it defines. Now the discussion of the last chapter eventually fixed on the Translational Truth Constraint as the master constraint on intendedness, and the problem with the Eliteness Constraint, construed as a constraint on intendedness, is that it gives results at odds with that master constraint. For, however worthy the natural properties and the elite sets which they subtend may be, there is a regrettable human tendency to ignore these cleavages in nature, and prattle in terms devised to suit our own menial ends. Illustrations are tendentious, failing some fuller explanation of just how natural properties work. But, by any standard, it seems that a functional term like 'seat', including as it does in its extension a heterogeneous collection of objects ranging from thrones through beanbags to upturned boxes and conveniently placed and shaped treestumps, fails to correspond to any natural property or elite set. Hence, the Eliteness Constraint excludes from intendedness any interpretation assigning the set of seats as the referent of any predicate. In this, it is at odds with the Translational Truth Constraint, which will permit such an interpretation to count as intended provided the object-language is so used as to license translation of the predicate in play by 'seat'. And here, surely, it is the Translational Truth Constraint which gets it right.

None of this is news to Lewis. His response[18] is to dump the Eliteness Constraint as it has so far been expressed (and, in doing so, as he sees matters, significantly to modify Merrill's approach), and to retreat to a new constraining principle stated in terms of a *comparative* notion of natural properties, according to which some properties are more natural than others (and some sets, accordingly, more elite than others, depending on the comparative naturalness of properties whose extensions they constitute). This new principle he sometimes[19] styles, following Grandy, the *Principle of Humanity*. It governs the construction of hermeneutic theory, and requires that we should prefer theories which, in addition to meeting the other hermeneutic constraints, seek to maximize the naturalness of the content assigned to the meanings and beliefs imputed to the subject interpreted. Lewis continues to speak as if this new principle functions as a constraint on intendedness, playing a similar role to the old Causal Reference Constraint and the rest. But, in fact, it occupies a rather different place in the logical geography; in terms of the framework of the present essay, it is better located not as a constraint on intended interpretations, but as a constraint to be met by hermeneutically adequate truth theories. And, so viewed, its formulation in terms of the comparative notion of naturalness does seem to achieve its desired effect, in not totally discrediting interpretations which deal with seats and other things which fall short of perfect naturalness. For, in constructing a hermeneutic theory, it directs us to select, out of truth theories otherwise equally suited by the principles of hermeneutic fit, a candidate whose specified interpretation, when it comes to predicate referents, makes more overall use of sets higher on the eliteness scale than does any competitor; and there is no reason why choice should not accordingly fall on a truth theory whose interpretation makes play with the set of seats, less than perfectly elite though that set may be.

Lewis's original idea, prompted by Merrill's work, was to use the Eliteness Constraint to counter the Argument from Completeness. Doubts were expressed above about this strategy, on the grounds that the Eliteness Constraint, like any other constraint on intendedness, should (Lewis's dismissal

18 'New Work', 48; 'Putnam's Paradox', 65–6; David K. Lewis, *On the Plurality of Worlds* (Oxford: Basil Blackwell, 1986), 38–9 and 107.
19 Ibid., 39 fn.; and 'New Work', 52.

notwithstanding) fall foul of the 'just more theory' manœuvre; but then the status of the Eliteness Constraint itself as a constraint on intendedness was brought into question. Following out that thought, in a way anticipated by Lewis, leads to the transmogrification of the Eliteness Constraint into a hermeneutic principle, the Principle of Humanity. In doing so, it is relocated in logical space to a place not prima facie in reach of the 'just more theory' manœuvre, so our previous misgivings no longer apply. We may seem to have travelled a fair distance from Merrill's original suggestion; still, might Lewis be right that the Argument from Completeness can be defeated by applying the Principle of Humanity?

It seems not. To see why, let us first reflect on the oddness of the soubriquet 'Principle of Humanity' for a principle requiring the assignment of content to match, so far as possible, the cold and impersonal cleavages inherent in nature. Where, after all, does mere humanity fit into such a picture? Presumably the idea is that it is somehow programmed into we humans that our classifications should broadly come into line with the joints of nature. But then, in particular, the natural properties have already constrained the contents of the attitudes of any interpreter. So it seems that reference to natural properties can be factored out; that requiring that the interpretee's contents be brought broadly into line with joints of nature has the same effect as requiring that they match, as much as possible, those of the interpreter. But then the Principle of Humanity really seems to add nothing to the old Principle of Charity; and, indeed, Lewis is happy at times to use this as an alternative title for his principle.[20] Now the effects of the Principle of Charity on the Argument from Completeness have already been taken into account in the argument of the last chapter, where it figured in section 3.5 as one of the constraints on hermeneutic theory, used to explicate the key notion of translation. As such, it served as a bastion of the Translational Truth Constraint; but that was found wanting as a weapon against the Argument from Completeness. A stronger hermeneutic principle could, perhaps, have altered this outcome by adding ginger to the notion of translation and, hence, to the Constraint; but this hope is lost if, as now appears, the Principle of Humanity really has nothing to add.

If, then, Merrill's proposal cannot be implemented by a constraint on intendedness (because then it is inconsistent with the master constraint of that ilk), nor by a hermeneutic principle (since that turns out to be too weak a tool for the task in hand), how should it be expressed? An obvious answer is that it should be formulated as a proposal that interpretations should take a different shape. But since Merrill interpretations are, after all, just a

---

[20] 'New Work', 52; 'Putnam's Paradox', 65–6; David K. Lewis, *On the Plurality of Worlds* (Oxford: Basil Blackwell, 1986), 38–9 and 107.

restricted sort of standard interpretations, it must be possible *somehow* to present the proposal as requiring standard interpretations to satisfy a constraint; and, if that is not a constraint on intendedness or a hermeneutic principle, it had best be a constraint of some other sort—a *metaphysical* constraint, to coin a term—set beside the master constraint on intendedness, and the hermeneutic principles under which it operates, and imposing an additional constraint on those interpretations, truth relative to which can be regarded as fully fledged truth.

We are, thus, led to re-articulate Merrill's proposal as follows. Satisfaction relative to an interpretation I is defined in the standard way. A notion of truth, though a mere shadow of the full-bodied one—we might style it *pseudo-truth*—then emerges from satisfaction in the standard way: a statement is pseudo-true on I iff satisfied on I by all sequences. Non-relative pseudo-truth comes from relative pseudo-truth by using the notion of intended interpretations: a statement is pseudo-true iff it is pseudo-true on I for some intended interpretation I (judging interpretations intended by the standard of the master Translational Truth Constraint, operating under the normal principles of hermeneutics). Then, finally, a statement is *full-bloodedly* true iff it is not only pseudo-true but some intended interpretation on which it is pseudo-true also satisfies the metaphysical Eliteness Constraint, and, hence, is not only an intended interpretation but a Merrill interpretation.

An intended interpretation, on this account, can mess with such inferior sets as the set of seats, though Merrill interpretations cannot; so statements about seats can be a best pseudo-true, never true full-bloodedly. But consequences of this sort are integral to Merrill's approach, however we choose to present it. We can soften, but not eliminate, this effect by taking a leaf out of Lewis's book and thinking of the primary notion of naturalness among properties, and, hence, of eliteness amongst sets, as a comparative one. Then the natural properties can be construed as those ranking high in the ordering induced by the relation 'is more natural than', in the way the hairy men are those ranking high in the ordering induced by 'is hairier than', and the vagueness so introduced may be exploited to allow statements to be full-bloodedly true even though the referents of their predicates are less than fully elite—though it is doubtful that this latitude could reasonably extend so far as to encompass statements about things as heterogeneous as seats.

But if Merrill's proposal can be presented in this fashion, then the serious question arises once more of how it is to meet the challenge of the 'just more theory' manœuvre. For it is revealed, after all, just as the proposal that standard interpretations must meet some constraints—a 'metaphysical' constraint, it now appears, as well as the old constraint on intendedness.

And, the taxonomy of constraints notwithstanding, surely the manœuvre, judged in section 3.6 to defuse the master constraint on intendedness, will also work to draw the fangs from the new-fangled metaphysical constraint as well. It seems, however, that that is not so, or at least that it is not clearly enough so for us to be confident the old manœuvre will suffice to dismiss Merrill's approach. The reason is that constraints on intended interpretations of the language L^* of ideal theory, though stated in a metalanguage, draw on no concepts not available in the object-language itself, beyond the compulsory set-theoretic extras and a domain-predicate. (The full gamut of these concepts, whatever they may be, are appealed to by the master Translational Truth Constraint, as examination of that constraint in its guise as the Homophonic Constraint makes clear. In the case of the other, reductionist constraints discussed in the last chapter, they will be more specialized concepts of a causal or psycho-behavioural cast; but, again, they will be concepts we may expect to be found in ideal theory, and indeed there put to considerable use.) It is this dependence between metalinguistic constraint and the conceptual content of the object-language which the 'just more theory' manœuvre exploits, arguing that it renders the constraints impotent to act as an independent arbiter on the legitimacy of an assignment of content and, hence, truth-value to statements of the object-language. What is less clear is that the metaphysical Eliteness Constraint shares a similar conceptual dependence on the object-language. We are familiar with the idea that a metalanguage must always contain some conceptual excess over its object-language, and have supposed this so far to be limited to the abstract minimum, a modicum of set theory. But Merrill's realist may argue that the notion of a natural property, and, hence, of an elite class, is an additional, metaphysical primitive required in any metalanguage which is to make sense of full-blooded truth as it applies to the language in which we discuss the physical world, so that the Eliteness Constraint does not share with constraints on intendedness that conceptual dependence on the object language needed for the 'just more theory' manœuvre to succeed.

We may, and with considerable justification, protest that the notion of an essentially metalinguistic metaphysical primitive is too murky to play the role it is called upon to do; but such protests will be met with stout denial, and it is not clear how the issue is to be cleanly resolved. Rather, then, than quibble about the legitimacy of the *status* here claimed for the concept of a natural property, let us concentrate rather on a more fundamental matter which has, for the sake of expository convenience, been allowed so far to pass without the scrutiny it deserves, namely the legitimacy of the concept itself. This will be the theme of the next chapter.

5

The Status of Natural Properties

5.1 NATURAL PROPERTIES AT WORK

As Merrill reminds us, the distinction between natural properties and the rest occupies an honoured and venerable place in traditional metaphysical realism. We may trace it back to Plato's distinction between predicates like 'just' and 'pious' which mark the Forms, and those like 'dirt' and 'hair' which do not; through Aristotle's contrast between predicates like 'man' which stand for substantial forms, and those like 'musician' or 'statue' which correspond to mere accidental unities or to artefacts; and on into the consequent doctrines of species, genera, and real essence which run through the scholastics to the moderns. But with Kant and the passing of traditional realism, and the more with the linguistic turn and the passing of traditional metaphysics in its entirety, doctrines of natural properties went rather out of fashion, and in the analytic tradition of the twentieth century they find few defenders. True, Quinton[1] and Quine[2] dabbled with the natural, but both ended up with an account too tainted with psychology to count as a true doctrine of natural properties in the present sense. Which left just a few isolated figures, such as the trope theorist Donald C. Williams,[3] as the last friends natural properties had.

Such, at any rate, was the situation until relatively recently. But, as the linguistic trend lost some of its impetus towards the end of the last century, and systematic metaphysics began to reassert itself within the analytic tradition, some realists turned again to doctrines of natural properties. David Armstrong[4] and Keith Campbell[5] are prime exemplars of the trend. But

---

[1] Anthony Quinton, 'Properties and Classes', *Proceedings of the Aristotelian Society*, 48 (1957), 33–58.

[2] W. V. Quine, 'Natural Kinds', in his *Ontological Relativity and Other Essays* (New York: Columbia University Press, 1969), 114–38.

[3] D. C. Williams, 'On the Elements of Being', *Review of Metaphysics*, 7 (1953), 3–18, 171–92.

[4] D. M. Armstrong, *Universals and Scientific Realism*, Vol. 1 (Cambridge: Cambridge University Press, 1978).

[5] Keith Campbell, *Abstract Particulars* (Oxford: Basil Blackwell, 1990).

nowhere are natural properties put to more sophisticated use than in the metaphysical system of David Lewis, and across a far broader front than the deployment in hermeneutics upon which we have already touched. To the writings of Lewis we accordingly turn, seeking to evaluate the defence of natural properties proffered by their greatest champion in the contemporary literature. Such an evaluation involves, as we shall see, a detailed examination of the uses to which natural properties are put by Lewis, which will take us into the bowels of his metaphysical system—strange territory indeed, in the eyes of many. But the overall shape of Lewis's system is ably and eloquently defended in his writings, and it is not in any case part of the current brief to endorse it. Rather, our aim is to study natural properties in their natural habitat, where they may be presumed to flourish best. If even there they fail to survive scrutiny, they will certainly have no place in the less sympathetic environment of a non-Lewisean metaphysic.

What, then, are the ways in which Lewis appeals to the notion of a natural property in elaborating his metaphysics?

(a) There is the use of the notion to found the concepts of the *theory of duplicates*. Two things are defined as duplicates iff they have the same perfectly natural properties (NW, 27; *Plurality*, 61, treating the second clause as redundant).[6] Then intrinsic properties emerge as properties which can never differ between duplicates (*Plurality*, 62; NW, 26). Generalizing this definition beyond the monadic case gives the category of internal relations[7] (NW, 26 fn. 16; *Plurality*, 62). And events are properties of regions which are predominantly intrinsic (NW, 44–5).[8] Thus these categories, arising through duplicate theory out of the perfectly natural properties, become available for use in familiar dilemmas and theses of Lewisian metaphysics. So, for example, the problems of accidental and temporary intrinsics (*Plurality*, 201–2), central to his doctrines in the metaphysics of identity, make essential use of duplication-theoretic terminology. So, too, does the dilemma posed for the exponents of 'magical ersatzism' (*Plurality*, 179 ff.), whom Lewis seeks to embarrass by a demand to classify as internal or external a relation of 'selection' playing a crucial role in their position. Duplicate theory is used to frame the ban on 'backtracking counterfactuals' critical in the celebrated analysis of causation (NW, 33; and see the

---

[6] The references are to 'New Work' and *On the Plurality of Worlds*, respectively. These are the main sources for Lewis's views on the present topic, and so will be referred to frequently in this chapter; hence, the adoption of these abbreviated styles.

[7] In expounding Lewis, we adopt his terminology, and use 'relation' as the many-place analogue of 'property'—that is, to mean the same as 'relational property' in the preferred terminology of the bulk of this book.

[8] See also, § 7 of David K. Lewis, 'Events', in his *Philosophical Papers*, Vol. 2 (Oxford: Oxford University Press, 1986), 241–69.

references there cited). And it figures in the formulations of some of the central supervenience claims which shape debate in the Lewisian system, such as materialism—the doctrine that 'among worlds where no natural properties alien to our world are instantiated . . . any two . . . that are exactly alike physically are duplicates' (NW, 37); or the even more fundamental thesis of 'Humean supervenience'.[9]

(b) Natural properties also play a role in the *analysis of legality*. It will not quite do, according to Lewis, just to say Ramsey-style that laws are those regularities which are entailed by a systematization of the truths which combines maximal breadth of coverage with maximal simplicity. For the simplicity of the systematization will depend in part on the vocabulary in which it is stated, and without some prior constraint on permissible vocabulary the simplicity requirement is too easily satisfied to have any real bite. The solution is to constrain the vocabulary by requiring that its primitive predicates must stand for perfectly natural properties (NW, 41–3).[10] It follows that perfectly natural properties are implicated not only in the analysis of laws themselves but also in other concepts into whose analysis laws enter—most notably, causation, since laws are involved in spelling out its counterfactual analysis (NW, 43). (There is, however, some overkill here, since duplicate theory has already entangled causation firmly in the web of natural properties, through the formulation of the ban on backtracking and the analysis of the events which cause connects (NW, 43–4).)

(c) Finally, there is, of course, the appeal to natural properties in the *assignment of content*, through their use in framing the hermeneutic Principle of Humanity. We have already (section 4.2) observed this Principle used in a direct attempt to combat the Argument from Completeness, and found it wanting, concluding that if natural properties are to defuse that argument, they will need to be rather differently deployed. But there are other puzzles Lewis seeks to solve by applying the same Principle. One is the Wittgensteinian rule-following conundrum (in Kripke's formulation), the problem of whether an agent is to be interpreted as adding or quadding (where to quadd is just like to add, until the sum reaches some limit which our agent's additions have, in fact, never yet reached; after which limit quadding diverges from adding, and always yields 5 as the result of the quaddition). For though attributing to the agent either the desire to add or the desire to quadd is equally consistent with the principles of fit, because adding is a more natural property than quadding, the Principle of Humanity forces interpretation to regard the

---

[9] 'Introduction', in David K. Lewis, *Philosophical Papers*, Vol. 2, ix ff.
[10] See also, David K. Lewis, 'A Subjectivist's Guide to Objective Chance', in his *Philosophical Papers*, Vol. 2, 123–4.

agent as an adder rather than a quadder (NW, 53–4). A second application uses the Principle of Humanity to turn a nasty cardinality objection to modal realism coming from David Kaplan and Christopher Peacocke. This objection rests on the assumption that any proposition can be the object of a legitimate belief; but Lewis feels safe in rejecting the assumption, on the ground that propositions involving grotesquely unnatural properties could never figure in belief-attributions legitimized by the Principle of Humanity (*Plurality*, 104–8).

Natural properties, then, play a crucial role in Lewis's metaphysics, alongside the more obvious and showy modal paraphernalia—the plurality of worlds and their inhabitants, and the relations of 'counterparthood' between world occupants, and of 'closeness' between worlds themselves. But what is the logical status of the notion of the natural in Lewis's system? He vacillates between two alternatives (*Plurality*, 63–9): whether it is best treated as primitive; or as defined within a deeper underlying metaphysic.

Suppose first it is a primitive. Then a subsidiary question arises: precisely *what* is the primitive required? As we noted in section 4.2, one of Lewis's refinements of Merrill was to urge the utility of a comparative notion ('more natural property than') in shaping the Principle of Humanity. But, in framing duplicate theory and analysing legality, it is an absolute concept ('perfectly natural properties') which is deployed. Which, then, is the more basic of the two? The obvious approach is to treat the relative notion as the more fundamental. Then we may take as our primitive the two-place predicate 'P_1 is at least as natural as P_2' (where P_1 and P_2 are properties, i.e., in Lewis's terms, classes of this- and other-worldly individuals), and define a perfectly natural property P as one which is at least as natural as any property P_1. Alternatively, we can treat the absolute notion as the more basic, taking as our primitive the one-place predicate 'P is perfectly natural'. Then we can introduce a measure of the complexity whereby other properties are definable out of the perfectly natural ones, and explain the relative concept 'P_1 is more natural than P_2' as meaning that P_1 is definable out of perfectly natural properties in a less complex way than is P_2. This second alternative is clumsier than the first, but seems to be the one Lewis himself prefers (NW, 53; *Plurality*, 61).

(One complication. Properties, it was just said, are classes for Lewis; but, in fact, his most recent work he advocates reducing use of specifically class-theoretic apparatus to an absolute minimum, and mereology and plural quantification are made to do much class-theoretic work. This means that in the most up-to-date presentation of his theory, the primitives would not be predicates of properties/classes as here, but would rather be 'multigrade' predicates of individuals with no fixed adicity. So the primitives would be '$x_1 x_2 x_3 \ldots$ are jointly at least as natural as are $y_1 y_2 y_3 \ldots$' if the relational notion is taken as basic; or '$x_1 x_2 x_3 \ldots$ are jointly perfectly natural' if the absolute notion is favoured. We shall, however, continue to talk class-theoretically for the sake of perspicuity; if Lewis's strategy works, applying his techniques will eliminate such talk here as in other contexts.)

What of the alternative to taking natural properties as somehow primitive, namely somehow to found them upon an underlying metaphysics? Specifically, what Lewis has in mind is that the underlying metaphysics should take the shape of an ontology either of universals, or of property-instances or 'tropes'(*Plurality,* 64–9). The version of the theory of universals he considers is one which posits universals corresponding precisely to the perfectly natural properties, so that to each perfectly natural property there corresponds a universal and vice versa. Then a perfectly natural property can be defined as a maximal class of individuals all of which instantiate some one universal. Similarly, his preferred theory of tropes is one which posits, for each perfectly natural property, a class of duplicate tropes, precisely one of which is present in any individual displaying the property in question. Then call a class *trope-unified* if in each member of the class there inheres a trope which is a duplicate of some trope inhering in any other member of the class, and we can define a perfectly natural property as a maximal trope-unified class. Notice how, in both cases, it is the absolute, nonrelative notion of natural property which emerges with most ease from the underlying metaphysic. This perhaps is why Lewis seems to favour this as the more basic notion, even though, as we noted two paragraphs back, it would otherwise seem more attractive to take the relative concept as the more fundamental.

Though Lewis is officially undecided as to which of three ways of treating natural properties—assumption as primitive, or metaphysical foundation in either the universal or the trope version—is the best ('I think the honours are roughly even, and remain undecided' (*Plurality,* 64)), there is also evidence that his preferences lie on the side of ontological underpinning, if that can in any way be made to work, and that his reluctance to come out on that side outright is due to misgivings about the solidity of the underpinnings—about the possibility of fully articulating and defending a theory of tropes or universals in detail irrelevant for present purposes, but crucial for its ultimate metaphysical credentials. Thus, he writes: 'I would willingly accept the distinction as primitive, *if* that were the only way to gain the use of it elsewhere in our analyses'

(*Plurality*, 63, emphasis added), and the structure of his sentence betrays his preference for a version which avoids primitive predicates in favour of defined ones. But the grounds for this preference are unclear. For the ontologically underpinned versions of the theory merely replace a primitive predicate with equally primitive ontological assumptions of the existence of appropriate metaphysical entities. The definitions canvassed of the primitive predicate involve no dismantling of murky conceptual components, offer no insight into the metaphysically obscure.

A speculative explanation for Lewis's preferences here may be that the ontologically based versions have, in his eyes, the merit of providing a firmer basis for the 'objective' character of the classifications which natural properties enshrine. 'Objective' is, in fact, a word whose use has been carefully avoided until now in describing this feature of natural properties, because it is a loaded term in the present work, having been gradually levered in Chapter 1 into the status of a semi-technical expression whose primary employment is in talk of the objective obtaining of facts or (preferably) the objective truth of sentences. But this can hardly debar *Lewis* from using the term to describe the divisions natural properties reflect, and he does so: they are, as he puts it, 'carved at the joints, so that their boundaries are established by *objective* sameness and difference in nature' (*Plurality*, 227, emphasis added). This is, of course, an entirely reasonable use of a familiar philosophical term; but, as bowled by Lewis, it has its own spin, and one moving in an opposite direction to our own. For Lewis connects realism always with the *existence of objects*: 'For me, the question is of the existence of objects—not the objectivity of a subject-matter' (*Plurality*, p. ix). Assuming, then, the commitment to the objectivity of the boundaries which natural properties mark is a form of realism, it should be underwritten by the existence of appropriate entities—and these the ontologically based versions oblige by providing. From the perspective of our own preferred account of objectivity, however, which makes objective truth the central thing, the existence of such entities is beside the point. The important thing is, rather, that it be objectively true whether or no an object instantiates a natural property, and primitive natural properties can subserve such an account of natural truth every bit as well as any which come accompanied by metaphysical baggage.

Mention just made of the connection between perfectly natural properties and 'objective sameness and difference in nature' might suggest that exploiting this connection could lead to the sort of insightful conceptual analysis of natural properties which, it seems, the metaphysics of universals or tropes are impotent to provide. Lewis toys with this idea in a footnote (NW, 15 n., translating out of multigrade terminology). It turns out that, to make it work even at a formal level, we need to help ourselves to a complex relation of *property contrast* to record the facts of objective sameness and difference, namely, the relation

> the elements of P_1 resemble one another and do not likewise resemble any of the elements of P_2

or $R(P_1,P_2)$ for short. Then we can define 'P is a perfectly natural property' as

$$\exists P_1 \forall x (\mathbf{R}(\{x\} \cup P, P_1) \leftrightarrow x \in P).$$

But Lewis is surely right in judging that we have too little independent grasp of this *outré* relation $\mathbf{R}$ of property contrast to regard this definition as marking any real progress in conceptual elucidation.

In sum, it seems that a version of Lewis's theory which takes natural properties somehow as primitive suffers not at all by comparison with any alternative. For no viable analysis of natural properties is yielded either by alternative primitives such as property contrast, or by metaphysical reduction to universals or tropes; nor does anchoring natural properties in ontology genuinely secure the objectivity of the natural in a way taking it as primitive does not. For concreteness, we shall accordingly regard the primitive treatment as canonical; more specifically, the treatment which takes as primitive the non-relational predicate of properties 'P is perfectly natural', that evidently being the version of the primitiveness option favoured by Lewis himself, the merits of a relational alternative notwithstanding.

5.2 GROUNDS FOR BELIEF?

Why believe in this division of properties into the perfectly natural and the rest? Lewis gives us two distinguishable, but related, reasons: the division is needed to accommodate Moorean facts of common sense (NW, 20–5); and it is indispensably presupposed by systematic philosophy (*Plurality*, 63).

What are the Moorean facts which can be accommodated only by appeal to the division? Lewis's discussion of the point is complicated by the fact that it is intertwined with his assessment of Armstrong's views on universals. So he takes over Armstrong's examples and terminology, and accepts part of the Armstrongian mix whilst rejecting other elements; and a little care is needed to keep track of just which elements are being endorsed. Certainly, Lewis thinks, and convincingly argues, that Armstrong's beloved One over Many Problem is a pseudo-issue. Accordingly, he rejects Armstrong's attempts to connect accommodation of Moorean facts with solving the Problem. Still, that there are Moorean facts to be accommodated is common ground, and Lewis evidently also goes along with Armstrong's identification of what these facts are: they are facts of 'apparent sameness of type' (NW, 20 ff.).[11] Here 'apparent' does not mark any connection with the phenomenal, nor is it meant to imply that the Moorean 'facts' might only seem to obtain; rather, it signifies that the 'sameness' in question is less than absolute or complete, being a sameness holding between particulars which are uncontroversially distinct. So the Moorean facts in question are of the form 'a and b are of the same type', or 'have some common property' (NW, 25). Giving an account of these Moorean facts is, in words Armstrong uses[12] and Lewis endorses, 'a compulsory question in the examination paper'. And we can give such an account only by helping ourselves either to a primitive notion of naturalness (so that we can explain that 'a and b are of the same type' means 'there is some natural property which is instantiated by both a and b'), or else to other apparatus which can be used, by the techniques of the last section, to underpin the natural.

Or so Lewis puts it, at any rate (NW, 21). Evidently there is some simplification going on. For the canonical version of Lewis's theory, as we saw, takes as its primitive not the simple predicate 'is a natural property', but the more sophisticated 'is a perfectly natural property'. Now in Lewis's view, the perfectly natural properties are few in number, and, in paradigmatic cases at least, they apply not to the medium-sized objects of common sense but to the point-particles of science; typical examples he gives are properties of mass, of charge, and of quark flavour and colour (*Plurality*, 66–7).[13] Hence, we can directly explain what it is for a and b to be of the same type using the canonical primitive of perfect naturalness ('a and b are of the same type iff there is some perfectly natural property which is instantiated by both a and b') only in the special cases where a and b are point-particles, or similar arcane items. Explananda like these are, however, odd examples of Moorean facts, if these are to bear any resemblance at all to the sort of facts which interested the Moore who once held up his hand in Cambridge. For the resemblance to hold, we should rather expect Moorean facts to be statable in the everyday language of ordinary folk and to relate more directly to their interests—to be such facts as that a (Pharlap) and b (Tulloch) are of the same type (horses). Explaining facts like these in terms of the perfectly natural properties (or of apparatus apt to underpin them) will be a messy indirect business—'Pharlap and Tulloch instantiate some property definable in some not-too-complicated fashion out of perfectly natural properties'. Lewis's point remains intact; these Moorean facts, he will maintain, can be accommodated only by invoking perfectly natural properties

---

[11] And see Armstrong, *Universals and Scientific Realism*, i. 12 and 16.
[12] Ibid., 17.
[13] See also Lewis, *Philosophical Papers*, i. pp. ix–x.

or apparatus apt to underpin them. Still, the genuinely Moorean facts are accommodated less directly and more messily than are pseudo-Moorean ones concerning point-particles.

To Lewis's own Moorean facts of apparent sameness of type, borrowed from Armstrong, we may suggest adding some more, namely, those of 'comparative communality'. Examples are such facts as that horses have more in common than can-openers, green things than blue-or-green ones, and so on. For these evidently fit the bill for Moorean status, as common-sense truisms of ordinary folk; and the claim that they can be accommodated only by appeal to perfectly natural properties or apparatus apt to underpin them seems every bit as strong as in the case of facts of apparent sameness of type. They would, of course, be most neatly and directly accommodated within that version of Lewis's theory which we have deemed noncanonical, and which takes the relation 'is more natural than' as its primitive. But other versions of the theory will also serve to accommodate them, each in their own clumsier and less direct fashion.

If accommodating these Moorean facts is a compulsory question on the philosophical examination paper, then Lewis's first ground for insisting on the division of properties into the perfectly natural and the rest—that the division must be invoked for the facts to be accommodated—is really just a special case of the second ground, that there can, in general, be no good answer paper to the philosophical examination which does not invoke the division. Although the first argument from Moorean facts is thus in a sense subsumed under the second argument from the general demands of philosophy, it is helpful to have it separated out as of special importance. For, as we shall see, its specificity enables a sharper debate than is easily conducted over the sweeping general claims of the second argument.

5.3 A VEGETARIAN ALTERNATIVE

Despite the air of judicious neutrality we have tried to affect so far, this chapter comes to bury natural properties, not to praise them. In describing natural properties as those which 'carve nature at the joints', we have faithfully echoed the words of their adherents; but the present author must confess he finds this whole idea of a prejointed nature utterly mysterious. It is proposed, accordingly, to leave carnivores like Lewis, Armstrong, and Merrill to quarrel over the joints the natural properties carve, and in their place to propose that systematic philosophy make use of a strictly vegetarian alternative—the *cosy* properties, or, more precisely, the *T-cosy* ones, those which are cosy relative to a particular theory *T*. These we envisage as defined in terms of a more primitive notion, that of the T-cosy *predicates*. The basic idea is that these are the predicates playing the more central and fundamental classificatory roles within T.

One method, and the one preferred here, for trying to make this idea more precise is to attempt to explicate it in terms of the deductive connections between predicates revealed in an axiomatic formulation of T. This method, in turn, could be implemented in a number of ways. The one we shall try depends on the idea that a primitive predicate F of T is to be deemed more central to T (or T-cosier than) another primitive predicate G if, by T's lights, G can be instantiated only if F is; whilst nonprimitive predicates will derive their cosiness from the primitives out of which they are constructed.

Descending to details: let *the atom* of an n-place predicate F of T be the formula $\exists x_1 \ldots \exists x_n F x_1 \ldots x_n$. Say that atom a *T-implies* atom b iff $a \vdash_T b$, and that a and b are *T-equivalent* iff a T-implies b and b T-implies a. Form equivalence classes of atoms under the relation of T-equivalence, and call these the atom-classes. Then the atom-classes are partially ordered by the relation $\leq$, where $x \leq y$ iff every atom in x T-implies every atom in y. Now take a primitive predicate F as T-cosier than a primitive predicate G iff F's atom belongs to an atom class higher in this partial ordering than G's atom does; and take a primitive predicate F as perfectly T-cosy iff its atom belongs to an atom-class which is a maximal element in the partial ordering. (There will be some of these, of course, assuming there are only finitely many primitive predicates in T.) Notice that it follows from these definitions that primitive F is T-cosier than primitive G iff the atom of F T-implies the atom of G; and that primitive F is perfectly T-cosy iff it T-implies only atoms by which it is itself also T-implied.

(Two wrinkles on this. The idea is that a predicate earns its cosiness rating by being treated in the proof theory of T as comparatively more fundamental than other predicates. But it will be too easy for any predicate to become perfectly cosy simply by T deeming its atom an axiom. Therefore the relation $\vdash_T$ appealed to in the above definition of T-implication should more accurately be taken as $\vdash_{T-}$, where $T-$ is T minus any existential axioms. For similar reasons, the identity predicate, with its special quasi-logical status, had better be excluded from any place in the ranking. Else it will count trivially as the only perfectly T-cosy predicate, no matter what T should happen to be.)

Now we can extend the notion of cosiness to predicates beyond the primitive using a move similar to one we have seen Lewis employ. Thus, begin by defining a metric of T-cosiness over the primitive predicates, based upon the partial ordering just established. (As a starter, we might suggest taking a predicate's degree of T-cosiness as the number of atom-classes which, in the partial ordering, intervene between its own atom-class and a maximal element. This will give the perfectly T-cosy predicates a degree of T-cosiness of 0, and higher ratings as T-cosiness decreases.) Then take the degree of T-cosiness of a nonprimitive predicate as a function of the complexity of its definition in terms of primitive predicates and of the degree of T-cosiness of those primitives. For present purposes, nothing will depend on the details of the way this is done, though we shall assume that a complex predicate always has a lower degree of T-cosiness than does any primitive predicate involved in its definition. It will follow that only a primitive predicate can be *perfectly* T-cosy. But notice that nothing prevents a complex predicate from being merely T-cosy—all that is needed is that the extended metric rates it as having a degree of T-cosiness at least as high as that awarded to some primitive predicate already counted as T-cosy.

And now, by semantic descent, we can reflect this terminology onto the ontological level. To facilitate our descent, we may fairly avail ourselves, at least *pro tem*, of the general apparatus to hand in Lewis's system; for if our account is to be a real alternative to his, it should in the first instance at least be capable of playing on Lewis's home ground, and we can take account of the facilities available there. So we may take a *T-cosy property* as the class of all this- and other-wordly things of which is true some T-cosy one-place predicate; and a T-cosy relation of degree n as the class of n-tuples of this and other-wordly things of which are true some T-cosy n-place predicate.

The theories to which cosiness is thus relativized are intended, of course, to be formalized ones; otherwise it is unclear what are to count as the 'primitive predicates' of our definitions, nor will the proof-theoretic relations on which those definitions depend be properly defined. This means it is difficult to illustrate the notions just introduced in detail, failing detailed elaboration of proposed sample formalizations. Still, relative to any reasonable formalization of the theory of common sense, we may confidently predict that 'horse' will be less cosy than 'animal', and 'coloured' than 'extended', since in each case the atom of the former will imply within regimented common sense the atom of the latter. And within regimented physics, and unified science if that elusive theory ever gets regimented, 'quark' and the properties and relations of point-particles will rate as very cosy indeed, plausibly as perfectly cosy.

It was claimed earlier that there are other ways in which one might try to explicate the intuitive idea of the cosy predicates as the central and fundamental predicates of a theory, besides this attempt to do so in terms of the deductive relations holding within the theory. One such alternative would be to appeal to the way in which predicates are used by the adherents of the theory. And one way of implementing this strategy would be to emphasize the importance of the uses of predicates in acts of inductive projection, and to identify the degree of cosiness of a predicate of T with its degree of entrenchment in the sense of Goodman.[14] We have preferred not to take this as our first explicatory option, since it introduces temporal complications and needs development if relational predicates are to be properly incorporated. But it will do as a strong fallback position.

Like Lewis's division of properties into the natural and the rest, the cosy/noncosy divide, however explicated, separates properties in a way roughly coinciding with their felt importance. There the resemblance ends. The cosiness division is relative; the naturalness divide is absolute. More importantly, cosiness is grounded in human classificatory practices, being nothing more, in fact, than a systematic enshrinement of the familiar; naturalness is grounded in the nature of things, the purported joints of reality. The author confessed already to finding these joints entirely mysterious, and it is submitted that an unmysterious dichotomy like the cosiness divide must be preferable, if only on the ground that it can, one way or another, be analysed and explained rather than taken as primitive. Provided, of course, that with its aid Lewis's arguments in favour of his own division can be countered.

5.4 THE COMPULSORY EXAMINATION

First: can we, armed only with the paltry vegetarian distinction, meet Lewis's challenge, and answer Armstrong's compulsory question on the philosophical examination paper, the one about the Moorean facts concerning apparent sameness of type?

Good examinees always read the question carefully before attempting an answer. In this case, however, neither Armstrong nor his co-examiner, Lewis, has bothered to spell the question out. Setting the question seems to be part of the exercise.

Looking at the works of the historical Moore for clues, what we primarily find is a claim rather than an interrogation; the claim, namely, that certain basic precepts of common sense are true, and are known with certainty

[14] Nelson Goodman, *Fact, Fiction, and Forecast*, 4 edn. (Cambridge, Mass., and London: Harvard University Press, 1983). Mention of Goodman prompts the question of the rating on the cosiness spectrum of 'grue', one of Lewis's paradigms of the highly unnatural. Obviously, with cosiness explicated as entrenchment, it will for Goodman's reasons also rate lowly on the score of cosiness. Our preferred explication, on the other hand, allows it to count as pretty cosy relative to a T which treats it as primitive and adopts appropriate axioms; but here the point is that no such T can fairly claim to be a proper representation of any theory we take seriously.

by ordinary people to be so. Perhaps, then, the question our examiners have in mind demands that we provide a defence of Moore's claim, taking the relevant precepts as everyday judgements about apparent sameness of type. If so, it is doubtful that they have been entirely fair in making the question compulsory—venerable though Moore and his views may be, it remains philosophically entirely respectable to maintain that his heroic attempt at the refutation of global scepticism does not, in the end, come off. A fairer question, accordingly, is one which demands not that we actually defend Moore's claim but only that we explain its attractiveness, by so explicating the precepts in question as to make it at least highly plausible that they should be true, and should be confidently believed to be true by ordinary folk.

Cosy properties are all we need to answer the question as thus phrased. To start with, we may construe a common-sense judgement of the apparent sameness of type of objects a and b as meaning that a and b share a property which is cosy relative to common sense. (So Pharlap and Tulloch are of the same type because they share the property of being a horse, a property which is cosy relative to any reasonable regimentation of common sense.) The theory of common sense has stood us in good stead for many a long century, enabling us efficiently to hew wood and draw water. So there is every reason to believe that judgements made by experts in its use are true, especially when the judgements concerned are simple ones involving the more familiar of the categories common sense employs. But ordinary folk are experts in the use of common sense, judgements of apparent sameness of type are simple ones, and the cosy predicates are those which mark the more used and familiar categories. So there is every reason to think that the common-sense judgements of apparent sameness of type made by ordinary people are true. And since all of this is itself just common sense, not only do we have reason to believe these judgements true; so, too, do the ordinary folk themselves. Similar points can be made about judgements of comparative communality, suggested above as worthy of setting in the same Moorean class as those of apparent sameness of type. Treating 'Fs have more in common than Gs' as meaning that, according to common sense, being F is cosier than being G, considerations parallel to those just adduced will again yield the result that common-sense judgements of this form are almost certainly true, and can be known to be so by ordinary people.

Indeed, now that the examination question has been explicitly set, it is not entirely clear how Lewis himself has provided an answer to it. Suppose, with Lewis, that 'Pharlap and Tulloch are of the same type' is to be explicated as 'Pharlap and Tulloch instantiate some property definable in a not-too-complicated way out of the perfectly natural properties'; how does that help us to explain why the original judgement is likely to be true, or that ordinary folk have good reason to think that it is? Of course, Lewis is as free as anyone else to advert to the nature of common sense and our everyday expertise in order to account for these facts; the point is, however, that his explication, unlike that in terms of cosiness, will be idle in such an account, because his natural properties are in no direct way connected with common-sense expertise.

Indeed his explication may even seem to be directly at odds with the possibility of folk expertise on facts of apparent sameness of type. For if perfectly natural properties are the arcane properties of point-particles which Lewis evidently thinks they are, they are beyond the ken of ordinary folk; so too, *a fortiori*, are the details of any definitions which link the perfectly natural properties to the classifications of common sense; hence, if Lewis is right about what it takes for Pharlap and Tulloch to be of the same type, knowledge of this simple fact would appear to involve considerations well beyond the comprehension of we ordinary types.

This last point is, however, unfair. Moore[15] was at great pains to distinguish between the (ordinary) *meaning* of the critical propositions of common sense, and their *analysis*. The former is transparent, known to all competent in the language, and gives the content of the certainly known judgements of ordinary people; the latter is highly controversial, often difficult to discover, the subject of the legitimate doubts of philosophical theorizers. There are, of course, well-known difficulties with the distinction, centring largely on the question of how meaning and analysis should relate. But difficulties notwithstanding, some such distinction seems to be constantly presupposed by analytical philosophy. To free himself from any objection based upon conflating the content ordinary users judge to be true with that imputed to their judgements by philosophical theory, all Lewis need do is insist that his explication is along the lines of a Moorean analysis.

But this defensive sword cuts two ways. Lewis and Armstrong appear to see one of the great virtues of their explication of judgements of apparent sameness of type as being that it emphasizes the totally objective nature of the facts such judgements concern; indeed, that they regard it as part of the core Moorean meaning of such judgements that they are in this way totally independent of human minds and classifications, so that accounts such as that in terms of cosiness, which ground these facts in the classifications imposed by human theory and habit, can be rejected out of hand as incompatible with core meaning. Against any such view, we should reply that it depends on misplacing the alleged commitment to the objective; that

---

[15] G. E. Moore, 'A Defence of Common Sense', in his *Philosophical Papers* (London: Allen & Unwin, 1959), 37, 53 ff.

the question of whether there is any such commitment properly belongs to problematic analysis rather than uncontroversial core meaning, and so is up for legitimate debate. For what it is worth, this response can claim some endorsement from the authority of the historical Moore himself.[16] For among his live candidates for the analysis of 'This is a human hand' is a Millian account in terms of possibilities of sensation, and this finds at the level of analysis a hidden subjective component in a judgement which is, prima facie, as objective as any.

5.5 CAN VEGETARIANS SURVIVE?

Suppose we have now turned Lewis's first argument in favour of his property dichotomy, the argument from Moorean facts. What of his second argument, that from the alleged indispensability of the dichotomy to systematic philosophy in general?

The claim involved in the argument is sweeping. It is also vague, in the absence of any agreed criteria as to what should count as adequacy in a proposed alternative philosophy. These factors combined mean that stubborn obstinacy will always ensure at least the formal show of defence for Lewis's position against any counterargument, at any rate against any counterargument which tries to meet his claims head-on and rebut them by developing an adequate philosophy which eschews his dichotomy. For it can always be maintained that the proposed alternative is less than adequate in its treatment of at least some topics, by some austere unstated standard of adequacy; or that, though it may fare more or less well over the topics it discusses, further unspecified topics lurking over the philosophical horizon will necessitate the invocation of natural properties. For the purposes of discussion, however, let us assume that the burden of proof will be cast back on Lewis if it can be shown that the uses he himself makes of natural properties can be bypassed, where the adequacy of an alternative is to be assessed by doctrinally neutral criteria, which do not presuppose that adequate philosophy must take some predetermined stance on subjects of philosophical controversy. And here 'bypassing Lewis's uses of natural properties' does not mean reaching a similar conclusion to Lewis himself on all issues, though without benefit of natural properties. Sometimes, indeed, this may be the way to go; on other occasions, and particularly when Lewis's application of the notion is to address questions highly internal to his own metaphysic, the foe of natural properties may just dismiss Lewis's position as irredeemably tainted by false ideology. The question is

---

[16] Ibid., 57 ff.

whether the sum of the positions thus adopted on specific issues constitutes (or can be embedded in) a coherent, prima facie adequate, alternative to Lewis's philosophy.

In attempting to construct such an alternative, we shall permit ourselves to make free with the other apparatus of Lewis's system—his worlds and their inhabitants, and the relations of counterparthood and world-similarity. In doing so, we construct an alternative to Lewis's own system, differing only over the existence of natural properties. This brings into sharp focus the main point presently at issue; still, the question of the status of the rest of this paraphernalia remains unanswered in the background. Now Lewis's main argument for the existence of the worlds and their inhabitants parallels that for the existence of natural properties currently under consideration—their alleged indispensability for systematic philosophy; and a full investigation of the case accordingly requires, once again, the construction of an alternative, equally systematic, philosophy in which worlds are eschewed. The general thrust of the rest of this book will make it clear that it presumes that some such alternative is indeed viable (to be specific, where invocation of world apparatus is inevitable, that *pace* Lewis some form of ersatzist construal can be made to work). But actually presenting the detail of such an alternative is beyond the scope of the present work. More to the point, it is not required to resolve the matter under discussion, the status of natural properties; and we can freely invoke all the rest of Lewis's paraphernalia in constructing an alternative to his theory differing over this critical issue.

Consider first Lewis's use of natural properties to found the concepts of duplicate theory—of duplicates themselves, of intrinsic and extrinsic properties, of internal and external relations. The literature contains no alternative systematic treatment of these notions free of a similar appeal to natural properties. True, there is the option of sacrificing systematicity, and simply adopting the whole family of notions as primitives. But whilst that option apparently avoids entanglement with natural properties (because there is no evident way of reversing Lewis's analyses and defining natural properties in terms of these other concepts (NW, 27–8)), it is hardly consonant with the spirit of present approach. For example, to accept a primitive, objective extrinsic/intrinsic distinction is to allow the world directly to determine which properties are relational and which are not, a line which sits ill with an approach whose emphasis has been to derive the characteristics of properties rather from the theoretical formulation and use of corresponding predicates. We do best, accordingly, to take a more heroic line, to deny outright the existence of true duplicates, and to accept that with them we lose the legitimacy of the distinctions between intrinsic and extrinsic properties and between external and internal relations. Of course, this means bidding farewell to old friends from traditional metaphysics, but that in itself hardly establishes that no systematic philosophy can make the break and survive. We have, after all, got on fairly well for a long time without the relying on the real darling of traditional metaphysics, the apparatus of ideas; and the notions currently under scrutiny have, in any case, been used only with sparing suspicion by most philosophers in the analytic tradition, with renegades like Lewis who want to resuscitate them being the exception rather than the rule.

Though the suspect notions themselves must go, we can, of course, find vegetarian substitutes for them, by parodying Lewis's definitions but this time using cosy predicates as our base. Thus, objects are *T-duplicates* iff they share all properties which are T-cosy; a property is *T-intrinsic* iff any two objects which are T-duplicates must agree in either both possessing or both lacking the property; and so on. Then these vegetarian substitutes become available for use in framing analyses which parallel those of Lewis, and sometimes at least the analyses so framed can apparently be defended as embodiments of Lewisian insights purged of his overweening adherence to an inherently structured nature.

A simple example is the use of duplicate theory in framing the ban on backtracking counterfactuals in the analysis of causation. Lewis's requirement is, in a nutshell, that actuality and relevant counterfactual alternatives should be duplicates up to (very near) the time of the causing event (NW, 33; and see the references there cited). A formally analogous constraint is obtained by replacing this by the requirement that they be T-duplicates merely—though, of course, this will serve only in the analysis of a weaker notion of causation, similarly relativized to a theory T.

Again, Lewis analyses an event as a (predominantly) intrinsic property of regions, the point of the restriction to intrinsic properties being to rule out as events such properties as *Xanthippe's being widowed* (= *being a region at which Xanthippe is located when someone married to her dies*), whose instantiation at a region is entirely independent of that region's qualitative character.[17] We may parody this analysis, and define an event relative to T as a property of regions which is (predominantly) T-intrinsic; and—assuming T is anything like a straightforward regimentation of common sense or some more embracing physical theory—the restriction will serve a parallel purpose of preventing the same renegade property from counting as a parameter-relative event. Now choose a sufficiently salient T—say, contemporary physics, or, even more grandly, an ideal theory like the T^* of earlier chapters. Then events relative to T can be

---

[17] Lewis, 'Events', 262.

proffered as hygienic analogues of Lewis's own red-blooded metaphysical excesses.

But other applications Lewis makes of the notions of duplicate theory depend essentially on the more carnivorous features of his metaphysical underpinning or of the context in which the notions are deployed, so that there is no analogous move for would-be vegetarians to make. Recall, for example, his explication of materialism as the doctrine that 'among worlds where no natural properties alien to our world are instantiated . . . any two . . . that are exactly alike physically are duplicates'.[18] Were there no alien natural properties—natural properties neither instantiated in our world, nor analysable in terms of natural properties so instantiated—the restriction of the quantifier over worlds in this explication would be idle, and the whole equivalent to a version Lewis has already seen reason to reject (see *M1*, at *NW*, 35; Lewis rejects it because it renders materialism a non-contingent thesis). But, relative to many a reasonable *T*, there are no alien cosy properties, since the only primitive predicates in *T* are instantiated in this world and, hence, not alien. So this time we cannot reduplicate Lewis's manœuvre within the vegetarian framework. Again, Lewis's argument from dilemma against magical ersatzism (based, it will be recalled, on the demand that a relation of 'selection' crucial for the position be classified as internal or external) depends for one horn on the thought that any relation holding necessarily between two things must hold in virtue of the intrinsic natures of those things. That thought may be reasonable if the intrinsic natures are, as Lewis conceives them to be, rich repositories of the intrinsic properties handed out by a bountiful nature. But it is not reasonable if the natures are at best thin creatures, perforce limited to containing only properties specifiable in some theory, as niggardly vegetarians must think of them. Further (to take an application not reviewed in our opening catalogue of Lewis's uses of natural properties), vegetarians must do without Lewis's definition of the *analogically spatiotemporal relations*, which unite the members of a single world (*Plurality*, 75–6). These are defined as relations which are, *inter alia*, external and natural; the role of the latter condition is indispensable, but it can only work if natural relations can be singled out even in worlds so bizarre as to differ from ours even in spatiotemporal framework. There is, accordingly, no chance that merely cosy relations could fill any analogous role, since no matter what the theory to which they are relativized it will perforce be too entangled with the details of this world to be able to supply the relations required.

It may be argued that these consequences follow only from an unwarranted restriction of theories to those which are either already at hand, or

---

[18] Lewis, *Philosophical Papers*, i. p. ix ff.

which we can, at any rate, envisage as extrapolations from such theories; and that we could at least go further towards reconstruction of Lewis's positions if we allowed ourselves to consider also *alien* theories, constructed to describe other worlds entirely from an other-worldly perspective. Then alien natural properties and relations could be reconstructed as those generated by the predicates which are cosy relative to some such alien theory. But this is not a path we should be keen to tread. These alien theories are shrouded in too much mystery, and invoking them means surrendering the bluff robustness which is intended to be one of the more endearing features of the alternative we are out to construct.

Nor is there any real need to head down this unattractive path. For, even if we admit we have no way of echoing these moves of Lewis, there is still a long way to go to establish that our evolving alternative to his position does not constitute a basis for a sound and systematic alternative philosophy. If materialism can only be sharply formulated with the aid of suspect apparatus, perhaps that just goes to show what many have suspected all along—that there is here no single and coherent doctrine at all. Lewis's dispute with magical ersatzism is very much his own highly contentious business, and many will find it a positive virtue of our vegetarian alternative that it leaves the door still open on one way of avoiding his stark realism about worlds and their inhabitants. Similarly, Lewis's problems defining the boundaries of his worlds arise urgently in the context of that same realism; but solving them is a lower priority for those of us who hope that such use as we make of the apparatus of worlds will admit of eventual reduction, which can be safely left to settle details about world-boundaries and the rest.

Likewise, we shall also be unable to follow Lewis in a final deployment of duplicate theory, perhaps that dearest to his heart—its use to bolster his views on the metaphysics of identity through discussion of the problems of temporary and accidental intrinsics. In the temporal case, which, for present purposes, entirely parallels the modal one, the problem is to explain how temporal nature of continuant things is consistent with the possibility of change; where a thing is said to change when it swaps one apparently intrinsic property (say squareness) for another inconsistent one (say roundness). One solution to this problem is to maintain that a continuant thing *endures*, that it persists through time by being wholly present at successive times; but to deny that purportedly intrinsic properties like shape are genuinely properties at all, and to take the lesson the problem teaches as being that these are properly speaking relations to times. Thus, the very same enduring thing wholly exists at t_1 and t_2, and changes by bearing the squareness relation to the former but the roundness relation to the latter. Lewis rejects this solution out of hand: 'This is simply incredible . . . If we know what shape is, we know that it is a property, not a relation' (*Plurality*, 204). From any perspective, this dogmatic response is rather thin, inviting rebuttal by equally dogmatic counterassertion. But, more than that, it is simply unavailable from a standpoint which replaces natural properties by *T*-cosy ones, and thereby emphasizes that, on a proper construal, the whole apparatus of duplicate theory is entirely relative to the syntactic forms which theory finds convenient. Which shows no defect in the alternative standpoint; only that it is sympathetic to entirely arguable positions which Lewis does not favour.

There remains one complication before we pass on from duplicate theory to other applications which Lewis makes of natural properties. The systematization of duplicate theory considered so far is the fully developed one featuring in Lewis's major works, most notably *On the Plurality of Worlds*. But latterly, in combination with Rae Langton,[19] Lewis developed a fallback, alternative method of systematizing duplicate theory; and we should pause to consider whether the appraisal made above needs modification in the face of the existence of this fallback.

The new systematization is based on the key notion of a *lonely* object, that being one which is the sole inhabitant of its world. An *accompanied* object is one which is not lonely. A property is *independent of loneliness* (or, respectively, *of accompaniment*) iff there are lonely (respectively, accompanied) objects which both possess and lack it. A *basic intrinsic property* is a property which is independent of both loneliness and accompaniment, which is not a disjunctive property, and which is not the negation of a disjunctive property. Objects are *duplicates* iff they have the same basic intrinsic properties. Then (unqualifiedly) intrinsic properties, internal relations and the rest emerge out of duplicates in the old way.

Natural properties still enter into this new systematization, via the definition of 'disjunctive' properties, which are said to be those properties which are not themselves natural, but can be expressed by a disjunction of (conjunctions of) natural properties.[20] So the fallback position remains as unashamedly dependent on natural properties as does its forebear. One significant difference is that it need not appeal to *perfectly* natural properties: 'all we need is enough of a distinction to sort out the disjunctive properties from the rest',[21] and for this the 'natural-enough' properties will do, rendering the new systematization available for more timid metaphysical souls than Lewis himself, people less prepared to embrace the natural with the same enthusiasm as he. The authors even suggest[22]

---

[19] Rae Langton and David K. Lewis, 'Defining "Intrinsic"', in Lewis's *Papers in Metaphysics and Epistemology*, 116–32.
[20] Ibid., 120.   [21] Ibid., 131.   [22] Ibid., 119–20.

that a vegetarian distinction, like that between the T-cosy properties and the rest, is all that this fallback position requires. But this is a throwaway remark, one which they never develop. Certainly it seems that the fallback systematization, if developed on such a vegetarian basis, will yield only vegetarian versions of the key notions of duplicates, intrinsic properties, and internal relations, since the relativity to theory and its language which infect the T-cosy properties must infect notions introduced on the basis of them. But then it yields no sharper tools than those we have already supposed available in constructing a vegetarian alternative to Lewis's theory. So the judgements we have already reached on the merits of Lewis's deployment of natural properties in duplicate theory on the basis of his core development of that theory should stand, the existence of a fallback systematization notwithstanding.

As noted in our preliminary survey of the way natural properties work in Lewisian metaphysics, another use Lewis finds for natural properties is to solve a problem in the analysis of lawhood. Lewis favours a 'best-system' theory, according to which—roughly—laws are those regularities which are entailed by an axiomatic systematization of truths which simultaneously maximizes both simplicity of axiomatization and breadth of coverage; the idea being that a true regularity will be dismissed as merely accidental when the added breadth achieved by adding it (or the resources to derive it) as an axiom is outweighed by the loss of simplicity the addition entails. The caveat 'roughly' is eliminated, and natural properties come into their own, when it is further required that the best system be so formulated as to take only predicates referring to perfectly natural properties as primitive. Without that restriction on the form of the best system, Lewis holds, the identification of laws will vary overmuch with the way we choose to systematize 'the same content'.

Here much depends on the strength of 'overmuch'. Certainly, it would spell disaster for the whole best-system approach if it could be shown, as Lewis claims (NW, 41–2), that without the restriction any bunch of truths is guaranteed a systematization of utter simplicity, so that the critical tradeoff between simplicity and coverage becomes nugatory. But Lewis himself indicates how this result is avoided if we insist that the axioms of a best system should 'entail' the laws via deducibility in a specifiable respectable system of proof theory, not just by strictly implying them (NW, 42). And if total global disaster can be averted, there is no apparent reason why one should not just bite the bullet and accept that laws are relative to a suggested formulation of best system, even if differing formulations do in some intuitive sense seek to capture the 'same content'. The resulting relative notion of law may not be Lewis's, but it needs to be demonstrated that it cannot do the respectable philosophical work to which the concept of a law is usually put.

(Further, it may be added that it is unclear that Lewis himself really avoids the need to thus relativize the notion of a law. For, even with his restriction in place, the vocabulary of a best system is not entirely fixed. Moreover, different axiomatizations will play off breadth against simplicity in different ways. So, even for Lewis, different regularities may emerge as laws relative to different, but equally respectable, best systems.[23] His preferred solution is to reserve the title 'law' just for those regularities which are laws relative to all such systems. But there is no watertight guarantee even that there are any laws, thus defined; and certainly not that there will not be an uncomfortably large number of regularities left in limbo because of the varying judgements of different best systems.)

Actually, a sympathizer of the alternative position being developed here will probably prefer to eschew the best system approach to laws altogether. For the best-system approach presupposes a fixed body of predetermined truths which the best system systematizes; and this doctrine of a presystematic body of truths sits ill with the emerging tendency of our vegetarian position to relativize all concepts to the perspective of a theory. Perhaps, then, we do better to attempt to disentangle the accidental generalizations of a theory from its lawful ones in some quite different way—say, by using Goodman's notion of entrenched predicates, a notion clearly close to the spirit of our cosy predicates, even if not selected as the first choice for actually explicating them. We need not decide here between these and other alternatives to conclude at least that there are a number of plausible avenues for attacking the analysis of legality outside a framework of natural properties.

There remains to be considered Lewis's final deployment of natural properties, in framing the Principle of Humanity as a supplementary hermeneutic constraint to govern the assignment of meaning and content. One of Lewis's main applications of that Principle, its use to defuse the Argument from Completeness, was examined in section 4.2, and judged to be wanting. That verdict depended largely on the point that the Principle of Humanity appeared, even in Lewis's own system, to impose no genuinely stronger constraint on hermeneutics than the familiar Principle of Charity. Certainly, that same point must hold from the vegetarian standpoint, where the Principle of Humanity can amount to no more than the requirement that interpreters seek to read conceptual structure similar to that in their own favourite theory into the language and thought of the interpretee.

---

[23] Lewis, 'A Subjectivist's Guide', 124.

We may conclude that natural properties, acting through the Principle of Humanity, succeed in this application neither in their red-blooded nor their vegetarian embodiments; so on this score the two positions stand even.

A similar verdict seems warranted in the cases of the other two of Lewis's applications of the Principle of Humanity. The first of these, it will be recalled, is to refute an objection to modal realism due to Kaplan and Peacocke (see *Plurality*, 104–8), resting on the assumption that any proposition (class of worlds) can be a legitimate object of belief. But here the Principle of Charity, uncontroversially available to both positions whatever its relation to the Principle of Humanity, is all that is needed to refute that assumption, since among the indenumerability of propositions there will be a vast subclass with content so bizarre that the Principle of Charity will rule them unfit to figure in any interpretative scheme (because, whenever there is a pattern of behaviour these contents can be made to fit, some more familiar contents can be made to fit the pattern, too). Thus the two positions stand even, both containing the resources required for a successful resolution of the problem along Lewisian lines.

This equality is preserved in the final application Lewis makes of the Principle of Humanity, the resolution of Kripke's Wittgensteinian puzzle about adding and quadding. This is, perhaps, the least promising of all Lewis's appeals to natural properties. For, whatever the case about the physical world, the idea that mathematical reality is inherently jointed—that what makes the addition function more natural than the quaddition one is something intrinsic to mathematical reality, rather than the way we think about it—is peculiarly unappealing. Here, then, it is even more implausible than in general that the Principle of Humanity has anything to add to the Principle of Charity. And the latter Principle is impotent against Kripke's puzzle, since the whole point of this puzzle is that it can be applied self-reflexively to raise questions about the identity of our familiar concepts—are we interpreters ourselves adders, or do we quadd?—rendering any application of Charity here entirely question-begging. Again, then, Lewis's own theory and the vegetarian alternative come out equal; this time, equally unsuccessful.

With this go the last grounds we have for belief in the apparatus needed to frame the metaphysical Eliteness Constraint which Merrill and Lewis deploy against the Argument from Completeness. In place of that apparatus, we have the homely paraphernalia of the T-cosy properties; and these palpably will not suffice to frame a modified Eliteness Constraint capable of taming the Argument. For such a modified form of the Constraint would be used to select among the intended interpretations of an ideal theory T^*, preferring those which assign to predicates relatively elite classes and relations as their referents, where the rank of classes on the eliteness scale is determined by the T-cosiness of the predicates of which they are the extension, relative to the best available T — i.e., relative to T^*. But this condition is vacuous: since the eliteness of an extension, thus construed, varies directly with the T^*-cosiness of the predicates which subtend them, it imposes no additional constraint on interpretations. So the Merrill response to the Argument from Completeness fails, leaving that argument in command of the field.

PART III

REALISM WITHOUT CORRESPONDENCE?

6
Taking the Hierarchy Seriously

The argument of Part Two has been that no firm basis for the account of objective truth, which, by the lights of Part One, is required to defend realism, can be found in the notion of correspondence, even after that notoriously vague notion is clarified by precise model-theoretic techniques. Now correspondence is, indeed, the staff upon which realists have traditionally relied when pressed to defend their conception of truth. Nevertheless, perhaps some other basis can be found, after all, to provide the footing that conception needs. It is certainly beyond the ambitions and scope of the present work to carry out an exhaustive survey of all the possible foundations for objective truth the realist may attempt to invoke; indeed, in the absence of any clear limitation on the cunning devices which the realist may exploit, the very idea of such an exhaustive survey makes little sense. There are, however, some obvious candidates, arising out of the framework of this discussion and the literature which has inspired it, which demand attention. In particular, the centrality of Putnam's negative case against correspondence-based truth in the preceding pages demands that we should assign some priority to evaluating his further, more positive, ruminations on the nature of truth and its connections with realism. To these matters this concluding Part Three is, accordingly, devoted.

6.1 TRUTH AND SUPERASSERTIBILITY

Section 2.3, the last section of Part One, was devoted to a discussion of the status of the account of objective truth, in terms of the Hierarchy of Certification, which had been the burden of many of the preceding pages. It was there suggested that the account given is best viewed as an analysis of lower grade, aiming less to establish the credentials of the concept analysed than to clarify its logical characteristics, with an eye to subsequent Quinean explication. At the same time, it was acknowledged that there was room for a more heroic course, which would attempt to use the hierarchical account, or some interpretation thereof, as the basis of a fully fledged, respectability-establishing analysis of objective truth. Correspondence and model theory having proved weak reeds, it is time this possibility was examined.

A considerable debt to the work of Crispin Wright was acknowledged as the hierarchical account was developed. Now Wright certainly takes a version of the hierarchy seriously as a suitable basis for high-grade analysis, putting it to work, indeed, to advance 'superassertibility' as the analysis of one notion of truth. So a thought worth exploring—not, we must hasten to add, one we attribute to Wright—is that this may constitute the hierarchy-based analysis of objective truth which we seek. A moment's reflection, however, suffices to dismiss the idea. For it seems fair to represent super-assertibility[1] as stable certifiability from some standpoint in a hierarchy *like* the full Hierarchy of Certification of Part One, but more limited; specific-ally, a hierarchy limited to *humanly accessible* individual standpoints and *finite* unions thereof, and with certifiability freed from the requirement that it be based on public certifiability at the base level.

The second of these deviations means that superassertibility, as Wright defines it, evidently fails the publicity criterion for objective truth. This is, however, a superficial failing, which can be overcome by modifying superassertibility in its pure, Wrightian, form by reimposing the requirement that all certifiability be publicly based. But the limitation of the standpoints to the human ones and, in particular, the eschewing of levels beyond the finite ones, mean that superassertibility falls short of objective truth on the scores of both bivalence and epistemic independence, traits which, on the hierarchical conception, arise only out of extending the levels into the infinite and the consequent construction of the Total View. There may thus be much to be said for superassertibility as a concept of truth, perhaps even as the preferred concept of truth; but not, in the terms of this book, anything to be said for its claims as a concept of *objective* truth.[2]

---

[1] As defined by Wright in Crispin Wright, 'Can a Davidsonian Meaning Theory Be Construed in Terms of Assertibility?' in his *Realism, Meaning and Truth*, 414–15.

[2] It might seem doubtful that superassertibility passes muster as a truth-concept at all. For, surely, any decent concept of truth should distribute across the connectives. Yet we found in section 2.1 that establishing distributivity, e.g., for negation and disjunction, depended on acknowledging the existence of a Total View; so it would seem it could not be established within the truncated hierarchy which accompanies superassertibility. In fact, however, Wright is at some pains to establish that superassertibility does exhibit the formal properties of truth (ibid., § 3; *Truth and Objectivity*, chs. 1 and 2). The trick is that Wright assigns to the biconditional in the statements of distributive equivalence, as to other metalinguistic connectives, a nonclassical reading derived from the truncated hierarchy, whereas we read metalinguistic connectives as classical functions of objective truth—see above, § 2.1, in the text immediately following the introduction of [CONJ]. Should we later come to fall back on superassertibility as a replacement for objective

6.2 TRUTH AS IDEALIZED RATIONAL ACCEPTABILITY

Another candidate replacement for correspondence-based truth, highly salient from the present perspective, can also be represented as an attempt to found a notion of truth on a literal construal of the Hierarchy of Certification, at least in a modified form. This is the conception which Putnam himself proposes in *Reason, Truth, and History*, following the demolition of correspondence-based truth we have charted and defended in Part Two: the conception, namely, of truth as idealized rational acceptability. Truth so conceived, he there contends, enshrines a 'kind of objectivity', though not 'metaphysical objectivity'.[3] Accordingly, to hold that some set of sentences S is true in this sense is to adopt a kind of realism about them, a realism which Putnam styles 'internal' because of his emphasis on the theory-relative nature of rational acceptability, be it idealized or mundane. Admittedly, it is far from obvious how this conception is to be construed as involving a literal interpretation of the Hierarchy of Certification, as just claimed. But it is worth making the effort to construe it in these terms, to facilitate comparing it with the other concepts of truth in play.

The clue to connecting this Putnamian conception of truth with the Hierarchy of Certification lies in turning to the complications that arise if we reject a simplifying assumption imposed on the discussion of the Hierarchy back in section 2.1, namely that it be based on a molecular epistemology. To recapitulate: according to such an epistemology, the certifiability of a core atomic sentence from an epistemic standpoint s is settled by rules based on the meanings of the predicates and terms out of which the sentence is constructed, and utilizing observational information available at s, and the results of specifiable epistemic manipulations carried out at s; boundary rules then determine which noncore atomic sentences are certifiable at s, on the basis of the certifiability or otherwise at s of core atomic sentences; and, finally, the formal principles of certification settle which nonatomic sentences are certifiable at s, on the basis of the certifiability, at s and elsewhere, of their parts. How is the structure of certifiability affected, if this molecular epistemology is abandoned for a more holistic alternative?

One immediate consequence is clear: the certifiability of atomic sentences form a standpoint s will no longer be straightforwardly determined

truth, we may well also come to accept Wright's version as giving the preferred statement of the desirable properties for truth to possess.

[3] Putnam, *Reason, Truth, and History*, 55.

simply by their structure, along with observations to be garnered at s or calculations there made. Rather, a whole set of sentences—a whole *theory of s*, as we shall put it—will be deemed certifiable at s according as it efficiently systematizes the observational data available at s, according to familiar methodological canons whereby efficiency of theoretical systematization is to be judged.

The canons in question operate against the background of an assumed discernment of structure within the theory of s: among the sentences it certifies, some are denominated highly *observational*, and a subset of these *directly* observational; and a set of *laws* is identified among the less observational generalizations which it certifies. (The details of how these discriminations are to be made are both complex and tendentious, but fortunately make little difference from our present lofty perspective. Importantly, however, there is no commitment to saying that observationality, directness, and legality are any more than matters of degree; nor, further, that they be any more than distinctions internal to the theory they inhabit.) Then among the conditions that a theory of s should meet are that its laws should be no more complex than those of any competitor. Again, it should match any competitor in predictive power, by some measure that increases with the size and complexity of the total set of observational sentences that the theory certifies, relative to the size and complexity of its laws and of the set of directly certified observation sentences.

But these conditions, even after the considerable supplementation with which a fully fledged philosophy of science will equip them, are not guaranteed to whittle down the contenders for a theory of s to a single candidate, if for no other reason than that it can be equally as reasonable to favour a theory scoring better on predictive power, but less well on legal simplicity, as to have the opposite preference. Thus, the single Hierarchy of Certification of molecular epistemology gives place, in the context of holistic epistemology, to a *family* of hierarchies, each embodying its own distinct theory of the given standpoint s.

Suppose T_s is a theory of s earning a place on a hierarchy H in this family of hierarchies. Theories of other standpoints will cohabit with T_s on H, and it is natural to conceive of all such theories as having broad features in common. (One suggestion is that theories on H not disagree fundamentally on matters of law. Thus if $s \subseteq s'$ and $T_{s'}$ is a theory on H, then the laws of T_s should follow, at least as approximations, from those of $T_{s'}$.) And the presence of T_s on H will also constrain H in other ways; for example, observational sentences certified by T_s but not directly so certified, had better in general be certified directly by some $T_{s'}$ in H.

As for the formal principles of certification—[CONJ], [NEG], and their ilk—which loomed large in former discussions of the Hierarchy of Certification, they will remain in operation in its holistic incarnation, but with a somewhat altered status. No longer do they determine the certification of molecular sentences from a predetermined atomic base. Rather, they form an additional set of constraints on the theories figuring in a hierarchy of certification, constraining the certifications which a theory of a given standpoint may make in terms either of other certifications it is prepared to issue from that same standpoint, or certifications it can make about what can be certified in theories of other standpoints in its hierarchy. Thus [CONJ] requires that $T(s)$ be prepared to certify a conjunction iff it is prepared to certify both conjuncts; and [NEG] requires that a theory be prepared to certify a negation iff it is prepared to certify that no theory in its hierarchy based upon a more enriched observational base than its own will certify the sentence negated.

Each of the family of Hierarchies of Certification which holistic epistemology sanctions thus shares the structure of the single Hierarchy of Certification of molecular epistemology; and just as the latter can be extended so as to incorporate a Total View, so, too, presumably with each of the former. And this brings us at last back to the topic which, it was claimed some pages back, these reflections on holistic certification would illuminate, namely Putnam's proposed identification of truth with idealized rational acceptability. For one way to interpret his suggestion is to take it as the proposal that truth is certifiability from the theory of the Total View of some favoured hierarchy **H**.

Certainly this interpretation has the merit of preserving Putnam's emphasis on the theory-relativity of rational acceptability; and the Total View, taking into account, as it does, the observational data of all possible standpoints, has impeccable credentials to count as an idealization. Further, it provides a concept of truth meeting our requirements for objectivity—it will be public, provided we build in sufficient restrictions on acceptable certifiability of observation sentences by a theory; it will be bivalent, since certifiability from the Total View of any holistic Hierarchy of Certification has the same structural features as the molecular Hierarchy; and it will be epistemically independent, in the sense that the ideal theory may turn out false by its lights. (For the last, consider the best humanly constructible theory. Based, as it is, on the sum total of evidence ever to be available to the human race, this is a theory of a finite union of human standpoints—the Human Total View, as we dubbed it back in section 2.2. As such, if it figures on the favoured hierarchy **H** at all, it is at a rank well below that of the Total View of **H**, so its deliverances need not correspond to those of the theory of the Total View, and may indeed be at odds with it, being overruled by the superior preponderance of evidence available at the higher level; whilst if it is unfortunate enough not to figure on **H** at all, there is clearly no ground at all for thinking its pronouncements will march in step with those of the favoured Total View.)

But the trouble with this construal is obvious: its idealization of everyday rational acceptability is too extreme. The reservations which led us, back in section 2.3, to shrink from claiming that a fully fledged analysis of object-ive truth can be founded on the Hierarchy of Certification in its molecular version, surely apply, with additional force, to any attempt to found such an analysis on its bells-and-whistles holistic version. Thus, in addition to confronting the vagueness of the notion of epistemic standpoints, includ-ing those possibly alien to we mere humans, and facing the issue of making detailed sense of what may be involved in certification from infinite uni-ons of such standpoints such as the Total View—problems confronted by any attempt to take the full Hierarchy seriously as the basis for a high-grade analysis of objective truth—the current proposal faces as well the problem of how the favoured hierarchy H is to be singled out from other members of the family which holistic epistemology regards as equally legitimate. In the context of Putnam's discussion of what idealized rational acceptabil-ity might entail, it is clear that there is no distinction to be made between H and its competitors on epistemic or metaphysical grounds; rather, it is singled out because our own theorizing somehow makes it our own. But it is hard to see how this can be. We can, of course, require that H must at some lower level embody our own current best theory, a theory of some finite set of human standpoints. Perhaps we can make sense further of the idea that some theory of the Human Total View is somehow implicit in our current best theory (though we may not as yet be able to say what that is), and so may require that H should embody this implicit theory of the Human Total View as well. But these requirements will fall well short of singling out any single hierarchy as favoured; and the problem is that we seem to have no way of indicating what requirements could ever suffice to do so, given that the differences between the various candidates depend on observations no human will ever make, and calculations involving infinite surveys which no human could ever undertake.

Although the above does, indeed, seem to be one natural way of inter-preting Putnam's proposal, it seems certain that it is not an interpretation he would favour, precisely because it overdoes the idealization of rational acceptability. (Thus, for example, he is at pains[4] to disassociate his favoured conception of truth from 'the God's-Eye View' and, hence, presumably would disavow any entanglement with the Total View of our hierarchies.) Another, less thoroughgoing, idealization, prompted by our recent discus-sion, is probably much closer to what he has in mind. This is to take truth as

---

[4] Putnam, *Reason, Truth, and History*, 55.

certifiability by the theory of the Human Total View in a hierarchy which embodies that version of the theory which is implicit in our own current best theory (a version we are not, of course, yet in a position to specify, but which is gradually revealed as our theory is refined in the light of further experience). Some such story as this can be told within the framework of a truncated version of the Hierarchy in which there figure only human epistemic standpoints, and in which the complexities of certification arising from infinite unions are avoided; hence, within a framework much more plausibly touted as suitable for the framing of a proper fully fledged analysis of truth. There may be much to be said for the ensuing analysis of truth, as for the earlier proposal to analyse it as superassertibility; the trouble is that, as with superassertibility, there seems little to be said for it as a concept of *objective* truth. For, once again, no structural features of the concept of truth, as thus defined, ensure that it will be bivalent, that being a characteristic the hierarchy guarantees only through connecting truth with the repudiated Total View. And again, epistemic independence is repudiated, since the ideal theory—that is, the theory of the Human Total View—is, on this conception, by definition trivially true.

7

Formal Theories of Truth and Putnam's 'Common-sense Realism'

7.1 COMMON-SENSE REALISM EXPLAINED

A *substantial* concept of truth is one which regards truth as connected essentially with some, typically relational, nontrivial property of things in the world beyond language; a *formal* concept, by contrast, is one according to which an exhaustive account of truth can be rendered by drawing attention merely to the formal or structural properties of truth-predicates or truth-operators. The concepts of truth we have examined hitherto are to be classified, accordingly, as substantial ones: correspondence concepts because they connect truth essentially with the relationship between sentences and some external structure, superassertibility and idealized rational acceptability because they connect it with the epistemic states of hypothetical or real observers (epistemic standpoints). The paradigm of a formal concept, on the other hand, is afforded by Ramsey's redundancy theory, which sees the key to the concept of truth as lying in the formal equivalence between 'it is true that p' and p. Also to be counted as formal concepts are the various versions of the 'minimalist' or 'deflationary' theories, which, in their own different ways, elaborate the central redundancy insight to accommodate truth-ascriptions involving descriptions or quantification ('Carnap's last statement is true', 'Everything the Pope says is true').

Formal concepts of truth attract attention in the present context particularly because one such features as an essential component of 'Common-sense Realism', the latest position adopted by Putnam on the realism issue—the latest, that is to say, at the time of writing. Putnam has figured in the foregoing pages largely in the role of hero, though it is true that the last section greeted his invitation to construe truth as idealized rational acceptability with less enthusiasm than that accorded to his ideas hitherto. But he is a mercurial philosopher, and many staunch adherents to the views expressed by one Putnamian temporal stage have been confounded when presented with the doctrines espoused by a later one; hence, the plaintive title of one of Michael Devitt's old papers, 'Realism and the Renegade Putnam'.[1] We are about to follow down this well-worn trail of disaffection. But let us first set out the principles of Common-sense Realism.

Common-sense Realism, as articulated by Putnam in his Dewey Lectures,[2] is a heady Wittgensteinian draught, brewed according to a recipe much influenced by John McDowell and J. L. Austin. Putnam develops it as a position about representational systems in general, mental as well as linguistic; and, whilst our present concerns will be primarily with his doctrines as they apply to language, we do well to follow him in elaborating them in these more general terms. Then his position can be fairly presented as consisting principally in two theses about the content of a representation system: the Thesis of Internality, and the Thesis of World-Embeddedness.

A. THESIS OF INTERNALITY. The elements of a representational system are internally related to their content.

Traditional paradigms of representational systems make content extrinsic to the representing elements, which are identified by means of their niche within the system, and which then assume content by entering into descriptive relations ultimately dependent on extrinsic causal ties. So a mental image of a deer, for example, represents a deer because extrinsic, and ultimately causal, relations sustain so viewing it; it embodies no representation intrinsically, but acquires it through warranted interpretation, just as a nonmental picture does. Opposing this view of the way mental images work, Putnam invites us to consider the case of a mental image of Wittgenstein's duck–rabbit drawing.[3] That external drawing can be legitimately interpreted as of a duck or a rabbit; so a mental image of the drawing, if it is on a logical par with the drawing itself, ought accordingly to prove ambiguous and sustain legitimate dual interpretations: as being an image of a drawing of a duck; or an image of a drawing of a rabbit (an image of a picture-duck, or of a picture-rabbit, in Wittgenstein's terminology).[4] In fact, however, Putnam claims, any such mental image proves on in(tro)spection to be not to be ambiguous at all; rather, it will generally be either an unambiguous image of a picture-duck, or an unambiguous image of a picture-rabbit, though, with practice and

---

[1] Michael Devitt, 'Realism and the Renegade Putnam', *Nous,* 17 (1983), 291–301.

[2] 'Sense, Nonsense, and the Senses: An Inquiry into the Powers of the Human Mind', Part One of Hilary Putnam, *The Threefold Cord: Mind, Body, and World* (New York: Columbia University Press, 1999).

[3] Ibid., 45.

[4] Ludwig Wittgenstein, *Philosophical Investigations*, 2nd edn. (Oxford: Blackwell, 1958), ii. 194.

effort, it may also prove possible to form an image which is unambiguously of a duck–rabbit drawing (i.e., an unambiguous image of an ambiguous object). Thus, it seems the mental image does not await interpretation as the external drawing does, but somehow has its interpretation inbuilt.

(Just how sound are Putnam's Wittgensteinian credentials here? At first sight, his claims may seem to run quite counter to the well-known passage at *Philosophical Investigations*, i. § 139, where Wittgenstein argues that the meaning of 'cube' could not be an inner picture of a cube, since the inner picture itself stands in need of interpretation via a method of projection. On second thoughts, however, this is entirely consistent with Putnam's insistence that a mental image must be quite different from an ordinary picture. In discussing the duck–rabbit at *Philosophical Investigations*, Part II, Section xi, Wittgenstein seems *inter alia* to make Putnam's points, but he makes them about 'visual impressions' rather than 'mental images' of the duck–rabbit drawing. (See especially pp. 194–6, and 199: 'Of course we can say: There are certain things which fall equally under the concept "picture-rabbit" and under the concept "picture-duck". And a picture, a drawing, is such a thing.—But the *impression* is not simultaneously of a picture-duck and a picture-rabbit'.) Since Putnam is clear that his 'mental images' are not perceptual items, he accordingly seems to go beyond anything explicit in Wittgenstein, to the extent of invoking a category of nonperceptual images having the logical characteristics which Wittgenstein attributes to visual impressions. But the extension is not an implausible one.)

If the elements of a representational system are internally related in this way to their contents, then, since mere expressions are not so related—since, for example, 'snow is white' might have had the meaning of 'the carburettor is clogged'—it follows that the elements of a Putnamian linguistic representational system are not mere expressions. Rather, we should think of them as expressions-in-use,[5] and of the elements of a mental representational system as mental analogues of such expressions. And, accordingly, the key to understanding how expressions assume representational significance is to concentrate on the way they are used, rather than on descriptive relations into which they may enter or truth-conditions they may assume.

It seems we may further clarify the issues involved here by pursuing an obvious analogy, drawn from the work which provides Putnam's chief inspiration in these lectures,[6] and construe an expression-in-use on the model of a chess piece. A certain piece of wood is the White King of set

---

[5] A new coinage, intended to capture the sort of idea expressed by Putnam at, e.g., Putnam, *Threefold Cord*, 46, and 197, n. 52.

[6] Wittgenstein, *Philosophical Investigations*, i. § 108; see also i. §§ 31 ff.

S because it is the piece in set *S* which is standardly used to play the White King role. The 'White King role', in turn, we might identify by referring to the rules of chess. Alternatively, we might identify it demonstratively, pointing to a particular use of a specific piece in a specific set: 'the White King role is the use to which these players are putting that piece now'. Proceeding the first way, it is both contingent and a posteriori that any piece in any set is the White King; proceeding the second way, it is contingent but a priori that the paradigm piece in the paradigm set is the White King, or at least that it was on the occasion of the paradigm use. (The case parallels a familiar Kripkean one: we 'fix the reference' of the designator 'the White King role' via contingent properties of the paradigm piece, just as the reference of '1 metre' is fixed through contingent properties of a stick in Paris; it is then a priori that the paradigm piece fits the White King role, just as it is that the stick in Paris is 1 metre long.[7]) Thus, chess pieces, if considered in the second way, do provide the model we seek for the elements of a Putnamian representational system, inasmuch as the paradigm chess pieces at least are related internally (more specifically, a priori) to their roles, and, hence, to their significance.

The analogy carries further once we appreciate what is involved in the conception of linguistic use which Common-sense Realism links with content. An earlier Putnam conceded the relevance of use, but conceived of it reductionistically, as describable in austere terms of causation and functional role. On the new, Wittgensteinian, conception, however, there is no reductionist account of use possible; instead, 'the use of words in a language game cannot, in most cases, be described without employing the vocabulary of that game, or a vocabulary internally related to the vocabulary of that game'.[8] In particular, the description of the use of many everyday expressions must link them to usages in which those same expressions are ineliminably deployed in reports of perception. The last is a detail of some importance, to which we shall return. For the moment, however, the critical point is that there can on this conception be no noncircular, independent circumscription given of the use of a linguistic expression, to match the independent account of the White King role which can be given by appeal to the rules of chess. Apparently, then, when circumscribing linguistic use, there is no alternative to proceeding demonstratively, and indicating the use in question by pointing to the way paradigm expressions are used in a paradigm language by paradigm speakers. Obvious candidates for the paradigms are to hand, in the shape of the familiar expressions of our

[7] Saul A. Kripke, *Naming and Necessity*, rev. and enlarged edn. (Oxford: Blackwell, 1980), 54 ff.

[8] Putnam, *Threefold Cord*, 14.

mother tongue, and their deployment by the community with which we share it. The upshot, then, is that these expressions are for us related internally to their significance, as the White King of the paradigm set is related to its role according to the second of the two conceptions we entertained above; and that these expressions, or their mental analogues, are suitable items as elements of a Putnamian representational system.

So much for the Thesis of Internality, the first of the planks of Commonsense Realism. Now for the second:

B. THESIS OF WORLD-EMBEDDEDNESS. The representational content of the elements of a representational system depend on the state of the world, in a way which is not merely causal.

It is Wittgenstein, once more, whom Putnam acknowledges as a principal source for this doctrine, too, citing a typically oracular text: 'When we say, and *mean*, that such-and-such is the case, we—and our meaning—do not stop anywhere short of the fact; but we mean: *this—is—so*.'[9] Apparently, this commits Wittgenstein to the view that the content of a linguistic act or mental state *is*, or at least includes, a fact; that is, a bit of the totality which constitutes the world, assuming (in the absence of any reason to the contrary) that his terminology still at least roughly matches that of his earlier *Tractatus*. John McDowell, to whose views on these topics Putnam awards a general and ringing endorsement,[10] formulates the point, in what he rightly terms 'a style Wittgenstein would have been uncomfortable with', as being that 'there is no ontological gap between the sort of thing one can mean, or generally the sort of thing one can think, and the sort of thing which can be the case'.[11]

For both Putnam and McDowell, what turns the trick in thus welding representational content onto the world is perception, which both insist is properly viewed in the manner of the J. L. Austin of *Sense and Sensibilia*[12] i.e., as involving direct engagement of the perceiving intellect with the facts, unmediated by intervening appearances, sense-data, or ideas—in short, unmediated by 'the Given'. It is McDowell who develops the issue in the fuller detail. It is essential to perception, he argues,[13] that it provides a rational constraint on world-directed thought. The Given is posited as this

---

[9] Wittgenstein, *Philosophical Investigations*, i. § 95; cited by Putnam, *Threefold Cord*, 47–8.

[10] Putnam, *Threefold Cord*, 10, and 192, n. 16.

[11] John McDowell, *Mind and World* (Cambridge, Mass., and London: Harvard University Press, 1994), 27.

[12] J. L. Austin, *Sense and Sensibilia*, 2nd edn. (London, Oxford, and New York: Oxford University Press, 1964).

[13] McDowell, *Mind and World*, Lectures 1 and 2.

constraining influence; but it is conceived as purely sensuous, and devoid of conceptual content, all such content being confined to an internal domain on which the world impinges only be presenting the Given. But *rational* constraint depends on conceptual relations between the constraining factors and the item constrained, relations into which a nonconceptual Given is incapable of entering—the best the Given can do is constrain thought *causally*, thereby supplying mere exculpations when what is needed are justifications. The way out is to abolish the Given, and with it the picture of a divide between a conceptualizing mind and an unconceptualized world: in perception, the mind takes into itself facts which, thus being mental contents, are *ipso facto* to be regarded as having conceptual content. Two points about this account of perception are worthy of remark. First, since the facts available to perception are not limited to those suited to be elements of the purely sensuous Given, its perceivable facts may be a rather more comprehensive class than traditionally conceived. Second, it faces a problem about how to accommodate *mis*perception, when the world fails to supply facts to constitute its content. But it is a problem of which McDowell is dismissive, insisting that it does nothing to undermine his account of veridical perception: 'there is no good argument from fallibility to what I call "the highest common factor conception" of our subjective position—the idea that even when things go well, cognitively speaking, our subjective position can only be something in common between such cases and cases in which things do not go well'.[14]

Thus, according to both Putnam and McDowell, some elements of a mind, its perceptions, assume as their content the facts with which they engage. Other, nonperceptual mental elements derive their content from the way the mind manipulates them in thinking, in the broadest sense, about the perceptual data—in forming predictions about perception's future course, for example, or taking decisions designed to influence its future shape. The mind thus acquires representational content through the way it is embedded in the world: its peripheral states (perceptions) assume a content which is actually *identical* with bits of the world it inhabits, whilst its interior states assume content through connections with each other and, ultimately, with the periphery. Notice how, because of the identity of the content of peripheral states with facts in the world, this conclusion delivers, as promised, a supercausal dependence of content upon world.

Similar considerations to these yield an analogous conclusion about content which is linguistic rather than mental. We saw above reasons for saying that the content of linguistic expressions arises from their use; that is, from the way our usage of them makes them relate to each other and to our nonlinguistic activities. It was noted, too, that in charting the content-bestowing use of typical everyday expressions, it would be necessary to link them to usages in which those same expressions were used in reports of perception. But the content of a perception-report, within this framework, is surely the same as that of the perception it reports; and we have seen how Putnam and McDowell identify the content of a perception with the fact which it engages. It follows that linguistic content also is inextricably and supercausally dependent on the facts of the world it attempts to describe.

True to the tradition of the latter-day Wittgenstein, to whom these theses about content owe their inspiration, Putnam also associates his Common-sense Realism with adherence to a formal theory of truth. Wittgenstein wrote: '[W]e have : "p" is true $= p$; "p" is false $=$ not p',[15] thereby making what is normally taken to be an explicit commitment to Ramsey's redundancy account.[16] Though endorsing Wittgenstein's view enthusiastically, Putnam rejects this standard interpretation of his position; the redundancy theory, and other 'deflationist' accounts, he claims, treat truth as a predicate of bare sentences, whereas the Wittgensteinian account predicates it rather of sentences-in-use.[17] Whatever the subtle ramifications Putnam may read into this point, it seems clear, at least, that he conceives of his Common-sense Realism as involving what is to be classified, in terms of the distinction introduced at the beginning of this section, as a *formal* concept of truth.

But if the truth of Common-sense Realism is thus conceived purely formally, there is no reason for regarding it, its title notwithstanding, as involving any essential commitment to real realism, construed by the lights of Part One. Whether truth-in-L is bivalent, for example, reduces under Wittgenstein's Ramseyan equivalences to the question of whether the Law of Excluded Middle holds for L. This will be a question of the meaning of the logical connectives in L, and that, in turn, given Common-sense Realism's linkage of meaning with use, to the inferential practices of L-users. But there is no apparent reason why the users of some language L, functioning as a representational system according to Common-sense Realism's canons, should not choose to argue intuitionistically; so Common-sense Realism can apply to languages which fail of true, fully fledged realism—the global pure realism of Part One.

---

[15] Wittgenstein, *Philosophical Investigations,* i. § 136 (formatting adjusted); see also, Ludwig Wittgenstein, *Remarks on the Foundations of Mathematics,* rev. edn. (Cambridge, Mass.: MIT Press, 1978), i. Appendix 1, 6.

[16] Saul A. Kripke, *Wittgenstein on Rules and Private Language: An Elementary Exposition* (Oxford: Blackwell, 1982), 86; Michael Dummett, 'What Does the Appeal to Use Do for the Theory of Meaning?', in his *The Seas of Language,* 111.

[17] Putnam, *Threefold Cord,* 64 ff.

To this it may be retorted that Part One's account of realism, setting out as it did to be a faithful refinement of traditional conceptions, is old-fogy stuff, suitable for consumption only by flies still buzzing around the fly-bottle, the product ultimately of the traditional illusion that some sort of chasm exists between representing system and the world. The truth is that the elements of a representational system are internally related to their content, and that that content, in turn, is directly embedded in the world; so that the very possibility of representation presupposes the reality of the world represented. Here is the only realism worthy of the name, the realism of the brave new Wittgensteinian order, freed of the cobwebs of fusty traditional metaphysics.

We shall turn in the next chapter to examining these claims of Common-sense Realism (or, rather, of a modified and improved version thereof) to constitute realism of a shiny new kind. But first we shall consider an objection applying to it or any other position committed to a formal account of truth: the objection that no such position has the resources to explain the systematic functioning of language.

7.2 USE, MEANING, AND FORMAL NOTIONS OF TRUTH

This objection concentrates on the ability of Common-sense Realism to account for the systematic nature of the way the elements of a representational system assume their content.

To sharpen the discussion, let us concentrate henceforth on the case where representation is linguistic.[18] Then the primary way in which systematic complexity is manifested, much stressed in the literature, is through *compositionality*: we somehow learn in a systematic way to assign content to sentences of ever-increasing complexity, on the basis of their composition. And another layer of structure in our linguistic competence is revealed in *transferability*: the way we manage, having been introduced to a sentence deployed as, say, a question, to use it, or some trivial syntactic derivative, without benefit of further instruction, in another mode (say, as a command or assertion).

How are we to account for these facts of systematicity? A familiar model, deriving from Frege, sees the theory of meaning for a language L as having at its core a recursive theory of truth for L, assigning content-giving

---

[18] The discussion to come is heavily influenced by Dummett. See especially Dummett, 'What Does the Appeal . . . ?'; but all of the first nine papers in his *The Seas of Language* are also relevant.

truth-conditions to sentences of *L* on the basis of their syntactic structure.[19] If, accordingly, we regard this core theory as somehow recording knowledge available to an *L*-speaker, the compositional abilities of such a speaker are accommodated. The model can now be extended to stretch its basic account of content as adhering to *sentences* to an account of the content of *utterances.* This it does by distinguishing two components in the content of an utterance: its *sense,* which is identified with the content of the sentence uttered (or an indicative form thereof, if the uttered sentence itself is nonindicative), as given by the truth-condition assigned to the sentence by the core theory; and its *force,* i.e., its classification as an utterance of a certain kind (question, command, assertion . . .) as determined by the circumstances of the utterance, and conventions which it is the task of the theory to articulate. Assuming, once again, users' knowledge of these principles of classification and conventions, these resources clearly equip the model with the resources to explain transferability. Notice, however, that the model naturally singles out assertion as the distinguished mode of utterance, because of its direct connection with truth, the key notion of the core theory. For assertion purports to aim at the truth, it being the fundamental sin of an asserter *qua* asserter to assert a sentence whose truth-condition the asserter has insufficient ground to believe to obtain.

There are obvious questions raised by this model, most notably concerning the status of the knowledge of core and subsidiary theories to be attributed to speakers. Perhaps it is *implicit* knowledge: speakers really know the theories in their entirety, despite the fact that they are unable to articulate what they know. Perhaps it is *inchoate* knowledge: speakers explicitly know in part what the theories articulate in full. Perhaps it is *potential* knowledge: the theories spell out knowledge which speakers could, in principle, possess, and in doing so explain how the abilities of speakers are possible by pointing to one possible way in which they could be acquired. Or perhaps some further account still for the status of this knowledge is favoured. Once some position on this matter is settled upon, there arises the further question of how the knowledge thus attributed to speakers is related to linguistic use. Is knowledge of the theory entirely manifest somehow in linguistic use, so that examination of the use enables us to recover in its entirety the knowledge which underlies it? Or is there an inner core of that knowledge which resists manifestation, a part of what makes usage possible which is not recoverable from use?

---

[19] The hermeneutic theories of earlier pages are designed to play this core role. But we here abstract from the broader hermeneutic context within which the Fregean model may be set, concentrating more on its internal structural features.

The theoretical possibility of a positive answer to the first of these questions—the possibility of the position that the knowledge attributed to speakers in a theory of meaning constructed on the Fregean model is fully manifest in use—means that there is nothing in the Common-sense Realism commitment to the link between meaning and use which is in itself incompatible with the Fregean model. At the same time, the later Wittgenstein, the main inspiration for Common-sense Realism, appears to reject the Fregean model on all counts. Thus he denies the possibility of decomposing an utterance into components of sense and force,[20] he denies that assertion is in any way central among the patterns of usage;[21] more radically, he apparently goes so far as to deny there is any such thing as unadorned assertion (telling, *Mitteilung*) at all.[22] These, perhaps, are Wittgensteinian doctrines which Common-sense Realism need not share. But it is explicit, as we have seen, in endorsing Wittgenstein's acceptance of a formal concept of truth; and this marks a repudiation of the central feature of the Fregean model. For if truth is a formal concept, statements of truth-conditions reduce to tautologies (' "Snow is white" is true iff snow is white' has the content of 'snow is white iff snow is white') and, hence, are incapable of functioning as ways of conveying substantive information about linguistic content, in the way the Fregean model construes them as doing. Common-sense Realism is thus committed to the thesis that content can somehow be explained in terms of features of use *directly*, that is, without detour through the truth theory of the Fregean model. Then sentences-with-content (= sentences-in-use) can be used to explain truth, rather than truth figuring in the explanation of content. The trouble with this is that the Fregean model is the principal one extant for explaining the systematicity of content, so we are left with the problem of explaining how Putnam and Common-sense Realism may hope to accommodate it.

7.3 SEEING FACES: A WITTGENSTEINIAN ANSWER

Cora Diamond is one of Putnam's favourite readers of Wittgenstein.[23] From her writings we can glean an answer to the problem of explaining systematic complexity which may well be one which Putnam himself would favour.

In his well-known review of Wittgenstein's *Remarks on the Foundations of Mathematics*,[24] Michael Dummett presented an influential interpretation

---

[20] Wittgenstein, *Philosophical Investigations*, i. § 22.   [21] Ibid., i. § 23.
[22] Ibid., i. § 363; see also i. § 356.   [23] Putnam, *Threefold Cord*, esp. 59 ff.
[24] Michael Dummett, 'Wittgenstein's Philosophy of Mathematics', in his *Truth and Other Enigmas*, 166–85.

of Wittgenstein's notion of mathematical proof, according to which accepting a proof is a matter for free decision; rather than the antecedent meanings of the constituent terms determining inexorably whether conclusion follows from premises, the decision to adopt the proof modifies the meanings of the constituent terms. This is a conception Dummett finds entirely unconvincing. He makes his case by examining what is involved in addition. Someone who learns to add learns, *inter alia*, a new proof for 'there are 12 children in the room', namely, how to deduce it from 'there are 7 girls and 5 boys'; and thereby learns a new criterion for having miscounted (having counted 7 girls, 5 boys, and 13 children). But this 'new' criterion is not wholly new, since the miscount must have already counted as a mistake by the criteria for counting in force before addition was learned. There is, then, a connection between old and new, one which Dummett thinks Wittgenstein obscures, and which is, in his view, to be elucidated by articulating the ties between truth-conditions and the criteria by which they are judged to obtain—in short, to be elucidated by reference to the Fregean model.

In response, Diamond[25] offers an alternative interpretation of Wittgenstein, along the way introducing a notion of relevance to our present concerns about the structural features of linguistic competence. The notion in question is introduced in terms of a simplified version of Dummett's counting example (the present version is, in turn, simplified a little further, but preserves the essentials). Consider, first, what we may call the Primitive Counting Game. A player is confronted with some rows of pencils; it is clear throughout the time the game is played that no pencils are added to, or subtracted from, any row, and that no pencil changes its position in the array. The player plays the game by starting from the left-hand end of a row, tapping each pencil in turn, and uttering the numerals in order from 1 as they do so. When the end of the row is reached, the player cries: 'Outcome: *n*!' (*n* being, it will be no surprise to learn, the numeral which was uttered when the last pencil was tapped). A refinement is that if a player notices that they have tapped the same pencil twice, or missed a pencil, or not started at the left, or not started with the numeral 1, or left out a numeral, or recited the numerals in the wrong order, they are to cry 'Miscount!'; such a cry aborts the procedure with the given row, rendering invalid any future or past announcement of outcome.

Compare this with the Sophisticated Counting Game (though admittedly, its degree of sophistication remains pretty moderate), which is just like the preceding except that the player is to cry 'Miscount!' under

[25] Cora Diamond, 'The Face of Necessity', in her *The Realistic Spirit* (Cambridge, Mass.: MIT Press, 1991), 243–66.

the earlier conditions, and also when they recognize that an announced outcome is different from one previously announced for the same row.

Then Diamond's claim is this: whilst it is possible for a player to be taught the two games and see them as unconnected, or to see them just as two slightly different games, it is also natural to see the sophisticated game as already implicit in the primitive one. Seeing this she compares to seeing that two picture-faces have the same expression: 'This is not like saying that the mouths are the same length, the eyes the same distance apart: it is not that kind of description. But it is not a description of *something* else, the expression, distinct from that curved line, those two dots, and so on.'[26] In the same way, seeing the Sophisticated Counting Game as implicit in the Primitive Counting Game is seeing something 'in a different dimension from comparisons of rules for an activity, or psychological accompaniments of an activity, or behavioural dispositions';[27] seeing something (to put it in emphatically nonDiamondian terms) which supervenes on such mundane facts without being reducible to them.

Clearly, Diamond has provided herself with the apparatus to frame an answer to Dummett's challenge; for she will claim that Wittgenstein's true position is that, in accepting a mathematical proof, one merely extends the language game to another which was already implicit in the original. So connections between the old language game and the new can be properly respected; and adopting the proof need involve no alteration to the meanings of the constituent terms of the sort Dummett found objectionable. More to the present point, it provides materials for addressing the phenomena of the structural complexity in linguistic competence. The ability of a speaker to understand new sentences composed out of a familiar vocabulary and using familiar grammatical constructions is easily accommodated: the speaker sees the new usage as implicit in the old language games. Just as easily dealt with is the ability to use the one sentence in various modes: the one usage is seen as implicit in the other.

The evident difficulty with this recourse to Diamond's apparatus to account for the structural features of linguistic competence is the mysterious nature of the ability to see one language game as implicit in another, which makes it less than transparent when it is reasonable to declare that this ability is in operation. It would, however, be quite unfair to charge that, because it is an ability irreducible to facts about linguistic rules and their mastery, or to introspectible psychological facts or facts about behavioural dispositions, it is, therefore, a magical matter outside the bounds of scientific investigation. It is, for example, perfectly consistent with anything Diamond says that the ability to see one language game in

[26] Ibid., 249.   [27] Ibid.

another should be explicable as a connectionist neural network; indeed, in the light of her comparison between it and the ability to recognize a pattern of shapes as a given facial expression, such a construal recommends itself rather readily. It is, however, of the essence of Diamond's proposal that it precludes any articulation of the ability involved into facts about linguistic rules, introspectible psychology, or behavioural dispositions—in short, into anything which a speaker might cite as a *reason* justifying an interpretation of new sentences, or for discerning common content in an order and an assertion. The best Diamond's speaker will be able to do is to claim 'I just see it!'

With Dummett,[28] we should find this situation entirely unacceptable, and the contrast with the Fregean model strikingly to the favour of the latter. For language is a rational activity if anything is and, accordingly, any acceptable account of our use of it must make it clear how it fits into our normal pattern of explaining rational action in terms of knowledge, purpose, and intention. Above, we spoke of the core recursive theory of truth-conditions of a Fregean meaning theory as 'somehow recording knowledge available' to a speaker. As we have noted, this does not mean that the core theory must be regarded as articulating knowledge actually possessed by a speaker. Still, it does display a pattern of knowledge which is, in principle, available to the ordinary speaker, and which may be regarded as supplying inchoately grasped principles which render our understanding of language rational, in much the same way as an algorithm for the Rubik cube, though not one a given solver may be able to articulate, may nevertheless be recognizable as that which, in principle, guides their manœuvres and renders their solution a rational procedure. In failing to provide a similar rational model for our grasp of linguistic complexity, Diamond's solution must be rejected.

The case just mounted against Common-sense Realism has seized upon its endorsement of a formal account of truth. It is, at the same time, a case against *any* view which holds that truth is a merely formal concept; for we have argued, in effect, that structural facts about language cannot be accommodated without adopting some form of the Fregean model, with an accompanying substantial conception of truth apt to do duty in the core theory. As such, the case, both against Common-sense Realism and against the more general target, is incomplete. For though Diamond's alternative account of the structural phenomena has been examined and found wanting, it remains possible that some Third Way can accommodate

---

[28] See e.g., Michael Dummett, 'What Do I Know When I Know a Language?', and 'Language and Truth', both in his *The Seas of Language*, 94–105 and 104 f. and 131 ff, respectively.

those phenomena more adequately whilst eschewing the Fregean model. There is, perhaps, no conclusive proof that no such Third Way is possible; at any rate, no such proof will be provided here. But the Coda to this essay will bolster the case against construing truth formally by showing in more detail the difficulties which Third Ways confront; it will examine, and find wanting, the recent ambitious attempt by Robert Brandom to develop a detailed use-based theory of meaning, eschewing the Fregean model but claiming to accommodate compositionality in the context of a formal concept of truth.

Even if this case against formal accounts of truth be conceded, it may be urged that it is unsatisfactory as providing a final judgement on Common-sense Realism. For could not that position be reformulated by somehow strengthening and rendering more substantial its formal conception of truth, thus restoring the availability of the Fregean model for its account of meaning? The question is a delicate one, since the notion of truth chosen, combined with the Fregean model, must yield an account of meaning which remains faithful to the Wittgensteinian conception of meaning as manifest in use, lest the credentials of the crucial Thesis of Internality of Content be undermined. The best chances would seem to lie in a minimal strengthening of the formal concept; and in the second half of the next chapter, we shall return to the possibility of a reformulated version of Common-sense Realism, in the context of a more general discussion of the best candidate for the role of such a minimal strengthening of the formal conception of truth: namely, truth as delineated by Tarski's theory.

8

Tarskian Truth and the Views of John McDowell

8.1 THE STATUS OF TARSKIAN TRUTH

The status of Tarski's theory of truth in the terms of the dichotomy between formal and substantial concepts of truth is, at first sight, moot.[1] Ramsey himself suggested that the elaboration of the redundancy insight necessary to accommodate truth-ascriptions involving quantification should depend upon discerning and classifying all the possible shapes which might be assumed by the sentences to which truth is ascribed; and it is, accordingly, natural to read Tarski as carrying out this Ramseyan programme, showing how subsentential structure contributes to truth as formally conceived. Tarski shows us how to construct a host of individual truth theories for specific languages, where a truth theory for a language L is an inductive specification of truth-conditions for the sentences of L, each such specification taking the form of a (truth-theoretic) *T-sentence*, i.e., a sentence of the form

    ** is true-in-L iff____

where '**' is replaced by a structural description of a sentence S of L, and '____' by a statement of the truth-conditions of S, as rendered in the metalanguage of L in which the truth theory is written. (The terms 'truth theory' and 'T-sentence' are familiar from section 3.5. They there defined model-theoretic analogues of the notions they embody here; thus, for example, they involved the model-theoretic truth-predicate 'A is true on interpretation I of L' rather than the present 'A is true-in-L'. Their incarnation in those earlier pages, in fact, is an adaptation from their present truth-theoretic, Tarskian home.) Each of these truth theories exhibits a common inductive structure, apt for conversion into an explicit definition of the truth-predicate it characterizes in the presence of appropriate set-theoretic resources in the metalanguage. Moreover, they share important conditional

---

[1] See Lecture 1 of Davidson, 'The Structure and Content of Truth', which is the basis of the present discussion.

properties. Let a *translational* T-sentence for S be a T-sentence for S in which the sentence on the right-hand side of the biconditional is a translation of S into the metalanguage. Then every truth theory has the property that it is adequate if it has as a theorem a translational T-sentence for every sentence of the object-language (this being the property utilized in Tarski's Convention T); further, it is adequate if and only if some translational T-sentence obtains for every object-language sentence. These structural and conditional properties are all that the various truth-predicates have in common, within the Tarskian framework. They look like formal properties, involving no relation to extralinguistic reality. This, combined with its apparent Ramseyan affinities, suggests Tarski's theory embodies a formal conception of truth.

But these appearances are deceptive, as becomes clearer when the concept of translation is subjected to further scrutiny. As we saw back in section 3.5, under analysis that notion is seen to belong to the domain of hermeneutics, with its key notion of a hermeneutic theory for a speaker U—a truth theory which assigns truth-conditions to the sentences of the language U speaks in such a manner that rational sense is made of U's behaviour if U is construed as having beliefs whose content is given by the truth-conditions appearing on the right-hand side of the T-sentences which the theory generates for U's believed-true sentences. The discussion there, cast in terms of model-theoretic truth theories, transposes straightforwardly into truth theories construed in the present, simpler Tarskian terms, the framework which, in fact, formed its original home. Thus, the conditional properties governing the adequacy of truth theories turn out to be more than formal, after all, for they contain covert reference to the extralinguistic world as manifested in the behaviour and psychology of speakers; whence the Tarskian conception of truth is revealed as a substantial one in the final analysis.[2]

Substantial it may be, but it does not appear to provide a basis for a concept of objective truth. To start with, there is no inherent reason why Tarskian truth should, in general, possess one key mark of the objective as Part One delineated it, to wit, bivalence. For whether bivalence holds for a given Tarskian truth-predicate will depend on the logic of the metalanguage within which its truth theory is set. And the only logical principles

[2] We here apparently depart from Davidson, by seeing hermeneutics as already implicit in Tarski's Convention T, whereas he evidently regards the connection as more remote (ibid., 295). This means that he has room for a reading of Tarskian theory as embodying a merely formal conception of truth (a reading in which the connection with hermeneutics is not made), though it is a reading he regards both as less true to Tarski's intentions, and as less defensible philosophically. But these divergences are minor, a matter principally of where the boundaries of conceptual content are to be drawn.

essential to any such metalanguage are those required for the primordial truth-theoretic task of recursive generation of T-sentences. These are limited in number, and are, primarily, substitution principles; in particular, no adherence is required to Excluded Middle, one of the crucial principles if bivalence for the object-language is to follow.

What are the chances for somehow extracting out of pure Tarskian truth, with its unfortunate neutrality on such crucial matters, some more committed concept which is guaranteed to underwrite bivalence and, ultimately, to share the other marks of objective truth? One striking feature of Tarski's work is the use of the notion of satisfaction in the analysis of truth. Now, satisfaction is a world/language relation, as is the correspondence relation beloved by adherents of the Correspondence Theory; so there is some temptation to construe the Tarskian use of satisfaction as licensing the classification of Tarskian truth as a form of the correspondence conception. This is a temptation to which Davidson succumbed, but later argued was ill-founded;[3] and certainly the satisfaction relation does, on reflection, look too thin and indiscriminating to be plausible as any version of correspondence (after all, it relates all true sentences to all sequences, and all false sentences to none). Still, it may well seem that Tarskian truth contains the seeds of a correspondence theory, seeds which can be made to flower by transplanting them into the rich potting-mix of a metalanguage of classical set theory, where Tarskian concepts can be recast into their model-theoretic counterparts, and semantic concepts are revealed as explicit relations to set-theoretic structures ('interpretations'), forming a whole network of interconnected world/language relations which may together be held to explicate the intuitive notion of correspondence. Then truth, as so explained, will be demonstrably bivalent as a consequence of the classical logic of the metalanguage; and that, in turn, will be justified as constituting the necessary framework for turning Tarskian truth into a fully fledged correspondence concept. But, whatever the attractions or merits of this approach, it is the lesson of Part Two that, though it may suffice to extract from Tarskian truth a concept which is essentially bivalent, the concept extracted falls short of fully fledged objectivity; for it lacks the further mark of epistemic independence.

Another way of extracting objective truth from a neutral Tarskian prototype might be to identify objective truth with a *particular* Tarskian truth-predicate, characterized in a metalanguage whose logic can be assumed to

[3] Donald Davidson, 'True to the Facts', in his *Inquiries into Truth and Interpretation*, 37–54; 'A Coherence Theory of Truth and Knowledge', and 'Afterthoughts', both in his *Subjective, Intersubjective, Objective* (Oxford: Clarendon Press, 2001), 137–53 and 154–7.

be classical (so securing the bivalence at least of privileged truth-predicate), and with other features which arguably ensure the other marks of objectivity. This, of course, prompts the question of just which truth-predicate is to be so singled out. One suggestion can be gleaned from the writings of Davidson, who, in a famous paper, introduces a notorious character, the 'Omniscient Interpreter'.[4] Using this device, we might take the objective truth of the sentences of the language L of an utterer U to be given by the truth-predicate of a hermeneutic theory for U constructed by the Omniscient Interpreter. We might then hope to argue somehow that the logic befitting the Omniscient Interpreter is classical, and thus to defuse our earlier worries that the Tarskian framework is unable to secure the essential bivalence of objective truth; and then to supplement this with arguments to show that the truth, as thus defined, also possesses the other essential features of objectivity.

The difficulty with this manœuvre is, of course, to explain the status of the Omniscient Interpreter. Presumably, this lofty being believes all and only the truths; but this leaves the problem of saying what this means, and how we are to envisage it coming about. One picture portrays the Interpreter as somehow endowed, by what process we need not care, with beliefs which just happen precisely to map the contours of a pre-existing reality; that is, it depends on a correspondence view of truth, which we have already judged inadequate as a foundation for objective truth.

A better picture sees the Interpreter as forming beliefs by an idealization of our own epistemic practices—that is, in terms of the current discussion, as advocating a theory formed at some high level of the Hierarchy of Certification in either its molecular or holistic incarnation. But then familiar difficulties arise once more. For if the idealization of our epistemic practices involved in constructing the Interpreter's theory is extreme, it becomes in effect the theory formed at the Total View of some hierarchy, and we face once more old problems endemic to taking the Hierarchy seriously, especially at its topmost levels—namely, the problems discussed above in section 6.2, in connection with the first, more idealized, way of construing Putnam's proposal to identify truth with idealized rational acceptability. If, on the other hand, the idealization is less extreme, perhaps no levels beyond the Human Total View need be invoked. But, then, there is a problem in accommodating the epistemic independence of objective truth, and explaining how a humanly accessible ideal theory can be false. For if the Interpreter recognizes the theory as ideal, its theses will become the Interpreter's beliefs. Hence, since the hermeneutic method of section 3.5 (particularly through the operation of the Principle of Charity)

---

[4] Davidson, 'A Coherence Theory of Truth and Knowledge', 150 ff.

requires that, in constructing a hermeneutic theory for a language of U, an interpreter should as much as possible assign truth-conditions he believes to obtain to sentences U holds true; and since, in this case, there is a perfect coincidence of the theses of the theory with the Interpreter's beliefs; it follows that the Interpreter's hermeneutic theory for the language of the ideal theory will assign truth-conditions to the theses of the theory which the Interpreter believes to be true. But truth-conditions the Omnipotent Interpreter believes to be true are indeed true (i.e., they are ideally rationally acceptable). Hence, the theses of the ideal theory do indeed possess the truth-property articulated in the Interpreter's hermeneutic theory; that is, they are objectively true.

The suggestions canvassed, then, fail to extract from the neutral Tarskian concept a notion of truth essentially possessing the hallmarks of objectivity. At the same time, it seems that the very neutrality of Tarskian truth itself means that it remains *compatible* with realism, in the sense that there is no reason why Tarskian truth for some particular language L should not satisfy the criteria for objectivity, not because of the nature of truth itself but because of the specifics of L, and of factors somehow determining the nature of an appropriate metalanguage for it. But, first, whilst this might count as realism about L by the letter of the definitions of Part One, it is a pallid version of the doctrine, out of tune with the spirit of that earlier analysis in counting truth objective only as a consequence of factors extraneous to the notion itself. And, second, it is entirely unclear what these extraneous factors might be; thus, it is unclear just when a Tarskian truth-predicate assumes the mantle of objectivity.

Finally, there are, in any case, powerful reasons for thinking that, initial appearances notwithstanding, a Tarskian truth-predicate can never really assume that mantle, at least if it is also to be capable of figuring as the core concept of a theory of meaning forged on the Fregean model. These reasons will emerge in the discussion of the next section.

8.2 JOHN McDOWELL AND 'QUIETIST REALISM'

Putnam's Common-sense Realism, expounded in section 7.1, was criticized for embedding a formal account of truth; for that, it was argued, cuts it off from appeal to the Fregean model in giving an account of meaning and, hence (it was more tendentiously urged), from giving any satisfactory account of meaning at all. It was conceded, however, that a place exists for a modified version of Common-sense Realism, one which replaces Putnam's favoured formal account of truth with a more substantial one, capable of bearing the theoretical burden required to figure in a theory of meaning constructed on the Fregean model. At the same time, if the spirit of Putnam's original position is to be preserved, it behoves the replacing concept of truth to be a modest one, formal in appearance if not in reality. Tarskian truth fits the bill. And supplanting formal truth in Putnam's Common-sense Realism by Tarskian truth leads to a position which, it transpires, is essentially the same as one which has achieved some prominence in recent literature. This is the position of John McDowell, which, for the sake of a convenient differentiating label, will here be tagged 'Quietist Realism'.

Not, let us be clear, that McDowell's views are derivative from those of Putnam; identifying his position in this way as a recasting of Putnam's Common-sense Realism is a piece of logical geography, not of philosophical genealogy. Indeed, as was made clear in the exposition of Putnam's views, he explicitly acknowledges the influence of McDowell in his adoption, in particular, of the Thesis of World-Embeddedness, so that, if anything, the historical dependence runs in the opposite direction. In fact, McDowell's views derive from his reading of Wittgenstein and Frege, in the context of a problematic defined by the views of Davidson, Dummett, and Gareth Evans; and it is in the attempt, *inter alia*, to locate Tarskian truth within this context that he is led to adopt not only the Thesis of World-Embeddedness but also the conception of the relationship of meaning to use which gives birth to the Thesis of Internality of Content. So for McDowell, the adoption of Tarskian truth is not, as the route by which we have introduced his views may misleadingly suggest, an optional add-on to the characteristic principles of Common-sense Realism; rather, those principles *permit* his adherence to Tarskian truth. More precisely, they permit his adherence to Tarskian truth as a conception of truth apt to figure as the corner-stone of a theory of meaning constructed according to the Fregean model, by playing an essential part in his response to attacks mounted by Dummett alleging its inadequacy for that task.

Observe, first, that nothing in the nature of Tarskian truth constrains the structure of the metalanguage in which it is characterized, beyond the bare requirement that it contain the expressive power of the object-language, so that it contains translations of object-language sentences apt to give the content of utterances in which they figure. In particular, there is no requirement that these translations in any way decompose or analyse the content of object-language sentences—bland restatements of the originals serve as well as any more spectacular or ambitious attempts to give their content, indeed, may well be reckoned preferable because so uncontroversially correct. Casting such a delineation of Tarskian truth in the role of the core of a theory of meaning on the Fregean model, we arrive at a *modest* theory of meaning, one which gives no account of the concepts expressed by the primitive expressions of the object-language.

But, Dummett contends,[5] such modest accounts of meaning are by their nature inadequate, though the grounds for his objection are less than clear. Superficially, his reasons are that a theory of meaning for *L* should be capable of conveying knowledge of the meaning of *L*'s expressions to one ignorant of any *L*-expressible concept. Upon reflection, however, it seems that this reading would impose an impossible burden on a theory of meaning for *L*. After all, no theory can convey knowledge to one ignorant of the concepts in which the theory itself trades, and it is hard to see how a theory of meaning for *L* could do its work if all trespass on *L*'s conceptual territory is to be forbidden. A more subtle interpretation suggests that Dummett's demand is rather that the theory of meaning for *L* be able to convey knowledge of the meanings of *L*'s expressions to one ignorant in general of the use of concepts, and specifically of the use of *L*-concepts, *in second intention*—that is, as they figure in the content-giving that-clauses apt to figure in attributions of psychological attitudes. And this demand, it seems, certainly does suffice to rule out any modest theory of meaning, if not directly because of its failure to offer analyses of primitive concepts, then because of the consequential blandness of the truth-conditions in which it is bound to issue. Consider, for example, a truth theory which modestly proclaims: 'The Old Quad is rectangular' is true-in-English iff the Old Quad is rectangular. To understand this as playing a role within the core of a theory of meaning requires that one understand it as carrying the significance: in English, 'The Old Quad is rectangular' has the content *that the Old Quad is rectangular*. And to attribute that significance, one must grasp the concepts of Old Quadhood and rectangularity as they figure inside a that-clause.

Dummett's objection, if valid, has implications beyond the present context evaluation of Tarskian truth and its ramifications. Whilst a commitment to Tarskian truth and the Fregean model entails commitment to the possibility of a modest theory of meaning, such an account may be independently deemed attractive anyway, even in the context of a richer account of truth; but the attractiveness is specious, if the objection carries. And if Davidson's framework entails a commitment to the viability of a modest account of meaning—as Dummett originally thought, and McDowell continues to maintain, despite a subsequent volte-face on Dummett's part[6]—then its implications extend to the legitimacy of that whole framework, and, hence, to the argument of earlier sections of the present work, in

[5] Michael Dummett, 'What Is a Theory of Meaning? (I)', in his *The Seas of Language*, 1–33; see also, 'What Do I Know . . .?', and 'What Is a Theory of Meaning? (II)'.
[6] See John McDowell, 'Another Plea for Modesty', in his *Meaning, Knowledge, and Reality* (Cambridge, Mass., and London: Harvard University Press, 1998), 108–31, § 6, and the references to Dummett there cited.

so far as that argument entangled itself with Davidsonian hermeneutics in its account of translation.

It is, therefore, some comfort to realize that Dummett has failed to articulate any clear alternative to a modest account of meaning. The matter is complicated by the fact that, for independent reasons to be investigated below, truth as it figures in the core of the version of the theory of meaning which Dummett ultimately favours will be nonclassical and nonbivalent. It is clear enough, however, that what he has in mind is that the core should always give truth-conditions in terms of procedures for the verification of sentences, with the difference between classical and nonclassical truth-conditions arising out of the extent to which these procedures are idealized. Many subtleties enter into the proper implementation of this idea, but a crude first approximation will suffice to bring out the issues of present relevance. Thus, let the Rectangularity Test be a procedure which can be applied by suitably trained speaker to sort presented objects into the rectangular and the rest; and let the Old Quad Identification be a procedure which can be used to track down and identify the Old Quad, so that it becomes a presented object. Then a Dummettian immodest theory of meaning will explain in detail how the Rectangularity Test and the Old Quad Identification work, working with the degree of idealization appropriate to the concept of truth in play. It thereby, as a good immodest theory should, gives an account of the meanings of the primitive expressions 'rectangular' and 'the Old Quad'; and if, in explaining how these procedures work, it chooses to use the concepts of rectangularity and Old Quadhood in first intention, outside content-giving that-clauses, it exercises a right to which it is entirely entitled. Then the core theory can use these notions to assign immodest truth-conditions to sentences, along such lines as this: 'The Old Quad is rectangular' is true-in-English iff the Rectangularity Test affords a positive result when applied to the object yielded by the Old Quad Identification. This much is straightforward enough. What is less clear is how this assignment of truth-conditions is to combine with the theory of force to issue in content-specifying descriptions of *utterances*, as the Fregean model requires it to do. Suppose Archie utters the sentence 'The Old Quad is rectangular', and his utterance in the circumstances fulfils the criteria for assertion. Then his utterance is redescribable as *an assertion that the Old Quad is rectangular*; but it is unclear how this is to be derived from the truth-conditions associated with the sentence by the immodest core theory. Evidently, if the task is to be achieved, the theory of force has more to do than merely to classify utterances into kinds; it must somehow also derive the content of the utterance from the immodestly stated truth-condition of the core theory. This is a task which the theory of force of a modest theory need not face, since its core truth theory already displays the content in its modestly stated truth-condition. And Dummett admits we have no model for how a theory of force can meet the demands which he thus imposes upon it.[7]

But even if Dummett has failed fully to articulate the structure of his full-blooded alternative to a modest theory of meaning, his strictures on modesty remain as yet unrebutted. To meet them head on, we need to inquire into the justification for the crucial requirement that an acceptable theory of meaning for *L* should be capable of conveying the meanings of sentences of *L* to one ignorant of the use of concepts in second intention. McDowell traces it to a repudiation of psychologism. For if the theory of meaning is not to accomplish this explanatory task, it must (McDowell's Dummett argues) fall to some fancied theory of the mind to explain what it is to grasp the thought *that the Old Quad is rectangular*, without presupposing either a prior understanding of the use of concepts in giving the content of thought, or of how sentences come to express meanings. The theory of meaning is then relegated to the task of describing how language operates as a method of encoding the thoughts thus delineated by the theory of mind. But such psychologism is unacceptable, since it renders one person's understanding of another's utterance 'no more than a *hypothesis*' about the hidden psychology of the other, whereas if genuine communication is to be possible, meaning must 'lie open to view, as Frege maintained that it does, in our use of language, in our communication in a common practice'.[8]

But this argument depends on the assumption that the project of explaining content, independent of a prior understanding of the use of concepts in second intention, is one which is possible, and therefore necessarily falls within the scope of one of the divisions of systematic inquiry. The obscurities already noted in Dummett's attempts to outline the shape of a theory of meaning conforming to his strictures serve to undermine confidence in this assumption, now revealed as their underpinning; and McDowell advocates that it be jettisoned entirely. An explanation of the meaning of the sentences of *L*, he suggests, is possible only if it presupposes an understanding of the use of concepts, and, more specifically, of the concepts of *L*, in second intention, deployed in the specifications of content. A modest theory of meaning for *L* constitutes such an explanation, its theorems *giving* the contents of *L*-sentences by the uses of an intelligible language. In such an account, '[o]ur attention is indeed drawn to the contents of the used sentences, rather than the mere words (which are possible

---

[7] Dummett, 'What Is a Theory of Meaning? (II)', 41. The point is discussed by McDowell in § 2 of 'In Defence of Modesty', in his *Meaning, Knowledge, and Reality*, 87–107.

[8] For this and the immediately preceding quotation, see Dummett, 'What Do I Know . . . ?', 102; both quoted in McDowell, 'In Defence of Modesty', 94.

objects of attention even for someone who does not understand the language they are in): but not as something "beneath" the words, to which we are to penetrate by stripping off the linguistic clothing; rather, as something *present in* the words—something capable of being heard or seen in the words by those who understand the language.' [9] Such a theory thus avoids psychologism, inasmuch as it construes content not as buried in a mind hiding behind used sentences, but present in them. In consequence, it is intelligible only to those with the eyes to discern the immanent content, namely those with an appropriate understanding of concepts deployed in the content-specifying role of second intention.

For us, the critical point to note here is how a crucial component of this position is the view of content as internal to sentences-in-use. This is precisely the linguistic form of the Thesis of the Internality, previously encountered as the first of the two major theses of Putnam's Commonsense Realism, and here invoked by McDowell in defence of the adequacy of Tarskian truth to serve as the key concept in the core of a theory of meaning constructed on the Fregean model. Similarly, the twin of this thesis, the Thesis of World-Embeddedness, is invoked by McDowell to turn another of Dummett's arguments.

This time, Dummett's target is not Tarskian truth itself, nor its use in the core of the theory of meaning; rather, it is the use of any *bivalent* concept of truth in this role. But this attack bears upon the present evaluation of Tarskian truth inasmuch as it further weakens the residual tenuous links between Tarskian truth and traditional realism as explicated in Part One. For the reflections of the last section left Tarskian truth at least neutral on the issue of bivalence, whereas Dummett's argument, if accepted, would mean that this neutrality must be firmed into a rejection if Tarskian truth is to be used to elucidate meaning.

The argument in question will be familiar to any with the most nodding acquaintance with Dummett's writings.[10] Suppose the core of the theory of meaning for L takes the form of a theory of bivalent truth. Then, for any sentence S of L, a speaker of the language must be credited with grasping a condition which determinately either obtains or fails to obtain, and whose obtaining is necessary and sufficient for the truth of S. When S is a decidable sentence, there is no mystery about how the speaker may

[9] McDowell, 'In Defence of Modesty', 99, emphasis added.

[10] See e.g., Michael Dummett, 'The Philosophical Basis of Intuitionistic Logic' and 'The Reality of the Past', both his *Truth and Other Enigmas*, 215–47 and 216–18 and 358–62, respectively; and 'What Is a Theory of Meaning? (II)', 42–62. Following the lead of the principal reference for McDowell's views on these matters (John McDowell, 'On "The Reality of the Past"', in his *Meaning, Knowledge, and Reality*, 295–313), we concentrate on the 'learnability' form of the argument. But the considerations advanced can be adapted to engage with the argument in its 'manifestation' form.

have acquired such a grasp; for in this case there is a verification procedure which will always succeed in determining whether the condition in question obtains or does not, and grasping the condition can be equated with learning the verification procedure. But matters stand differently when S is an undecidable sentence, on which no verification procedure can adjudicate, so that this model becomes unavailable. The problem emerges most clearly when S is a sentence regarded as 'barely' true or false, that is, as one whose truth-condition is not stateable in any terms more fundamental than those of S itself, rather than one whose truth-value can be displayed as dependent on the truth-values of sentences of some more fundamental reductive class. For the only model we have for a verification-procedure for such sentences is that of direct observation, immediately certifying whether or not the truth-condition obtains. Yet examples abound of sentences of which no reductive account is plausible, yet which cannot be settled by direct observation, in the shape of undecidable sentences of mathematics, or statements about past events which have vanished without trace, or statements about the contents of other minds unevinced in behaviour.

McDowell's response[11] is that this argument is wrong in a crucial premiss: at least for sentences about the past and about other minds, the correct model for the speaker's grasp of truth-conditions *is* that of direct observation. Thus, in favourable circumstances, memory can make us directly aware *that it rained yesterday*, or perception *that Higgins is in pain*, without benefit of intervening inference from present traces or observed behaviour. (The same move is not available for mathematical sentences, in McDowell's view; but this shows only that Dummett's argument goes through for mathematics as a special case.[12]) True, there is no guarantee that such direct perception of truth-conditions will be available whenever they obtain, as Dummett's argument would evidently require them to be; but this, McDowell argues, is a simple mistake—it is enough to show how truth-conditions for sentences of a given class can be learned, that one can learn how to associate truth-conditions with *samples* of the given class, and this the direct perception model is equipped to do.[13] Thus McDowell turns this second argument of Dummett's by appeal to direct perception; but it is a response which is available only by exploiting the idiosyncracies of his own account of perception, with its rejection of the Given and consequent breadth in the range of facts available to direct perception. And part and parcel of that rejection is, as we have seen, the second characteristic thesis of Common-sense Realism, the Thesis of World-Embeddedness.

[11] McDowell, 'On "The Reality of the Past" ', 305–6.
[12] John McDowell, 'Mathematical Platonism and Dummettian Anti-Realism', in his *Meaning, Knowledge, and Reality*, 344–65.
[13] McDowell, 'On "The Reality of the Past" ', § 7.

McDowell's position thus, as was heralded when it was introduced, combines the fundamental principles of Putnam's Common-sense Realism with Tarskian truth, invoking them to defend the fitness of the latter to serve in the articulation of meaning. The resultant cocktail thus has the advantage over Putnam's version, with its redundancy account of truth, in containing the resources for a systematic semantics. We have tagged this position 'Quietist Realism'. The first component of this sobriquet is meant to encapsulate the Wittgensteinian quietism characteristic of McDowell's approach. The second records a claim, emphasized by Putnam but also discernible in McDowell, about the metaphysical box into which the position fits—a tendentious claim, and one which it is now time to evaluate.

To begin with, let us note that, having turned Dummett's argument against the suitability of a bivalent truth-predicate to figure in the core of a Fregean theory of meaning, McDowell can claim to have preserved bivalence at least as an option for his Tarskian truth-predicate. Thus his position, apparently at least, remains compatible with traditional realism as explicated in Part One, in the sense noted at the end of the last section, that McDowell's Tarskian truth-predicate, for some suitable language L at least, might bear the hallmarks of objective truth. But mere compatibility with realism, in this sense, is hardly enough to warrant classifying the whole position as a form of realism, and we might well wonder if there are stronger grounds for placing it in that pigeon-hole. Such grounds, in fact, were foreshadowed at the end of section 7.1, after Putnam's Common-sense Realism was introduced. Then it was remarked that, whatever its status by the old-fogy standards of Part One, Putnam's position could fairly claim to be the true realism of the brave new Wittgensteinian order: by making content intrinsic to the representing element and embedding content in the world, it makes the very possibility of representation dependent on the reality of the world represented. And any entitlement to this claim possessed by Putnam's position is surely inherited by that position in its superior, McDowellian incarnation.

But a little reflection is enough to cast doubt on this case for classifying McDowell's position as a new realism. For if the representing mind is embedded in the world, then it seems that there is a danger that the world is thereby contaminated with mentality—so that, rather than a new realism, what McDowell has to peddle is a new idealism. This is a charge of which McDowell is well aware, and which he goes to some lengths to rebut. Articulating it with precision, and evaluating its status, is of the first importance in assessing the significance of McDowell's work for the issue of realism.

We may distinguish two ontological levels on which the charge of idealism can be urged against McDowell: the level of objects; and that of facts.

Facts, for McDowell, are given by content-specifying that-clauses—he gives as an example *that spring has begun*, and, as the generic form, *that things are thus and so*.[14] Perception, as we have seen, involves direct engagement with the world at the level of facts; and, indeed, the world as McDowell conceives it is, like the world of the *Tractatus*, a totality of facts rather than of things.[15] The difference is that McDowell's facts, being possible contents of thought as well as building-blocks of the world, belong firmly in the realm of Fregean sense,[16] whence they are equally describable as '(Fregean) thoughts' or as 'thinkable contents'.[17] (This location in the world of sense also differentiates McDowell's facts from the homonymous entities which figured in sections 1.2 and 1.3 of Chapter 1 in connection with the Correspondence Theory of Truth, of which the facts of the *Tractatus*, on a standard reading of that oracular work, are a species. It unfits them for the task, which those earlier facts were intended to fulfil, of underwriting the analysis of truth; at the same time, it bestows upon them logical characteristics of intensionality, rendering them immune to the Great Fact Argument which bore heavily upon facts of the earlier kind.) The charge of idealism, at the level of objects, then arises from the idea that there is no place for mind-independent objects in a world constituted of these thinkable contents.

This idea gives rise to the following argument:[18] McDowell's facts are Fregean thoughts; but such thoughts, being senses, can have only senses as their constituents; so objects cannot figure as constituents of such facts—in their place, there is room only for 'individual' or 'singular' senses; so humdrum objects have no place in McDowell's world. McDowell's response is, in effect, to deny the final step of this argument: objects, he maintains, *figure in* facts without being constituents of them. The key to understanding how this happens is to realize that singular senses are *object-dependent*—they are 'modes of presentation' of existing objects, and, as such, their existence and identity is conceptually dependent on the existence and identity of an object which they represent. So when a singular sense is a constituent of a fact, that fact is inevitably drawn into the figured-in relation to the concomitant object of the singular sense.[19]

[14] McDowell, *Mind and World*, 26–7.

[15] John McDowell, 'Comments: Response to Ian Lyne', *Journal of the British Society for Phenomenology*, 31 (2000), 339.

[16] See e.g., McDowell, *Mind and World*, 179 for an explicit statement of a point implicit in much of his writing.

[17] Ibid., 28.

[18] Cf. Julian Dodd, 'McDowell and the Identity Theory of Truth', *Analysis*, 55 (1995), 160–5.

[19] John McDowell, 'Singular Thought and the Extent of Inner Space', in his *Meaning, Knowledge, and Reality*, 237.

The charge of idealism at the level of objects, however, permits of other formulations, not obviously rebutted by similar considerations. McDowell himself puts such a formulation into the words of an imaginary objector:

You can make it look as if your drift is not idealistic, as long as you consider the world only as something whose elements are *things that are the case*. In that context, you can exploit the claim that it is no more than a truism that when one's thought is true, what one thinks *is* what is the case. But as soon as we try to accommodate the sense in which the world is populated by *things*, by objects (and there had better be such a sense), it will emerge that your image of erasing an outer boundary around the realm of thought must be idealistic in tenor, perhaps in an extended sense. Even if the image allows for a certain kind of direct contact between minds and facts, it obliterates a certain possibility that we should not be willing to renounce, a possibility of direct contact between minds and *objects*, which must surely be external to the realm of thought.[20]

On the face of it, this is rather a different objection from the one previously canvassed. But McDowell, responding to it in discussion immediately following the quoted passage, construes it as turning on similar issues. What motivates the objector, he argues, is a rejection of generalized descriptivism, according to which singular reference is possible only when the object of reference is specified in general terms. That rejection is entirely justified, but the objector mistakenly thinks that the only alternative to the rejected doctrine is to regard singular reference as involving a direct, extra-conceptual relation between thinkers and objects, conceived as lying beyond the outer boundary of the conceptual. This misses the true, and intermediate, position, that singular reference is mediated by object-dependent singular senses, in virtue of which objects come to figure in thoughts/facts. So the recognition of the role of singular senses is, once again, the crucial factor in explaining the place of objects in the world.

But it is questionable whether this response exhaustively answers the concerns raised by the imagined objector. Suppose we grant McDowell his apparatus of object-dependent singular senses—no small concession, incidentally, since the key notion is hardly pellucid. Then we can explain, perhaps, how 'objects', in some sense of the term, 'figure in' thought and facts. But the status of the objects thus figuring remains moot. In what sense do we regain a 'world populated by things' by invoking this apparatus? Or are McDowell's objects no more than idealistic shadows of the things with which realism fills the world? For there would seem to be no more to a McDowellian object than a locus around which singular senses cluster—as it may be, a permanent possibility of conceptualization. It might be right

[20] McDowell, *Mind and World*, 179.

that there is no more to an object than this; but it is doubtful that any red-blooded realist would agree.

An issue which arises in the interpretation of Frege may help to sharpen this point. In an article discussed by Dummett in his book on Frege's philosophy of language,[21] Ernst Tugendhat suggested that Frege's objects be construed as the 'truth-value potentials' of singular terms; that is, in effect, as equivalence classes of singular terms under the relation *corefers*, or, better—since, as Dummett points out, it would be ludicrous to identify Dr Tugendhat himself, as a sample object, with a class of linguistic expressions—as entities given only as elements standing in a one : one correspondence to these equivalence classes. In an article on the interpretation of the *Tractatus* to which McDowell refers with approval,[22] Brian McGuinness proposed applying Tugendhat's analysis to the objects of the *Tractatus*. Given McDowell's explicit comparisons of his own system with the *Tractatus*, it does not seem too long a bow to draw to suggest he would find congenial a similar account of objects, at the representational level of sense rather than of language. Then, if a singular sense 'determines' its associated object, McDowell's objects become equivalence classes of singular senses under the relation *codetermines*, or, more precisely, entities standing in one : one correspondence to these equivalence classes; and certainly such a construal of McDowell's objects is in line with that we have recently mooted. But Dummett insists that Tugendhat's interpretation fails to capture Frege's realism, at least if taken as embodying the Last Word about objects; for it offers only an 'ineradicably language-dependent' characterization of objects, whilst Frege's realism requires it should also be characterizable as the language-independent second terms of the name/bearer relation. Similarly, the mooted construal of McDowell's objects may seem too ineradicably thought-dependent for realism; but it is a construal which is inevitable, since to portray them also as the thought-independent second terms of some sense/object relation would be to invoke precisely the sort of relation, between thought and things outside some fancied boundary of the conceptual, which McDowell rejects. There is, of course, no ground for objection to McDowell here. But what it does suggest is that on one antecedent and independent conception of realism about objects, that attributed to Frege by Dummett, McDowell's views emerge as, if not outrightly idealist, at least well short of realist.

[21] Ernst Tugendhat, 'The Meaning of "*Bedeutung*" in Frege', *Analysis*, 30 (1970), 177–89; Michael Dummett, *Frege: Philosophy of Language* (London: Duckworth, 1973), 199–203.
[22] Brian McGuinness, 'The So-Called Realism of the *Tractatus*', in Irving Block (ed.), *Perspectives on the Philosophy of Wittgenstein* (Oxford: Blackwell, 1981), 70–3; McDowell, 'In Defence of Modesty', 92 n.

Still, this discussion warrants no more than a tentative conclusion, and needs to be supplemented by consideration of the charge of idealism at the level of facts. Here, indeed, we may expect to hope for more illumination. After all, it was argued in sections 1.2 and 1.3 of Chapter 1, it is at the level of facts (and, hence, of truth) that the realism issue emerges most clearly, at least if realism is construed in traditional terms; and, though we are now attempting to locate McDowell's position in terms of realism more fluidly conceived, it is at the level of facts that we might expect considerations to emerge which, through family resemblance to those relevant in the more traditional framework, will assist us in making the location.

Once again, McDowell himself is well aware of plausibility of the charge of idealism against his position, this time at the level of facts:

People sometimes object to positions like the one I have been urging on the ground that they embody an arrogant anthropocentrism, a baseless confidence that the world is completely within the reach of our powers of thinking. This looks at least akin to an accusation of idealism. Why should we be so sure of our capacity to comprehend the world if not because we conceive the world as a shadow or reflection of our thinking?[23]

The reason McDowell's world may seem to be 'completely within the reach of our powers of thinking', in a way giving rise to this charge, lies in the structure of thought within his system. The mind engages directly with the world in veridical perception, giving rise to perceptual beliefs whose contents are worldly facts. Further true beliefs—further facts—arise as the active mind (the 'faculty of sponaneity') fleshes out the perceptual ones into a systematic and total world-view. Thus it appears that the facts in general are available to the mind, either through perception or through the operation of the faculty of spontaneity.

Before we review McDowell's response, it is worth noting another which is *not* available to him. This is to suggest that perceptual facts may elude the mind because it is unable to discriminate with certainty between veridical and nonveridical perception, leaving the question of the true nature of the world irresolvable. When McDowell's views were first introduced in section 7.1, we suggested he owes an account of nonveridical perception. This is a debt he refuses to acknowledge, on the ground that the demand for it is premised on traditional views which he rejects, and presupposes the legitimacy of the Given; but he is insistent that no major issue turns on the point. Thus, whilst he says '[i]t is true that we could not establish we are open to the facts in any given case',[24] he goes on to say that the correct attitude to such sceptical questions is 'to ignore them, to treat them as unreal, in the way that common sense has always wanted to', and to reply to the sceptic 'I know why you think that question is peculiarly pressing, but it is not'. But if nothing of philosophical importance turns on the distinction between veridical and nonveridical perception, then in particular it cannot be made the bulwark against the charge of idealism.

The response which McDowell does make, in a passage immediately following that quoted above,[25] is that it is the epistemic duty of the faculty of spontaneity constantly to revise and improve its belief system—to 'reflect on the credentials of the putatively rational linkages that, at any one time, one takes to govern the active business of adjusting one's world-view in response to experience', as McDowell puts it; hence, '[t]here is no guarantee that the world is completely within the reach of a system of concepts and conceptions as it stands at some particular moment in its historical development.'

As a defence against the charge of arrogant anthropomorphism which McDowell has levelled against himself, this response seems entirely effective: the world may lie forever just beyond the best effort of the faculty of spontaneity at any given time. But there is another concern, familiar from the earlier pages of this book. For surely we can consider the ideal conceptual system formed by taking the limit of the best methods of the faculty of spontaneity, applied to the sum total of all possible veridical perception. Then there seems no way such an ideal conceptual system can fall short of the world as McDowell conceives it. Accordingly, if we encapsulate this ideal system in a suitable language L, its becomes an ideal theory, all of whose theses are true, in the sense given by the disquotational Tarskian truth-predicate for L. Hence McDowell's position denies epistemic independence, one of the key theses of traditional realism.

There is a response to this line of argument foreshadowed in McDowell. This is to deny the legitimacy of the very conception of an ideal conceptual system: 'it might well be argued', he writes, 'that even as an ideal of reason, this conception is suspect', the reason being that it involves 'a vestigial reflection of the unwarranted confidence in our powers' involved in the charge of arrogant anthropomorphism.[26] But this response seems to beg the question. Aspiring to carry out the rational operations of the faculty of spontaneity to the limit will involve an unwarranted confidence in our powers to embrace total truth only if the total truth is so conceived as to be guaranteed to be revealed in this way.

The doubts which were raised about the effectiveness of McDowell's rebuttal of the charge of idealism against objects, combined with this newly identified repudiation of a key tenet of traditional realism as explicated in

---

[25] McDowell, *Mind and World*, 40.   [26] Ibid.

Part One, surely suffice to dispel any claims his position may lay to constituting some new-fangled version of realism. Moreover, even the formal compatibility we have noted hitherto between Tarskian truth and the theses of explicated traditional realism is lost once it is embedded inside the wider framework of McDowellism. For then it preserves its adherence to Bivalence against the attacks of Dummett only at the expense of sacrificing epistemic independence. In sum, there may be much to be said for McDowell's quietism. But it is not a form of realism, traditional or new-fangled.

8.3 CONCLUDING REMARKS

Realism, we conclude, is dead: there is no defensible notion of truth which preserves the theses of traditional realism, nor any defensible position deserving the title of realism through inheriting the mantle of the traditional form. The closest we can come to defence of realism is to embrace Tarskian truth, which can at least claim compatibility with the traditional doctrine. But this will be at best a formal compliance with the letter of realist doctrine, insufficient to satisfy any red-blooded realist. And even it will not be available if truth is to be used in the explanation of meaning, unless some answer other than McDowell's can be found to answer Dummett's challenges to its use in that role; for McDowell's way involves sacrificing even this formal compliance.

The real choice, then, is between different varieties of antirealism. But this does not necessarily mean choosing between ways of rejecting Bivalence, as it may appear to those who view these matters through an exclusively Dummettian lens. For all this book has to say, less radical options remain on the table, options which hang on to Bivalence and classical logic, but reject epistemic independence. It is in the choice between these options that the future debate on the realism issue—perhaps better styled the antirealism issue—will lie.

The champions of these two options are, of course, Michael Dummett and John McDowell. If I may abandon the authorial 'we' and the lofty, if somewhat pompous, impersonal voice I have found myself adopting in this work (perhaps through some ironical subconscious wish to appear objective), and sound in this last paragraph a more personal note, I should acknowledge that I was privileged to have these two champions as supervisors of my work many years ago. I am, therefore, in a position to conclude that, though I may not know what the correct view on these matters may be, at least I was taught by someone who does.

Coda: Brandom, Compositionality, and Singular Terms

Robert Brandom, in his monumental tome *Making it Explicit*,[1] purports to offer a theory of precisely the kind which sections 7.2 and 7.3 of this book supposed to be impossible: a use-based theory of meaning, operating with a formal concept of truth and eschewing the Fregean model, but accommodating structural complexity and, in particular, compositionality. The purpose of this Coda is to examine Brandom's theory and, by finding it wanting, bolster the claims of that earlier chapter.

Inference is, for Brandom, the semantically critical feature of use, and he offers an inferentialist account of semantic content. This means that the first thing involved in the specification of the content of a sentence is to indicate its role, in relation to the contents of other sentences, in three different sorts of inferential structure: *committive* inferences; *permissive* inferences; and *incompatibilities* (*ME*, 188). In committive inferences, *commitment* to the premisses carries a further commitment to the conclusion; in permissive ones, *entitlement* to the premisses carries a further entitlement to the conclusion; and *incompatibility* arises when commitment to one claim precludes entitlement to another (*ME*, 168, 189). Importantly, the inferences involved here go beyond the formal and include *material* ones, such as the committive inference: *A* is west of *B*, so *B* is east of A; and the permissive one: thunder now, so lightning earlier (*ME*, 168); both of which, in Brandom's view, are incorrectly viewed as enthymemes. Further, as Brandom's examples make clear, the acceptable material inferences may vary from person to person; thus, it appears, the notion of content must be, at least in the first instance, person-relative. Beyond this intralinguistic inferential core, sentential content also comprises inferential links to the extralinguistic world (*ME*, ch. 4, cf. 674, fn. 38). First, there are language entry points: part of the content of

---

[1] Robert Brandom, *Making it Explicit* (Cambridge, Mass., and London: Harvard University Press, 1994). Referred to in the text as *ME*.

observation sentences is that commitment to them by a reliable observer is sufficient for entitlement to them (*ME*, 189). Next, there are language exit points; part of the content of a sentence is that it entitles various actions on the part of an agent entitled to deploy it as a premiss in practical reasoning (*ME*, ch. 4, § v). Importantly, for Brandom, such implications go through unmediated by Humean premisses concerning the agent's desires.

Construing sentence content in this way allows Brandom to explain how uttered sentences function in what, following Sellars, he regards as the fundamental linguistic activity, 'the game of giving and asking for reasons'. Thus, to utter a sentence assertively is to undertake commitments, and assume entitlements, in ways shaped by the inferential structures spelled out in the sentence's content (*ME*, 190–1). These include a commitment to produce, if challenged, a reason for the assertion, either in the shape of a prior entitlement to premisses related to the asserted sentence by permissive inference, or of a claim to entitlement to undertake commitment as a reliable observer. Further, they involve undertaking commitments, and assuming entitlements, to claims expressible by other sentences, which are (in the light of prior commitments and entitlements) related to the sentence asserted by committive or permissive inference; and assuming entitlements to actions related by practical inference to the sentence asserted, or to others to which entitlement is assumed as a result of the assertion. Further still, they involve a commitment to revoke prior commitments and entitlements to claims expressible by sentences incompatible with that asserted. Utterances of the sentence with auxiliary, nonassertive, force can be understood on a similar model; for example, a disavowal undoes the new commitments and entitlements associated with assertion, and reinstores entitlements it would cancel (*ME*, 192). Communication is a matter of 'score-keeping'; keeping track of the evolving commitments and entitlements of participants (*ME*, ch. 3, § iv).

Substitution is Brandom's key to extending content, as thus explained for sentences, to subsentential expressions. First, it is deployed at the syntactic level to make some key distinctions (*ME*, 367–70). He distinguishes two roles which expressions can play in a substitution: one expression is *substituted in*, which expressions within it are *substituted for*. Two expressions are *substitutional variants* iff one arises from the other by substitutions within it. A *substitutional frame* is what two substitutional variants have in common; where these variants are sentences, it can also be called a *sentence frame*. Frames are expressions only in an extended sense, and are better viewed as *patterns* ordinary expressions can exemplify. (So, when 'Cicero' is substituted by 'Tully' throughout in 'Cicero greatly admired Cicero' the result is a substitutional variant of that sentence, namely, 'Tully greatly admired Tully'; and the substitutional/sentence frame they share is 'α greatly admired α'.) Because sentence frames differ so from ordinary expressions, an exchange of sentence frames within a sentence (as when 'Cicero denounced Catiline' becomes 'Cicero orated') is not a substitution (a term reserved for the exchange of genuine expressions) but a *replacement*; the sentence obtained as a result of such a replacement is called a *frame variant* of the original. Finally, a *syntactic category* or *kind* of expression is a set of expressions, all of which are mutually interchangeable in any sentence without destroying sentencehood.

This syntactic apparatus permits the further deployment of substitution at the semantic (inferential) level, to extend the notion of content to subsentential expressions (*ME*, 370–6). The key idea is that of a Simple Material Substitutional Inferential Commitment (SMSIC) concerning a subsentential expression *e*. Paradigmatically, such a commitment is enshrined in the endorsement of a *substitution rule*,[2] i.e, of an inferential pattern endorsing an inference from a premiss containing *e* to a *substitutional* variant thereof obtained by substituting *e* by some specified alternative expression *e**. This paradigm is extended to allow an SMSIC concerning *e* to involve commitment not to a substitution rule but to a *replacement rule*, i.e., an inferential pattern endorsing an inference from a premiss containing *e* to a *frame* variant thereof, obtained by replacing *e* by some specified alternative expression *e**. Brandom acknowledges (*ME*, 373–4) that, in the light of well-known complications generated by modal and other contexts, both substitution and replacement rules will need some restriction to premisses in which the critical expression *e* occurs in appropriate position; these restrictions define the *primary substitution semantic occurrences* of expressions. The content of a subsentential expression can now be identified with the SMSICs in which it figures (*ME*, 374), and thus as given by the totality of substitution or replacement rules which govern it.

Does subsentential content, as thus defined, determine sentential content as compositionality requires? Brandom seems satisfied that it does, on the ground that 'the collaboration of all the SMSICs corresponding to subsentential expressions having primary occurrence in a sentence settles the correctness of the whole set of substitution inferences it appears in as premise or conclusion' (*ME*, 374). For this ground to suffice, it must be that settling these substitution inferences involving the sentence is enough to settle *all* the material inferences involving it, including its language entrance and exit links. The details of how this comes about are less

---

[2] Here, as with 'replacement rule' later, we follow Peter Graham, 'Brandom on Singular Terms', *Philosophical Studies*, 93 (1999), 247–64 in adapting Brandom's own, rather clumsy, terminology.

than entirely evident; still, it seems reasonable to concede that Brandom's subsentential content determines at least the core of sentential content as he construes it, even if some further tale needs telling as to how the core thus determined expands to content fully fledged.

Substitutional frames depend for their identification on a prior identification of a set of expressions as those which are substituted for. Thus, subject to an identification of 'Socrates', 'Cicero', 'Tully', and the like as expressions substituted for, 'Socrates is wise' will be parsed as comprising the sentence frame 'α is wise' together with the substituted-for expression 'Socrates'; but under identification of 'wise', 'foolish', 'vain', and their ilk as expressions substituted for, it will comprise the sentence frame 'Socrates is α' combined with the substituted-for expression 'wise'. Ramsey's well-known challenge[3] is to find grounds for preferring the more intuitive former parsing as more semantically well motivated than the latter. Whilst Brandom does not address the problem directly, a key result which he claims[4] to be able rigorously to prove constitutes just such grounds. This result is that, if a language is to be capable of enrichment by adding negation or the conditional, expressions substituted for must be governed by substitutional rules imposing a symmetric pattern of substitutional inferences on those terms (*ME*, 376–84). This requirement is satisfied by the first identification of substituted-fors, since a substitutional rule governing 'Cicero', allowing for substitution of its primary substitutional semantic occurrences by 'Tully', will always be matched by a rule governing 'Tully' allowing similar substitutions by 'Cicero'. The second identification of substituted-fors will, however, flout the requirement: for, absent logical connectives, a substitutional rule on 'wise' would allow for its substitution in normal contexts by 'ratiocinative', whilst no matching rule would license substitutions in the reverse direction; so the language would stand convicted of an inbuilt incompatibility to enrichment by the logical particles. The traditional parsing of 'Socrates is wise' accordingly emerges as the one to be preferred. Traditional terminology describes this as the segmentation of the sentence into a singular term ('Socrates') and a predicate ('α is wise'); Brandom adopts this terminology as well, defining a singular term within his framework as an expression which is substituted for, and which figures only in a symmetric pattern of substitutional inferences; and a predicate as a sentence frame formed from a sentence by deletion of singular terms, and figuring in at least some asymmetric

[3] F. P. Ramsey, 'Universals', in his *The Foundations of Mathematics; and Other Logical Essays* (London: Routledge & Kegan Paul, 1931), 112–34.
[4] But see Graham, 'Brandom on Singular Terms', for criticism of the claim.

replacement inferences (*ME*, 375–6). But these definitions lead to some very *non*traditional identifications of singular terms (and, hence, predicates) which raise serious problems for Brandom's whole account of subsentential structure.

Consider a language in which the letters 'c' and 'g' are interchangeable; the speakers choose to use syntactically distinct but related expressions to the same semantic end, perhaps because they value the variety on aesthetic grounds. Call this the *CG language*, and let expressions differing from each other only in the distribution of 'c's and 'g's be called *c/g variants*. For concreteness, let us suppose it contains, among others, the sentences 'the blob is green' and 'the blob is coloured' (with inferential content appropriate to equating them to their English counterparts), along with sentences 'the blob is creen' and 'the blob is goloured', each with the same inferential content as its c/g variant. Then 'c' and 'g' would appear to fit Brandom's definition of singular terms: each is an expression which can be substituted for, and the inferential substitutional patterns in which they are involved are symmetric. The Brandomian logical structure of 'the blob is green' in the CG language would accordingly appear to be the rather peculiar 'Reen(the blob, g)'.

An immediate objection to this conclusion is that 'c' and 'g' fail the test of being expressions substitutable for, since, though each may be substitutable for the other, replacement of either by other noncontroversial singular terms such as 'Cicero' will result in a nongrammatical sentence. All that this shows, however, is that Brandom's singular terms need not form a unitary syntactic category; rather, there can be many categories of singular terms, each based on a different group of mutually substitutable-for expressions, and each meeting the additional semantic criterion of symmetric substitutional inference. In fact, Brandom would seem to need, in any case, to split the uncontroversial singular terms into distinct categories, since his criterion for sentencehood is that of 'an expression which can be used to perform one of the fundamental kinds of speech act' (*ME*, 368); so, since '72 is an orator' seems to fail this test, numerals and personal names must perforce be assigned different categories. What *is* strange about 'c' and 'g' is that the range of mutually substitutable-for expressions on which their category is based is so restricted, being confined to these two alone; but complicating the example in obvious ways should serve to eliminate that feature.

A second thought might be that the difference between c/g variants can be simply ignored; what are apparently two expressions are, at a deeper level, one. But it is hard to find a nonarbitrary motivation for the identification. Certainly, by any ordinary phonetic or syntactic tests, 'c' and 'g', and, hence, expressions which contain them, are distinct. So, if they are to be identified, that must be because they are to be individuated semantically.

But the fact that whole sentences which are c/g variants share a semantic content is not enough to warrant any conclusion about the content of their subsentential parts; and the viability of an extension of the account of sentential content to subsentential parts is precisely the point now at issue.

A third idea might be that 'c' and 'g' differ from orthodox singular terms in being *everywhere* intersubstitutable, whereas for orthodox singular terms such substitution is limited to primary substitution semantic occurrences. But, though this does mark a difference between orthodox singular terms and our upstart candidates, it does not provide a ground for denying the latter singular-term status under Brandom's definitions, nor is it obvious that it provides any rationale for a revision of those definitions aimed at excluding the trouble-makers. Further, it seems easy enough to modify the example so that speakers of the CG language are portrayed as less promiscuous in permitting substitution, so that the difference just noted disappears. For why should not the brute facts of use be, for example, that speakers everywhere prefer to use the 'c' version of their vocabulary for all occurrences other than primary substitution semantic occurrences, and balk at any inference attempting substitution, in such occurrences, of 'g' for 'c'?

A fourth thought is that Brandom might expand his definition of singular terms to require that all such terms must *refer*, the thought being that this is a requirement which the aberrant 'c' and 'g' must surely fail. To add the further requirement, we must, of course, look to reference as that notion is to be explained in the framework of Brandomian inferential semantics, on pain of polluting his project with alien elements. Now Brandom favours a formal account of truth which is a modified version of the anaphoric theory of Grover, Camp, and Belnap, and which treats '. . . is true' as what he calls a 'prosentence-forming operator' (*ME*, 301–5). He builds on this account (*ME*, 305–22) to construct an analogous theory of reference in which 'refers' is treated as an operator forming complex pro*nouns* of a sort he calls 'indirect descriptions'; criteria are given for the identification of such an operator in inferential semantic terms (*ME*, 313–15), so the result can be claimed to be a thoroughgoing account of reference within Brandom's preferred framework.

Brandom's paradigm of an indirect description is

the one Joe referred to as 'that airhead';

the upshot of his theory being that this is not the definite description it appears, but a complex pronoun, which has as its anaphoric antecedent, and, hence, shares the content of, the indicated tokening by Joe of the words 'that airhead'. Likewise,

the one referred to by 'Leibniz'

is an indirect description, though this time no specific tokening of 'Leibniz' is indicated as the anaphoric antecedent; instead, there is a presupposition of 'invariance under cotypical intersubstitutions', so that *any* tokening of 'Leibniz' can be taken as the anaphoric antecedent to the same effect. In particular, then, the anaphoric antecedent can be taken to be that token which occurs on the right hand of the identity in

(1) the one referred to by 'Leibniz' = Leibniz.

Hence (1), and its more vernacular and more Tarskian equivalent

(2) 'Leibniz' refers to Leibniz

are trivial truths; and Brandom happily agrees with standard logic that from (2) we may derive

(3) $\exists x$('Leibniz' refers to x)

(on which more below). But as with 'Leibniz', so it appears with 'c' and 'g'. So Brandom's account of reference leaves no room for discriminating these from other singular terms on the grounds of not referring; though as we shall see, ghosts of this issue will return to haunt us below.

Even supposing it granted that consideration of the CG language shows there is a prima-facie case that Brandom's account of subsentential structure leads to some eccentric parsing by orthodox logical lights, one might ask why that should matter. After all, from the standpoint of the compositionality problem, all that matters it that the semantics of complex expressions should be systematically determined by their structure from finitely many subsentential components; there is, surely, no requirement on a satisfactory solution that those components should fit some predetermined pattern.

To this, Brandom himself supplies (*ME*, 414–15) a convincing, and very Dummettian, answer: as Frege came to realize through examination of the hard case of arithmetic, in which the inadequacies of alternatives are the more apparent, our cognitive grasp on objects is mediated not by mental pictures or by the causal influence of the world on thought, but by the singular terms of an articulated language. So the construal of subsentential structure is constrained at least to the extent that reading the right structure of singular terms into a language is critical to determining the objects its users cognize. That in itself does not, of course, mean that the singular terms discerned must be those of stodgy orthodoxy. But it is enough to show that the matter is no trivial one, and that deviations from orthodoxy (or coincidence with it) is something that matters.

Brandom's discussion of this point leads, nevertheless, to his revealing new facts about his construal of singular terms which may bear on the question of the entitlement of 'c' and 'g' to claim that status. To begin with, part of what is involved in being an object-determining singular term is to be associated with criteria of identity, in the sense that somehow or other the correctness must be settled of nontrivial identity statements involving the singular term in question. As Frege interpreted it, this is the requirement that the correctness of *all* such identity statements be settled; Brandom argues that it is sufficient that this hold just for *some* nontrivial statement of identity (*ME*, 416–26).

As for the status of identity statements in general, Brandom's general theory of logical vocabulary applies. This construes the function of such vocabulary as being to make explicit as claims what is implicit in the practice of material inference (*ME*, 116–17 and *passim*); the paradigm of such vocabulary is the conditional, which expresses as a claim a commitment to a material inference from the antecedent as premiss to the consequent as conclusion (*ME*, ch. 2, § 4). Applied to the case of identity, an identity statement makes explicit substitutional commitments permitting the intersubstitutivity of its terms in primary substitutional occurrences (*ME*, 416–19). It follows that the cash value of the requirement for a criterion of identity to be associated with each singular term is that, for any such term, there be at least one other such that there is a commitment to the mutual intersubstitutivity of the two in appropriate contexts. But this is a requirement which will be met by any singular term with nonvacuous content, as that notion has already been defined. It constitutes, then, no new condition for singular terms to meet, but rather expands and explains the account already given. And, importantly, it is a requirement which 'c' and 'g' quite evidently meet.

Brandom's discussion of identity nevertheless brings to light a further factor which, it seems, may bear upon the case. This is that each singular term should be associated with a *sortal*, on the familiar ground that judgements of identity make sense only against the background of a sortal presupposition (*ME*, 436–40). (The point bears on another made previously, where it was suggested Brandomian singular terms would need to divide into categories; these may be defined by a sortal common to all members of a category.) Perhaps 'c' and 'g' fall short of full singular termhood by failing to be associated with such a sortal? The question admits of no ready answer, since Brandom advances no precise criteria for identifying sortals or telling when they exist. There is, of course, a considerable literature on the topic, though it is a moot point whether that provides criteria sufficient to yield a definitive answer to our question. More importantly, what is required is an account of sortals which will jibe with the framework of Brandom's inferential semantics. So the sortal associated with a singular term should be recoverable from the way the term is embedded in a pattern of material inferences. Further, since, according to Brandom, the meaningful use of an identity statement turns on the association of its terms with sortals, and since further such a statement merely makes explicit a commitment to the mutual intersubstitutivity of those terms in appropriate contexts, it apparently follows that, wherever a commitment to such inter-substitutivity is intelligible, there must be some sortal associated with those terms (and so somehow recoverable, once a suitable story about sortals is finally told, from the pattern of material inferences in which they figure). But the description of the commitment to intersubstitutivity of 'c' and 'g' in the CG language is evidently entirely intelligible; it follows that some sortal is associated with each of them—though doubtless it will turn out to be a sortal only in some uninteresting, limiting-case sense of the term.

All this talk of identity raises the question of the correlative notion of quantification; and herein, many will doubtless have been thinking for some time, lies the solution to the problem of 'c' and 'g'. For surely, it may be urged, the singular termhood or otherwise of these must turn on the matter of whether or not, in the inferential practice out of which their content arises, the positions they occupy are regarded as available for quantificational binding.

Brandom's treatment of the quantifiers (*ME*, 434–6) is in line with his general treatment of logical vocabulary. Thus, a claim of the form $\forall x Px$ makes explicit a commitment to *every* claim of the form Pa (where a is a singular term), whilst a claim of the form $\exists x Px$ makes explicit a commit-ment to *some* such claim (with no obligation to an ability to specify which one). Brandomian quantification is, accordingly, a species of substitutional quantification; he hopes to turn well-known objections to such a construal, on the grounds of an inadequate supply of substituting terms a to meet the needs of quantifying over indenumerable domains, by allowing the substi-tuting terms to be not just those available at any stage within a language, but to embrace as well all those which could be introduced to it.

The upshot of this account of the quantifiers would, however, seem to be that the quantificational criterion cannot be used to disqualify the 'c' and 'g' of the CG language from the status of singular terms. For there is no doubt that a commitment to 'the blob is green' involves a commitment to 'the blob is $a$reen', for some as-yet-undisqualified singular term a, to wit, 'g'; and this commitment can be made explicit in the claim '$\exists x$(the blob is $x$reen)', revealing the position of 'g' to be accessible after all to the quantifiers. Of course, this possibility might not be exploited in the syntax and inferential practice of the users of the language, just as it was not explicitly foreshadowed in our introduction of the case. But any such failure to exploit the possibility would seem, on Brandom's principles, to reflect an imperfect grasp of its structure, demanding reform of artificially truncated practice. (Similarly, unreflective use might deny access of complex singular terms, constructed by means of a description operator—such as '$\iota x(x = c)$'—to the positions occupied by 'c' and 'g'; but the well-known connections between quantifiers and descriptions should lead also to descriptions being admitted to such positions, once access to the quantifiers is allowed.)

For Brandom, '∃' is the *particular* quantifier, not the existential one; the claim '$\exists x Px$' need not involve commitment to the actual existence of a P object. This is because not all singular terms need be treated as referring to actually existent objects—some singular terms merely *purport* to refer (*ME*, 431), and '$\exists x Px$' may make explicit a commitment only to the claim 'Pa' for some such term a. This may seem inconsistent with what has gone before; for our discussion of Brandom's views on reference made it seem a trivial consequence that each singular term refers, whereas now it seems some merely purport to do so. But the inconsistency is merely verbal: according to Brandom, all singular terms do, indeed, refer; those that are said merely to 'purport to refer' are those whose referents do not exist (*ME*, 444–5).

These considerations suggest a final avenue for denying 'c' and 'g' full status as singular terms, on the ground that they somehow lack a possible connection with an existent referent. Exploring the issue requires us to examine further distinctions between particular and existential quantification, and between terms with real and nonexistent referents. The key to both distinctions, as Brandom sees things, lies with the identification of a special category—or, more accurately, a range of special categories—of singular terms, known as 'canonical designators' (*ME*, 443–9). These are expressions which specify an address for each member of a range of entities, locating the place of each entity inside a structure which they inhabit. The paradigm canonical designators are the numerals: each natural number is uniquely located in its place in the number series by some numeral. 'Egocentric spatiotemporal co-ordinate descriptions' of the form 'the F at $\langle x, y, z, t \rangle$ from here' will do the same job for physical objects, locating each in physical space and time; names and singular terms constructed from material available in works of fiction will locate fictional objects in the structured worlds the works describe. Corresponding to each category of canonical designators is a category of existence—numerical, physical, fictional. A particular quantification '$\exists x Px$' is a claim of existence in some category if it makes explicit a commitment to some claim of the form 'Pd', where d is not merely a singular term but a canonical designator of the appropriate category. And to treat a singular term a as one with an existent referent is to undertake a commitment to a claim which can be made explicit as '$\exists x x = a$', where the quantifier has full existential force.

How, then, can 'c' and 'g' somehow fail of connection with an existent referent, and what bearing does this have on their status as fully fledged singular terms? First, they may, of course, be used as terms with an existent referent, but the existence presupposition fail to be satisfied; as happens when a commitment to '$\exists xx = c$' is undertaken, but the commitment that makes to some claim of the form '$d = c$' (for d a canonical designator) turns out to be unsustainable. In this case, however, 'c' is in no worse a boat than a seriously used 'the present King of France' (or 'Pegasus' as used by one mistakenly taking the mythical beast for a real horse); any failings it may have lie not in an intrinsic difference between it and other terms, but in a failure of the world to oblige by matching it. Second, they may be used as terms without being treated as terms with an existent referent. In this case, they correspond to 'the present King of France' as that may be idly used by one who believes that France has no current monarch, real, mythical, or fictional. (For the last to be reasonable, presumably some relatively fixed canon of fiction must be presupposed.) Again, this marks no real failure in these as singular terms, if such a use can be understood as parasitic on a use of the first sort. What *would* seem to make for a genuine difference is the third possibility: that 'c' and 'g' cannot be supposed ever to be used in the first way, and treated as having existent referents.

But this last possibility, damaging though it may be to the status of 'c' and 'g' as fully fledged singular terms, does not seem to be one which genuinely arises. It is equivalent to the view that 'c' and 'g' are such that no terms exist, or can be introduced, to play the role of canonical designators for them; but it is hard to see why that should be so. Canonical designators give the address of an object in a structure. That structure, in turn, arises out of a theory erected to account for a complex pattern of identifications and discriminations made over a range of objects, as these are revealed in the substitution inferences governing a set of singular terms. Now, 'c' and 'g' (and other singular terms in their substitution range, such as, perhaps, '$\iota x(x = c)$') figure only in the most trivial pattern of substitution. It does not follow, however, that there is no structure they inhabit; only that it will be a trivial and uninteresting one, for which a correspondingly trivial and uninteresting set of canonical designators will suffice. (So, for the CG language so far described, we could take the structure simply as $\langle =, \{c\}\rangle$; and the set of canonical designators just as $\{'c'\}$.) 'c' and 'g' may, accordingly, stand justly convicted of being peculiarly *uninteresting* singular terms. What is interesting, counterintuitive, and damaging, is that they should, according to Brandom, be singular terms at all.

Within the confines of a Fregean theory of meaning, singular terms are distinguished by the characteristic role they play in the inductive assignment of substantial truth-conditions made by the core theory. Nothing in the CG language as described provides the slightest impetus for thinking 'c' and 'g' will need to be distinguished as playing that singular-term role. By contrast, a use-based approach operating in the context of a formal theory of truth must perforce look to characteristic patterns of *use* to categorize its subsentential expressions. If, as our examination suggests, even Brandom's painstaking and detailed theory goes awry on this score, it must be doubted that any such approach can succeed in avoiding a misidentification of singular terms, and a consequently distorted account of the structure of objects which language embodies.

Bibliography

Armstrong, D. M., *Universals and Scientific Realism*, Vol. 1 (Cambridge: Cambridge University Press, 1978).

Austin, J. L., *Sense and Sensibilia*, 2nd edn. (London, Oxford, and New York: Oxford University Press, 1964).

Boolos, G., 'Nominalist Platonism', *The Philosophical Review*, 94 (1985), 327–44.

―――― 'To Be Is to Be a Value of a Variable (or to Be Some Values of Some Variables)', *The Journal of Philosophy*, 81 (1984), 430–49.

Boyd, R., 'Realism, Underdetermination, and a Causal Theory of Evidence', *Nous*, 7 (1973), 1–12.

Brandom, R., *Making it Explicit* (Cambridge, Mass., and London: Harvard University Press, 1994).

Campbell, K., *Abstract Particulars* (Oxford: Basil Blackwell, 1990).

Church, A., *Introduction to Mathematical Logic*, Vol. 1 (Princeton, NJ: Princeton University Press, 1956).

Davidson, D., 'Afterthoughts', in his *Subjective, Intersubjective, Objective*, 154–7.

―――― 'Belief and the Basis of Meaning', in his *Inquiries into Truth and Interpretation*, 141–54.

―――― 'A Coherence Theory of Truth and Knowledge', in his *Subjective, Intersubjective, Objective*, 137–53.

―――― *Essays on Actions and Events* (Oxford: Clarendon Press, 1980).

―――― *Inquiries into Truth and Interpretation* (Oxford: Clarendon Press, 1984).

―――― 'The Inscrutability of Reference', in his *Inquiries into Truth and Interpretation*, 227–41.

―――― 'The Method of Truth in Metaphysics', in his *Inquiries into Truth and Interpretation*, 199–214.

―――― 'Radical Interpretation', in his *Inquiries into Truth and Interpretation*, 125–40.

―――― 'Reality without Reference', in his *Inquiries into Truth and Interpretation*, 215–26.

―――― 'The Structure and Content of Truth', *The Journal of Philosophy*, 87 (1990), 279–328.

―――― 'True to the Facts', in his *Inquiries into Truth and Interpretation*, 37–54.

―――― *Subjective, Intersubjective, Objective* (Oxford: Clarendon Press, 2001).

Devitt, M., 'Realism and the Renegade Putnam', *Nous*, 17 (1983), 291–301.

―――― *Realism and Truth*, 2nd edn. (Oxford: Basil Blackwell, 1991).

Diamond, C., 'The Face of Necessity', in her *The Realistic Spirit* (Cambridge, Mass.: MIT Press, 1991), 243–66.

Dodd, J., 'McDowell and the Identity Theory of Truth', *Analysis*, 55 (1995), 160–5.

Douven, I., 'Putnam's Model-theoretic Argument Reconsidered', *The Journal of Philosophy*, 96 (1999), 479–90.

Dummett, M., 'A Defence of McTaggart's Proof of the Unreality of Time', in his *Truth and Other Enigmas*, 351–7.

――― *Frege: Philosophy of Language* (London: Duckworth, 1973).

――― 'Language and Truth', in his *The Seas of Language*, 117–46.

――― *The Logical Basis of Metaphysics* (Cambridge, Mass.: Harvard University Press, 1991).

――― 'The Philosophical Basis of Intuitionistic Logic', in his *Truth and Other Enigmas*, 215–47.

――― 'Realism', in his *The Seas of Language*, 230–76.

――― 'Realism and Anti-Realism', in his *The Seas of Language*, 462–78.

――― 'The Reality of the Past', in his *Truth and Other Enigmas*, 358–74.

――― *Truth and Other Enigmas* (London: Duckworth, 1978).

――― *The Seas of Language* (Oxford: Clarendon Press, 1993).

――― 'Truth', in his *Truth and Other Enigmas*, 1–24.

――― 'What Do I Know When I Know a Language?' in his *The Seas of Language*, 94–105.

――― 'What Does the Appeal to Use Do for the Theory of Meaning?' in his *The Seas of Language*, 106–16.

――― 'What Is a Theory of Meaning? (I)', in his *The Seas of Language*, 1–33.

――― 'What Is a Theory of Meaning? (II)', in his *The Seas of Language*, 34–93.

――― 'Wittgenstein's Philosophy of Mathematics', in his *Truth and Other Enigmas*, 166–85.

Evans, G., and McDowell, J., (eds.), *Truth and Meaning: Essays in Semantics* (Oxford: Clarendon Press, 1976).

Frege, G., 'On Sense and Meaning', in his *Collected Papers on Mathematics, Logic, and Philosophy*, ed. by B. F. McGuinness (Oxford and New York: Basil Blackwell, 1984), 157–77.

Goodman, N., *Fact, Fiction, and Forecast*, 4 edn. (Cambridge, Mass., and London: Harvard University Press, 1983).

Graham, P., 'Brandom on Singular Terms', *Philosophical Studies*, 93 (1999), 247–64.

Grice, P., 'Utterer's Meaning, Sentence Meaning, and Word Meaning', in his *Studies in the Way of Words* (Cambridge, Mass.: Harvard University Press, 1989), 117–37.

Hacking, I., *Representing and Intervening: Introductory Topics in the Philosophy of Science* (Cambridge: Cambridge University Press, 1983).

Hale, B., and Wright, C., 'Putnam's Model-theoretic Argument against Metaphysical Realism', in R. Hale and C. Wright (eds.), *A Companion to the Philosophy of Language* (Oxford: Blackwell, 1997), 427–57.

Hunter, G., *Metalogic: An Introduction to the Metatheory of Standard First-order Logic* (Berkeley and Los Angeles: University of California Press, 1971).

Kripke, S. A., *Naming and Necessity*, rev. and enlarged edn. (Oxford: Blackwell, 1980).

Kripke, S. A., *Wittgenstein on Rules and Private Language: An Elementary Exposition* (Oxford: Blackwell, 1982).

Langton, R., and Lewis, D. K., 'Defining "Intrinsic" ', in D. K. Lewis, (ed.), *Papers in Metaphysics and Epistemology*, 116–32.

Lewis, D. K., *Convention: A Philosophical Study* (Cambridge, Mass.: Harvard University Press, 1969).

_____ 'Events', in his *Philosophical Papers*, Vol. 2, 241–69.

_____ 'New Work for a Theory of Universals', in his *Papers in Metaphysics and Epistemology*, 8–55.

_____ *On the Plurality of Worlds* (Oxford: Basil Blackwell, 1986).

_____ *Philosophical Papers*, 2 vols. (Oxford: Oxford University Press, 1986).

_____ *Papers in Metaphysics and Epistemology* (Cambridge and New York: Cambridge University Press, 1999).

_____ 'Putnam's Paradox', in his *Papers in Metaphysics and Epistemology*, 56–77.

_____ 'A Subjectivist's Guide to Objective Chance', in his *Philosophical Papers*, Vol. 2 , 83–113.

McDowell, J., 'Another Plea for Modesty', in his *Meaning, Knowledge, and Reality*, 108–31.

_____ 'In Defence of Modesty', in his *Meaning, Knowledge, and Reality*, 87–107.

_____ 'Mathematical Platonism and Dummettian Anti-Realism', in his *Meaning, Knowledge, and Reality*, 344–65.

_____ *Meaning, Knowledge, and Reality* (Cambridge, Mass., and London: Harvard University Press, 1998).

_____ *Mind and World* (Cambridge, Mass., and London: Harvard University Press, 1994).

_____ 'On "The Reality of the Past" ', in his *Meaning, Knowledge, and Reality*, 295–313.

_____ 'Singular Thought and the Extent of Inner Space', in his *Meaning, Knowledge, and Reality*, 228–59.

_____ 'Comments: Response to Ian Lyne', *Journal of the British Society for Phenomenology*, 31 (2000), 338–40.

McGuinness, B., 'The So-Called Realism of the *Tractatus*', in I. Block (ed.), *Perspectives on the Philosophy of Wittgenstein* (Oxford: Blackwell, 1981), 70–3.

McTaggart, J. McT. E., 'The Unreality of Time', in his *Philosophical Studies*, ed. by Stanley Victor Keeling (London: E. Arnold, 1934), 110–31.

Mendelson, E., *Introduction to Mathematical Logic* (Princeton, NJ: Van Nostrand, 1964).

Merrill, G. H., 'The Model-theoretic Argument against Realism', *Philosophy of Science*, 47 (1980), 69–81.

Moore, G. E., 'A Defence of Common Sense', in his *Philosophical Papers* (London: Allen and Unwin, 1959), 32–59.

Newton-Smith, W., 'The Underdetermination of Theories by Data', *Proceedings of the Aristotelian Society Supplementary Volume*, 70 (1978), 71–91.

Peacocke, C., *Holistic Explanation: Action, Space, Interpretation* (Oxford: Clarendon Press, 1979).

_____ 'Truth Definitions and Actual Languages', in G. Evans and J. McDowell (eds.), *Truth and Meaning*, 263–84.

Putnam, H., *Meaning and the Moral Sciences* (London and Boston: Routledge & Kegan Paul, 1978).

_____ *Mind, Language and Reality: Philosophical Papers, Volume Two* (Cambridge and New York: Cambridge University Press, 1975).

_____ *Reason, Truth, and History* (Cambridge and New York: Cambridge University Press, 1981).

_____ 'Models and Reality', in his *Realism and Reason: Philosophical Papers Volume Three* (Cambridge and New York. Cambridge University Press, 1983), 1–25.

_____ *The Threefold Cord: Mind, Body, and World* (New York: Columbia University Press, 1999).

_____ 'What Is "Realism"?' *Proceedings of the Aristotelian Society*, 76 (1975/6), 141–62.

Quine, W. V., 'Natural Kinds', in his *Ontological Relativity and Other Essays* (New York: Columbia University Press, 1969), 114–38.

_____ *Word and Object* (Cambridge: Technology Press of the Massachusetts Institute of Technology, 1960).

Quinton, A., 'Properties and Classes', *Proceedings of the Aristotelian Society*, 48 (1957), 33–58.

Ramsey, F. P., 'Universals', in his *The Foundations of Mathematics; and Other Logical Essays* (London: Routledge & Kegan Paul, 1931), 112–34.

Russell, B., *Our Knowledge of the External World* (London: George Allen & Unwin, 1926).

Shapiro, S., *Foundations without Foundationalism: A Case for Second-order Logic* (Oxford and New York: Clarendon Press and Oxford University Press, 1991).

Strawson, P. F., 'Truth', in his *Logico-linguistic Papers* (London: Methuen, 1971), 190–213.

_____ 'Causation in Perception', in his *Freedom and Restraint, and Other Essays* (London: Methuen, 1974), 66–84.

Taylor, B., 'Dummett's McTaggart', in R. G. Heck (ed.), *Language, Thought, and Logic: Essays in Honour of Michael Dummett* (Oxford and New York: Oxford University Press, 1997), 183–99.

_____ ' "Just More Theory": A Manœuvre in Putnam's Model-theoretic Argument for Antirealism', *Australasian Journal of Philosophy*, 69 (1991), 152–66.

_____ *Modes of Occurrence: Verbs, Adverbs, and Events* (Oxford: Basil Blackwell, 1985).

_____ 'On Natural Properties in Metaphysics', *Mind*, 102 (1993), 81–100.

_____ 'States of Affairs', in G. Evans and J. McDowell (eds.), *Truth and Meaning*, 263–84.

Tugendhat, E., 'The Meaning of "Bedeutung" in Frege', *Analysis*, 30 (1970), 177–89.

van Cleve, J., 'Semantic Supervenience and Referential Indeterminacy', *The Journal of Philosophy*, 89 (1992), 344–61.

Bibliography

Wallace, John, ' "Only in the Context of a Sentence Do Words Have Any Meaning" ', in P. A. French, T. E. Uehling, and H. K. Wettstein (eds.), *Midwest Studies in Philosophy 2: Studies in the Philosophy of Language* (Morris: University of Minnesota Press, 1977), 305–25.

Williams, D. C., 'On the Elements of Being', *Review of Metaphysics*, 7 (1953), 3–18, 171–92.

Wittgenstein, L., *Philosophical Investigations*, 2nd edn. (Oxford: Blackwell, 1958).

—— *Remarks on the Foundations of Mathematics*, rev. edn. (Cambridge, Mass.: MIT Press, 1978).

Wright, C., 'Anti-Realism and Revisionism', in his *Realism, Meaning and Truth*, 433–57.

—— 'Can a Davidsonian Meaning theory be Construed in Terms of Assertibility?', in his *Realism, Meaning and Truth*, 403–32.

—— *Realism, Meaning and Truth*, 2nd edn. (Oxford: Blackwell, 1993).

—— *Truth and Objectivity* (Cambridge, Mass., and London: Harvard University Press, 1992).

—— 'Truth Conditions and Criteria', in his *Realism, Meaning and Truth*, 47–69.

Index

Aristotle, 101
Armstrong, David, 101, 107-9, 112, 114, 178
Austin, J. L., 135, 138, 178

Berkeley, George, 19-20, 23
bivalence
  required by pure realism, 39-42
  see also Dummett, Michael
Boolos, George, 88n., 94, 178
Boyd, Richard, 29n., 178
Brandom, Robert, 1, 7, 166-77, 178
  on identity, 173-4
  inferentialist semantics of, 166-9
  on quantifiers, 174-6
  on reference, 171-2
  on singular terms, 169-77

Campbell, Keith, 101, 178
Cardinality
  Argument from, 3, 53-3, 57-9;
    formulated, 52-3
  Constraint, 59
certification, 18-19 (notion
    introduced)
  corroborated, defined, 31
  second-order, 3, 34-7,
  stable, defined, 29
CG language, 170-7
Charity, Principle of, 73, 98, 122-3, 151
Church, Alonzo, 25, 65n., 178
Completeness
  Argument from, 3-5, 6, Part 2,
    pass.; formulated, 51
  Theorem, formulated, 51
COND, formulated, 35
CONJ, formulated, 33
Constraints, *see individual entries*
Convergence Thesis, 2, 28-9

Davidson, Donald, 4, 8, 25-7, 54, 58, 69-70, 72, 86-7, 150, 151, 153, 154, 178
Devitt, Michael, 1, 14-17, 21, 26, 78n., 135, 178

Diamond, Cora, 8, 143-6, 178
DISJ, formulated, 34
Douven, Igor, 78n., 179
Dummett, Michael, 8, 40, 84n., 140n., 141n., 153, 172, 179
  his critique of bivalence, 157-9
  his critique of latterday
    Wittgensteinianism about
    meaning, 143-7
  his critique of modest theories of
    meaning, 154-7
  as respected teacher of the
    author, 165

Eliteness Constraint, 5-6, 95-100;
    formulated, 95-6
epistemic standpoints, possible *see*
    possible epistemic standpoints
epistemology
  holistic, 129-33
  molecular, 33
Evans, Gareth, 77, 153, 179
existence
  objective, 14-21; defined, 18
  gold-class, 15-16

facts
  as correspondents of true
    sentences, 2, 24-8
  as thinkable contents, 160-5
  see also Moorean facts
frame variant, defined, 168
Frege, Gottlob, 25, 153, 156, 160, 162, 172-3, 179; *see also* meaning

Geach-Kaplan sentences, 88
God's-Eye View, 14, 39; *see also* Total
    View
Goodman, Nelson, 112, 122, 179
Graham, Peter, 168n., 169n., 179
Grandy, Richard, 97
Grice, Paul, 63, 179

Hacking, Ian, 85n., 179
Hale, Bob, and Crispin Wright, 54-6, 58, 78n., 84